LIVE A LIFE THAT MATTERS FOR GOD

WHAT PEOPLE ARE SAYING ABOUT JACK AND THE BOOK

JULIE WOODLEY

"From a clinical perspective the book has great value as a teaching and therapeutic tool for the soul. From a spiritual perspective it is a direct hit right to the heart of every Christian. This uplifting book will inspire you no matter what chapter you are reading. I love that you can pick up any chapter, anywhere, in any section in the book and be blessed immediately. Jack covers so many different topics that are relevant and critical to our growth as Christians, our happiness and our desire to walk closer with God. Jack's style is straight to the point and laser focused. Each chapter stands on its own as a lesson, reminder and encouragement for Christians to *Live A Life That Matters for God.* Jack doesn't just tell you to do it, he shows you how!

"You can read most chapters in 2 minutes or less so it's easy to dive in anytime and grab some spiritual truth. If you are hurting, hoping, praying, questioning, wondering or just in need of answers or encouragement, *Live A Life That Matters for God* is a life tool for you that you can use over and over again to remind you of God's great truths and purpose for you life. It will bless you tremendously.

"Jack, in his no holds barred, real talk style, exposes himself completely and shares with you many of the experiences and lessons God showed him to make sure He would *Live a Life That Matters for God.* I know Jack wants to make His life count for the Kingdom and I am sure you do too. So don't miss this wonderful, easy to read, fast moving book that will inspire you and direct you to make sure you get all God's best blessings and that your life truly matters and impacts the world for the God and His kingdom. I am honored to be Jack's friend and Colleague in Ministry."

JULIE WOODLEY, MA
DIVISION CHAIR, AMERICAN ASSOCIATION OF CHRISTIAN COUNSELING
FOUNDER/DIRECTOR, RESTORING THE HEART MINISTRIES

"Since 2011 Jack has traveled throughout the state of Florida ministering with me alongside other speakers and leaders. Jack has consistently stood out whether he was teaching an equipping workshop or ministering during a main session."

REV. DENNIS DEMAROIS
EXEC. DIR. FLORIDA MEN OF INTEGRITY

"Jack is a spiritually gifted teacher and counselor with a calling to share the eternal truths of God's Word for the purpose of transforming lives. Jack impacts individuals, couples, families, small groups, and congregations by sharing God's design for life and a message of love and hope in Jesus Christ with a simple, clear, and passionate style."

DAVID HECHT
PASTOR, FIRST BAPTIST CHURCH, HOLLYWOOD, FLORIDA

"His down to earth style and the everyday applications that he uses to teach the Bible really connect the people with Jesus in a special way."

VIC BATISTA
PASTOR, CALVARY CHAPEL, AVENTURA, FLORIDA

"The passion he brings is getting people to react and change immediately. Great results."

WILLIE ROMEO
DIRECTOR OF OPERATIONS, BURGER KING CORPORATION

"His eagerness for Christ and passion for others to draw close to the Lord is evident. Jack is a powerful voice for the gospel."

MICHAEL LoBRUTTO,
SENIOR PASTOR, BARWICK ROAD CHURCH, DELRAY BEACH, FLORIDA

"Jack Levine has a unique appeal because he has rubbed elbows with the rich and famous, yet his personality is humble and approachable. Everyone loves Jack and his message is pure gospel! Jack's presentation is passionate and powerful!

DALE FAIRCLOTH
PASTOR, FIRST BAPTIST CHURCH OF ROYAL PALM BEACH, FLORIDA

"Jack's message impacts lives. Above all else, Jack is the real deal!"

MIKE BUTZBERGER
SENIOR PASTOR, LIGHTHOUSE CHURCH, NORTH PALM BEACH FLORIDA.

"In 2006 I invited Jack to speak at a Christian business breakfast. He delivered a riveting talk that to this day has changed my life as a businessman! Then, I had Jack speak to the Fellowship Of Christian Athletes at Lake Sumter Community College. Jack spoke their language and many of them are still referencing the impact of that meeting!

"I pastored at a church in Oakland Park, Florida and then became the Associate Pastor of a fast-growing, youth-oriented, intra-denominational Church near Orlando, Florida. Jack spoke at all our Sunday services and was just awesome! Lives were changed."

SEAN LaGASSE
PASTOR, VICTORY CHRISTIAN CHURCH, OAKLAND PARK, FL AND THE CROSSINGS CHURCH, ORLANDO, FLORIDA

"Jack's conversion to Christ is a powerful testimony and he has been able to help people find hope no matter what problem or addiction they struggle with."

TRUMAN HERRING
SENIOR PASTOR, BOCA GLADES BAPTIST CHURCH

"Jack Levine preached often for me and he was always a tremendous blessing, with a clear word from God. His passion for the Lord was infectious."

WAYNE GILL
SENIOR PASTOR, CHANGED LIVES CHURCH, LAKE WORTH, FLORIDA

"People were challenged, encouraged and blessed by his message."

BOB DYSHUK
SENIOR PASTOR, NEW BEGINNINGS COMMUNITY CHURCH, BOYNTON BEACH, FLORIDA AND FLAMINGO ROAD CHURCH, HALLANDALE BEACH, FLORIDA

"Jack Levine is an exciting preacher. Jack cares! He is bold and there is no compromise. I wish there were more like him."

MANNY BARAHONA
SENIOR Pastor, WESTSIDE Church, Boynton Beach, Florida

"Jack Levine is an engaging and gifted communicator. He has a fresh and tangible approach in his delivery."

ROB TAYLOR
SENIOR PASTOR, FIRST BAPTIST CHURCH OF BOCA RATON, FLORIDA

"Jack is enthusiastic and heartfelt, with a passionate delivery and uncompromising devotion to delivering truth."

PAUL LUIS
SENIOR PASTOR, PALM SPRINGS BAPTIST CHURCH, PALM SPRINGS, FLORIDA

LIVE A LIFE THAT MATTERS FOR GOD

Jack Alan Levine

Live A Life That Matters For God
By Jack Alan Levine

Published by Great Hope Publishing, Coconut Creek, Fl

www.DontBlowItWithGod.com
www.LifeSolutionSeminars.com
www.GreatHopePublishing.com
www.JackAlanLevine.com

parklandjack1@aol.com
connect@LifeSolutionSeminars.com

© 2014 Jack Alan Levine. All Rights Reserved. Printed in the United States of America. Excerpt as permitted under the United States Copyright Act of 1976, no part of this publication may be reproduced or distributed in any form, or by any means, or stored in a database retrieval system, without the prior written permission of the copyright holder, except by a reviewer, who may quote brief passages in review.

Neither the publisher nor the author is engaged in rendering advice or services to the individual reader. Neither the authors nor the publisher shall be liable or responsible for any loss, injury, or damage allegedly arising from any information or suggestion in this book. The opinions expressed in this book represent the personal views of the author and not of the publisher, and are for informational purposes only.

Many of the various stories of people in this book draw from real life experience, at certain points involving a composite of stories. In some instances people's names have been changed in these stories to protect privacy.

ISBN 978-0-9904097-2-4 - paperback
ISBN 978-0-9904097-3-1 - ePub
Library of Congress Control Number: 2014951441

Scripture taken from the HOLY BIBLE, NEW INTERNATIONAL VERSION®. Copyright © 1973, 1978, 1984 Biblica. Used by permission of Zondervan. All rights reserved.

"Scripture taken from the New King James Version®. Copyright © 1982 by Thomas Nelson, Inc. Used by permission. All rights reserved."

Scripture taken from The Message. Copyright © 1993, 1994, 1995, 1996, 2000, 2001, 2002. Used by permission of NavPress Publishing Group.

TABLE OF CONTENTS

Foreword xix
Acknowledgments xxiii
Dedication xxvii
Introduction xxix

1
GOING ALL IN
(Commitment In The Christian Life)

The Fukishima 50 3
The Big Leagues 5
Pull Up 7
Wisdom from an NFL Coach 9
Seek with All Your Heart 10
Guitar Practice. 12
For Christ's Sake. 14
Integrity on a Lear Jet. 16
Keep Yourselves from Idols 19
The Truest Test 21
St. Louis Blues. 24
On the Field 26
Every Step 29
Popcorn Life 31
Every Single Day. 33

Foot Bath 35
I Know A Real Apostle 39
Doing Good 42
Return on Investment 45
Encouragement from a Renegade 47
Don't Miss It 52
Pouring Out Perfume 54
Eye on the Prize 57

2

THE FATHER AND HIS CHILDREN
(How God Relates To Us As A Father)

The Empty Home 61
The Face in the Crowd 63
What's the Problem? 65
Interrupted Blessings 70
Jump! 72
Wrong Turn 74
Ask for Directions 77
The Reptile Store 81
Pizza Detours 83
The Kidnapper 86
The Car Keys 88
Tell Daddy the Truth 90
Don't Be Troubled 92
Bad Company 94
A Father's Discipline 96
April Fools 98
Does God Know What He's Doing? 99
Dirty Diapers 102
Refusing a Gift? 104

Not Just One Pitch 106
The Refrigerator 109
A Child's Prayer 110
God's Kid 111
A Better Plan 112
Fishing Trip 114
Scared of the Ball 116
Consider it Joy 119

3
PLUGGING IN
(Accessing The Power Of God)

Power Flow 125
Power Now 128
Rooted and Established 130
Getting the Keys Now 132
The Power 134
Staring Contest 137
Just Shut Up 139
Pit Stop 141
The One Percent Army 143
Proof 145
A Face from the Past 148
One on One 151
All-Access 153

4

LIGHT ON THE PATH
(The Importance Of The Bible)

Which Stage? 159
What's For Dinner? 161
Love and Statutes 164
Have a Peace 166
Encouragement from Joel 169
The Gift of "Do Not" 172
When I Doubt 174
Don't Be Stupid 176
Words Have Meaning. 178
A Work of Art 180
The Devil's Plan 183
Great Reward 187
Lifting the Veil 190
Qualifying 193

5

GENEROUS GOD
(God's Overflowing Kindness Towards Us)

Help Me Choose. 199
Fill Up. 201
For Your Enjoyment. 203
Healing 206
True Riches 209
But for the Grace of God 212
A .300 Hitter 214

It's Finished 218
An "A" in the Class 220
Scot-Free 223
The Claim Ticket 225
Opening Gifts 227
Missed 230
A Fresh Breath of Perspective 232
Revealed for You 234
Angels Ahead 237
Ordering Food 238
He is Willing 240
Grants and Applications 242
Bloodbath 244
Getting to Know Him 246
Betrayed 249

6

DOING IT RIGHT
(Obeying God)

No Small Things 253
A Fine Line 256
Jumping for Joy 259
In Private 260
Frequent Flyer Points 261
Friends in Low Places 263
Reaping What You Sow 264
God's Requirements 266
Get Out of Jail Free 269
Set Apart 272
Knowing and Living 275
Tree and Fruit 276

Red Dye	278
Keep in Step	280
Practice Makes Perfect	283
Quizzing God	285
Whose Signature?	287
The Audit	289
Losing it All	291
You're a Teacher	293
Focused	295
An Order from the Commander	298
Good Fish	300
Prepared in Advance	303
The Players	305
No Free Pass	307
The Hall of Fame	310
Ambassadors	312
Going to Class	315
Stay Dressed	317
Get with the System	320
No Camping for Me	322
Smelling Like Garlic	323
Missing It	325
The Sweet Spot	327
Be Ready	329
Wakeup Call	331
Being a Picture	333
Trained and Ready	336
Choosing Teams	339

7
HEAVEN
(The Certainty Of Heaven For Believers)

No Closing Time 343
No Tears 345
Breath on a Cold Winter Morning 347
Raised from the Dead. 349
A Butterfly 352
Perishable to Imperishable. 355
The Great Separation 358
The Super Bowl Trophy 360
The Real Magic Kingdom 363
The Pilgrimage. 366
Pizza, with Everything 368
Seeing the Thorn 370
Homeless. 372
Revival 375
Your Name in a Book 377

8
HAVE A PIECE OF PEACE
(How To Have The Peace Of God In Your Life)

Air Conditioning 381
Tsunamis, Earthquakes, and Market Crashes 383
An Open Wallet. 386
Pressing Forward 388
Great Comebacks. 390
Faith in What?. 392

A Win-Win. 394
Being the Clay. 397
Some Thorns in My Side 399
Silver and Gold 402
Inflated Basketball. 404
No Pain 406
Consider the Lilies 408
A Snake in the Grass 411

9

STORIES FROM THE STORY
(Digging Into Biblical Stories)

Fake Power. 415
The Old Guy and the Young Guy 418
Gotta Serve Somebody. 422
The Patience of Job 425
Day and Night 429
Strength from Revelation 432
A Mighty Hand 434
The First Sign of Trouble 436
The Rescuer 439
Gratitude 442
It's Raining Bread 445
Fickle People 450
Being God's People 455
Who Did This?. 457
Keeping the Faith 459
Cain's Mutiny 463
Every Jar Full. 468
Whose Neighbor?. 471
A Cry is Heard. 474

The Right Team 477
A God Contest. 481
Missing a Shot 486
Getting Seconds 490
Just Two Things 493

Final Thoughts. 495
Special Thanks. 497

FOREWORD

Are you busy? Most people that want to make their life count for something important are busy. They are going somewhere, making changes, impacting lives, and do not have the time to waste on things that do not pay dividends and have value.

That is my friend Jack Alan Levine. As a successful businessman, he was on the fast track. Making quick decisions, not afraid to take risks- win some lose some- but then always seeking and moving on to the next project or opportunity. Conversations with Jack were friendly but short and to the point- a bottom line type of guy. Where is the opportunity- let's seize it quickly? What is the problem- let's solve it now and not wait. And always he is the eternal optimist. If the sky is falling then let's find a way to make it work for us.

So the question is with our busy lives, who has time for another book? I pray the answer is you! I urge you to make time for this book. *Live a Life That Matters* is a book that will jump start your day like a great cup of coffee. Each chapter is short enough to read between your sips of coffee. The chapters are motivational and practical and will inspire you and encourage you throughout your day.

Foreword

I first met Jack, a young Jewish businessman, when he stopped by our church in 1991. He was going through a personal crisis and came in just to pray. Our conversation that day began with Abraham the father of the Jews and ended with Jesus the Savior of the Jews and Gentiles. Jack became a Christian that day.

I watched the transformation and growth in his life over the next few months and years as he became a serious follower of Christ. Jack the businessman continued to run his company but his greater passion became that of ministry.

Jack came to Christ, like we all do, with lots of unwanted baggage. As he one by one overcame habits and addictions from the past, he had a passion to help other people find that same freedom in Christ.

It was not long after Jack accepted Jesus that he gave me three cassette tapes to listen to as I was driving out of state, "Just tell me what you think." They were sermons that he had felt compelled to preach in an empty room at his house. As I listened I knew that God wanted to use Jack as a Christian speaker or preacher. Those first tape sermons were not like a pastor from a pulpit but more like a man who had been around the block and knew what people were missing without Christ-just straight talk to the heart.

Later I asked Jack to become our Men's ministry leader and he built a great men's ministry in our church. I recommended Jack to some of my pastor friends to preach in their churches and he became a well sought after preacher. In 2002, Jack sold his business and made his ministry for God the priority in his life. In the years to follow His ministry has grown and he has

Foreword

become a successful Christian author (this book is his fourth) and accomplished conference speaker.

As a businessman Jack was full speed ahead. As a Christian, he has an even greater zeal to live a life of eternal purpose. *Live A Life that Matters* is written to challenge you to make your life count for God. Use it well.

Pastor Truman Herring
Senior Pastor, Boca Glades Baptist Church
Boca Raton, Florida

ACKNOWLEDGMENTS

Patrick Morley, one of my heroes, wrote the book *Man in the Mirror*. This book tremendously impacted and influenced my life, got me focused and brought me closer to God. Getting the opportunity to meet Pat and speak at the same confer-

PATRICK MORLEY

ence as him was a tremendous blessing for me. I've been so blessed by getting to speak to so many thousands of Christian men who are hungry for the Word of God. He's a selfless brother who works tirelessly on behalf of the Lord. His faith and his life are an inspiration to me.

Erwin McManus' book *Seizing Your Divine Moment* was the definitive life-changing book in my life. It opened my eyes, fired me up, and focused me, in a laser- like way, to make sure that I had my eye on the prize... God, His kingdom and His purpose for my life. I will always be grateful to Erwin for the inspira-

Acknowledgments

ERWIN MCMANUS

tional messages I heard him speak at Promise Keepers and for all his books. I don't know of any single author who has ever impacted me more greatly than he has. Erwin is an out-of-the-box thinker, a visionary, an innovator, who lets you see into his very soul as he walks this earth and lives for the kingdom of God. It's my hope and prayer that my books have even a fraction of the impact on people in the world that his have. That's why I wrote them. Because I saw the tremendous impact others' books were having on me. And I wanted to be sure that I had the opportunity to bless other people the same way.

Charles Carrin is a dear brother in the Lord. I am so grateful he chose to invest his time in my life and ministry. Equipping me, teaching me, and sharing with me the many experiences and truth's that God has shown him in his life. His book *The Edge of Glory* was another one of those life-changing books for me, which literally took the scales off my eyes and helped me see the mighty power of

CHARLES CARRIN

Acknowledgments

God. I was able to see firsthand many, many lives touched and transformed by his ministry, a ministry that depends solely on the Holy Spirit and power of God. Charles is the sweetest, kindest man you'll ever meet, and even in his 80's is still on fire for the Lord. I hope and pray I can finish my race strong like Charles is. It's so awesome to see him still impacting people for the kingdom of God, still writing, still preaching, still sharing his message of healing and hope through God's power and Spirit. Charles is all about the transforming power of Jesus Christ. The Holy Spirit working through Charles is an undeniable fact and millions throughout the world have been touched by it.

There are a couple of other guys who've inspired some books that I really want to meet. Guys like Moses, Daniel, David, Paul, Peter, James and a host of others. I look forward to the day when you and I are face-to-face with them, and with Jesus and God our Father. At that point I know there will be no need for any more pictures, any more words or any more explanations. But in the meantime, I am so grateful to God that He has given us His Holy Spirit and these other wonderful Christian brothers to help us, encourage us and equip us along the way as we fulfill our purpose for this life. Thank you Lord. To God be the glory!

DEDICATION

The problem with writing so many books is you run out of people to dedicate them to (smile!) I always dedicate everything I do to Jesus Christ. Even though I know I fall far short of the glory of God, I am so grateful for His love and the life He has given me. It is my honor and privilege to dedicate my life and certainly everything I write to God's glory. Thank you, Father. Thank you for salvation. Thank you for Jesus. Thank you for the Holy Spirit. I'm the luckiest man in the world to know You and to be Your son.

My life is made even better and more complete by my wonderful wife Beth and my three children Ricky, Jackson and Talia. It just amazes me that I have this wonderful family in my life. Thank you guys for putting up with my insanity, my humor, (which is much funnier than you give me credit for) my extremely quirky ways (quirky only compared to the rest of the world) and of course, most of all, for loving me. You guys are always an inspiration to me and the motivation for much of what I do.

Last but not least I dedicate this book to my friend Andrew Pitoniak, whom I have known for many years, who inspired

Dedication

me with his desire to walk closer to the Lord. He has inspired me with his faith during trials and tribulations that would crush other men, and with his love for God. He's inspired me by sharing his own heartbreaks, shortcomings, and issues that have impacted and affected his life. Over 50 years old now, my brother has experienced in his lifetime physical abuse, gambling addiction, drug addiction, and health issues - as he is at stage 4 with his battle with lymphoma, and does not know how much time he has left to spend here with us on earth. But he does know that when his time on earth is up he's going home to be with Jesus. His postings, letters, phone calls and rallying response to the cross and feet of Jesus Christ is an inspiration for every Christian. Andrew, my brother, you touch my heart and inspire me to cherish God each and every moment. You, my brother, are living a life that matters for God... I know of no greater way to inspire anyone. Love you man. Keep the train rolling!

Thanks everybody.
Jack

INTRODUCTION

Of all the books I've written, this is perhaps the one I'm most excited about. For I expect this one to have the greatest appeal and impact on today's generation. It's by far the easiest to read. I've made the chapters very short, concise and easy-to-understand. I wrote this book so that you can pick it up anywhere, at any time, read a chapter or two and get filled with the Spirit of God by the Word of God.

You don't have to start at the beginning; you can start anywhere you want. You can pick out any one of the sections that appeals to you and dive right in. Or, you can look at any chapter titles you like and start there. You can move around, bounce back and forth, do anything you want.

There are nine unique sections in the book and within those sections are hundreds of chapters. I believe each one can change your day, your thinking and your life in a heartbeat, and you can read many chapters in two minutes or less. You can pick it up any time, whether you're hurting, searching, praying, reflecting, hoping, walking in faith, walking out of faith, or just seeking God's will, this book will bring you closer to God. You will see some themes and verses that run through the book. Pay attention to them. They are important.

Introduction

They are principles and truths I believe God wants you to hear, embrace and be blessed by.

The purpose of the book is to make sure that you *Live A Life That Matters For God.* As I examined my own life I wanted to make sure I was not just talking the talk, but truly walking the walk. I am sharing with you the realizations, conclusions and wisdom I've learned and applied to my own life to make sure my life matters for God.

You'll see it chapter by chapter through personal stories, messages and God's truths, which I believe will have an extremely practical and personal application to your life today. I know with the help of the Holy Spirit you will be blessed tremendously by this book and it will encourage, inspire and direct you on how to live a life that matters for God. After all isn't that what's important? Isn't that what we all strive for deep down in our souls? Isn't that what we want? Isn't that why God created us? And isn't that what we should have?

Just know I wrote this book for you. As we know, the Holy Spirit speaks to us individually, each one receiving the message we need to, at that very moment, if we are attuned to the Spirit. So, I pray you will enjoy it and it is a blessing to you. I hope it's one that you'll refer to time and time again throughout the rest of your life, going back to certain sections and chapters when you need inspiration and encouragement from the Word of God and especially as a reminder to make sure that your life matters for God.

To God be the Glory! Keep the train rolling.

Your brother in Christ,
Jack

1

GOING ALL IN
(Commitment In The Christian Life)

The Fukishima 50

In 2011, there was a great tragedy in Japan—a massive earthquake followed by a killer tsunami. If that wasn't enough, there was also a nuclear meltdown. There's a group known as the Fukushima 50. They're the fifty or so guys who were told by management at the nuclear plant, "You guys are going in to fix it. You're going to be exposed to higher levels of radiation than anybody has ever been exposed to, and you're probably going to die within a few years."

Those men said, "It's our honor to go. We will save our country."

They were willing to lay down their lives for the purpose immediately and without question. They didn't say, "Let me think about it. Maybe I should. Maybe I shouldn't. Pick somebody else." All fifty of them said, "We're in. We're going. It's our honor."

Why isn't it our honor to lay down our lives and live for Jesus Christ? That is the purpose of our lives. That's why we were created—to bear fruit that will last, to make disciples, and to do the good works which God prepared in advance for us to do. We should be fulfilling this purpose of our lives.

1: Going All In

If you're not, don't wonder why you're not happy. You're not happy because you aren't fulfilling your calling, God's purpose for you.

I was talking the other day to a buddy of mine who is a great surgeon and is widely respected by the other doctors. I asked him, "What will people say about you at your funeral? Will they be talking about what a great surgeon you were?" Then I said to him, "They shouldn't be. It would be a tragic shame if I'm at your funeral and people are talking about what a great *surgeon* you were. They'd should be talking about what a great *Christian* you were."

What "sermon" does your life preach? If there was an American Idol like TV show for Christians, and we were sitting there judging you and rating you, what would we see? Would we say, "Oh, man, he was awesome for God! He was amazing. We all give him a ten." Or would we hold up the card and say, "Him? He stank for Jesus. He struck out for Jesus. He was a waste. We all give him a two."

What does your life show for Jesus Christ? It's not about perfection. It's about how you live your life. You don't have to be a minister or pastor to preach the Word of Jesus Christ. It's about what we do with our lives, if and how they reflect Christ overall.

The Big Leagues

God wants to grant you a favor. He wants to give you everything you will ever need. You say, "Well, how do I receive this?" The answer is found in 2 Peter 1:3 and 4:

> *His divine power has given us everything we need for life and godliness through our knowledge of Him who called us by His own glory and goodness. Through these He has given us His very great and precious promises, so that through them you may participate in the divine nature and escape the corruption in the world caused by evil desires.*

It's only by the saving grace of God that you receive His power. In Ezra 7:10, it says, "Ezra had prepared his heart to seek the law of the Lord and to do it." God called Ezra a man after His own heart because he prepared his heart to seek the law of the Lord and to do it. He didn't just *find out* what God's law was. He *did* it.

If God looks at you and me today, will He see our hearts that way? Will He see us seeking to know His heart and being imitators of Christ? God said we are to be holy because He

1: Going All In

is holy. We are to be imitators of Christ to the best of our earthly ability.

He's our coach. He's invited us to play for Him this season of our life we are living now on earth. Jesus was out there on the field playing the game of life just like we are. He dealt with the dust, the crowds, the curve balls, and the fast ones. And he hit the biggest home run the world has ever seen. That was on Calvary, when he took the game to a whole new level.

Now, God is our coach: pitching the balls to us, encouraging us to swing, to hit. He's practiced with us every day since we joined the team. And His vision for all of us—even though we might feel we're not cut out for it—is the big leagues.

God is there, ready to teach us and show us every step of the way. But, not only do we need to show up to hear the instruction, we need to practice it and put it into action. We should love the Coach, after all He created the game and created us to play it. He promises He will teach us how to play better. Not only does He teach us how to win if we let him, but He is personally rooting for us to win all the time!

There are people watching you. They see the times you strike out, and they see your attitude as you get excited about getting up to bat again. You don't get discouraged, and you don't quit because you struck out. This time you know you will get a hit! You know your team is going to win. You've seen the final score. God's kids win! Here on earth and forever in eternity! You know you are supposed to play the game joyfully, loving every minute of it like a little kid, and if you play with all your heart, you know at the end your Coach is going to say, "Well done!"

Pull Up

I was talking with a buddy of mine after men's ministry one day. He said, "Hey, I just got back from New Orleans on a flight, and I thought I was going to meet my maker."

I said, "What do you mean? What happened?"

He said, "We were coming into Ft. Lauderdale in this thunderstorm and it was crazy. The plane was going all over the place, and we were ten feet from landing on the runway when all of sudden the pilot pulls the plane straight up like a rocket and I've never been so scared in my life. Then we were flying around trying to come back and make the landing again."

I'm thinking to myself, "Well, the pilot was actually pretty smart because at least he did it again until he got it right. He was close the first time, about ten feet from the runway, but he obviously thought he was going to crash so he didn't land. He did it again until he got it right.

That's what we need to do. Why crash? We don't have to crash. Why don't we just keep trying until we get it right?

I believe God is saying to us very clearly, "I've given you all this. I'm not going to be satisfied with less than your best."

1: Going All In

It's like the parable of the talents (Matthew 25:14-30) where people are challenged to invest all they have been given and trusted with by their master for the benefit of their master. It's so simple. It is basically this, "Look, you've been given this gift, this life, from God. What are you going to do with it?" You can't la-di-da through your life and think it doesn't matter or that you're going to get to it later. Now is the time. This is when it all happens. So why crash? Why not be careful and diligent and make sure you get it right...like any good pilot would and any good Christian should!

Wisdom from an NFL Coach

At the end of the 2011 football season, the Pittsburgh Steelers were about to play in a playoff game. I was intrigued most by Coach Mike Tomlin of the Steelers. When he was asked about the poor performances and the injuries that his team was facing going into the AFC conference championship game, his response to those injuries and poor performances was, "We don't live in our fears. We live in our hopes."

I thought, *holy cow, this is amazing.* Here's this NFL football coach, and his team has not been playing well. They don't know if they're going to win or not, they've got injuries, and the coach is saying, "Look, we don't live in our fears. We live in our hopes."

Coach Mike Tomlin has it right. Sometimes we as Christians don't get it right. Sometimes we live in our fears, and we don't live in our hopes. We should be living in our hopes, not our fears. We know that faith is being certain of what we can't see and sure of what we hope for. We should live in that. It struck me as funny that an NFL football coach would have it right, but we as Christians struggle with it.

Seek with All Your Heart

Psalm 95:7-9 urges us:

For He is our God and we are the people of his pasture, the sheep of His hand.

Do not harden your hearts, as in the rebellion, as in the day of trial in the wilderness, when your fathers tested Me; They tried Me, though they saw My work.

Even though they were God's people, the sheep of His pasture, they didn't believe. They tested Him, even though they had already witnessed and experienced the great work of God.

Do we do that in our Christian life? Do we see God but still feel it's necessary to try and test Him, as if we're not sure and not certain that He is indeed God, that indeed He can do what He said He can do—past, present, and future? He's the Alpha and the Omega, the Beginning and the End. Oh, that our hearts would learn from these past histories. The next verses go on to say:

For forty years I was grieved with that generation and said, "It is a people who go astray in their hearts, and they do not know My ways." So I swore in My wrath, "They shall not enter My rest."

God freed them from captivity in Egypt. He led them step by step all the way, yet they sadly never entered into His rest because they went astray in their hearts. Rather than following God's purpose, they altogether missed why the Lord had brought them out. He wanted to bring them to Himself, but their hearts were far away from Him.

I pray that we may not be a people of whom God says, "They went astray," that grieved God with our generation, and that did not know His ways. God says that the wisdom and knowledge of the Lord is more valuable than rubies and gold. We're to seek it with all our hearts. And of course God promises when we seek Him with all our hearts, we will find Him.

Guitar Practice

When my son Jackson was almost ten, he was taking guitar lessons and I made him practice his guitar regularly. It was something that he did—not quite willingly, but he did it.

At one point he came to me and said, "Daddy, I want to quit guitar." He always said he wanted to quit. And I said, "No, Son, that's the one thing I'm not letting you quit until you are at least sixteen. You're going to keep playing guitar no matter what."

Before he went to practice one day, he looked at me (hoping to get out of practicing) and asked "Daddy, do I have to practice today?" I said, "Son, you have to practice."

He looked at me again and asked, "Why, Daddy?" *Why, Daddy?* As if I was torturing him and subjecting him to the gas chamber, not guitar practice.

I said, "Son, when you're sixteen years old you're going to put your arm around me—you'll be taller than me then, so you'll be looking down at me—and you'll say, 'Dad, I just want to thank you so much that you didn't let me quit guitar because you knew the benefits I would get from it.'"

(Commitment In The Christian Life)

He will be thankful when he's reaping those benefits, when he's enjoying the freedom and opportunities that come from using his talent and being able to play a musical instrument, when he's meeting people and getting other life opportunities—instead of playing video games or watching television all the time. He'll be out there in the world doing something and hopefully something that matters for the Lord.

So, he'll have those opportunities and I know when he sees those benefits (someday) he's going to thank me. The problem is, today he can't see the benefits. He doesn't see what they are, so he thinks it's torture. He's thinking, "Why am I doing this? Why do I have to learn this? This is a pain in the butt."

It's often the same way with us and God. We sit there and we ask, "Why God? Why are we going through this? Why do I have to do this?" We know what God's Word says, but we question that too.

Well, the Lord is saying right back to us, "Someday you're going to thank me for this. You don't know the benefits you're reaping in heaven and on earth through your obedience and your faith right now! You don't see the rewards you'll reap later in life and in heaven, but one day you're going to thank me, and you're going to be so grateful that I didn't let you quit."

We see it so clearly with our children, or sometimes with other people, but we often fail to connect the dots in our own lives. But God laid out clearly for me how it works in what I now call "The Parable of Jackson's Guitar Lessons."

For Christ's Sake

I was walking along the other day and I heard these guys talking. They were obviously not Christians, but you wouldn't know it by their language because every word out of their mouths was, "For Christ's sake!"

For Christ's sake this, for Christ's sake that. I'm thinking, *Oh, you going to preach it brother? Preach it!* Then I heard the rest, and I'm going, *Uh-oh, this isn't good.*

For Christ's sake this. Christ's sake that. Christ's sake, Christ's sake...

I began to think, you know what? We should be saying that—we the church, we Christians—every word that comes out of our mouths, every sentence should be, "For Christ's sake," and then we should *live like it.*

We should really do it *"for Christ's sake."*

We should live for Christ's sake. We should act and speak and do things for Christ's sake—not the way the world says it, almost as if it's a curse and a bad thing. But we should really live that way for Christ's sake.

The question I had for myself and the question I believe God has for each of us is: Who are we living for? Am I living for Jack's sake, or am I living for Christ's sake?

(Commitment In The Christian Life)

I think God wants you to ask yourself that question and honestly answer it. Who are you living for? Are you living for your sake, or are you living for Christ's sake?

Integrity on a Lear Jet

Our lives here on earth are like a ship sailing on the water. What happens when the water gets in the ship? The ship sinks. But when it floats on top of that water, it's fine.

That's how we're meant to live our lives here on earth. We're to be in the world but not of it. We're not to let the water of the world come into our ships, these godly vessels that God has given us. Why? Because it will sink you. Satan will sink you if you let him in. One way or the other, his desire and plan is to sink you.

The word of God says in 1 John 3:7-8:

> *Dear children, do not let anyone lead you astray. He who does what is right is righteous, just as He is righteous. He who does what is sinful is of the devil, because the devil has been sinning from the beginning. The reason the Son of God appeared was to destroy the devil's work.*

I've been involved in a solar farm deal. As such, I've been talking to a few people who are in the solar industry; I flew out to San Diego not long ago to talk to a solar company out there.

(Commitment In The Christian Life)

A week later, their owner flew into Ft. Lauderdale to meet with me. This guy is like a kazillionaire—two jets, five houses, made his first ten million dollars when he was thirty-eight years old and has just kept on making money since then.

When I went to San Diego, he had flown in on one of his jets from another town just to have dinner with us and talk. Now he was flying into Ft. Lauderdale just to see me.

My accountant and I talked with him over lunch and he amazed me by saying, "Listen, I don't know if we're ready to do a deal this big with the technology we have in our company. What you should probably do is go with a more established solar panel—and don't gamble on our new technology."

I'm sitting here thinking, Wow, this guy flew from all the way from California to sit here and tell me something he could have told me over the phone. He could have just called me up and said, "Hey, listen, I don't think we're ready."

So anyway, I said, "No problem. We'll talk about it internally and decide on the next step. But I'm just curious, why did you fly from California to tell me this?"

He said, "You came out to see me, and I owe you the respect of coming back to see you in person."

I was pretty much flabbergasted, thinking to myself, Where else do you find this kind of integrity today? Here's a guy who doesn't need to have integrity; he's got so much money. Now, of course, everybody needs to have integrity, but by the world's standards, he can afford to blow people off and do what he wants. He doesn't know me from Adam. We met one time at dinner in California and probably won't end up even doing a deal together. Yet he flew in from California,

1: Going All In

landed at 6:30 in the morning and left at 6:00 at night, just to talk with us and tell us it probably wasn't in our best interest to use his technology.

I spoke with him a little more that day and learned that he was brought up in the Lutheran church and believes in Jesus Christ. We were talking about business, and working hard, and getting ahead, and he said, "I don't believe it's about luck. Here's what I found. The harder I worked, the 'luckier' I got. I worked hard for everything I've got."

I thought to myself that this is how every Christian should behave in life. This is the kind of integrity we should have—not just in business, but in relationships as well. It should be that yes is yes and no is no. We should have respect for people and care for people. It's not about how much money we have or who we are or what our position is.

Jesus talks about that. He says that we're not to align ourselves with rich people for what they can give us. We're not supposed to take the first place at the table. We're to humble ourselves and not be afraid to associate with lowly people. As Christians, we're not supposed to get prideful and puffed up.

My take on this gentleman was, Man, that's how I want people to view me one day.

I hope and pray that I remain faithful in treating people that same way, so that, no matter if I'm broke or rich, healthy or ill, old or young, people are going to say, "There's a man of integrity and character." You can't buy that. And when Jesus says, "What does it profit a man to gain the whole world if he forfeits his soul." (Matthew 16:26) You can certainly apply that to your integrity. Don't sell yours for anything in the world.

Keep Yourselves from Idols

In 1 John 5, John begins talking about love, living for God, being obedient, making sure we don't get led astray, and a lot of other things. And finally in the last verse, he says: "Dear children, keep yourselves from idols." What's an idol?

An idol in your life is anything that is allowed to stand between you and God. An idol is anything that you worship ahead of God—whether it's money, a relationship, another god, a sports team, a golf game, an image—whatever. Anything that you put ahead of God is an idol in your life. And so important is it to keep yourself from idols that it's the last thing that John says to us: "Keep yourself from idols."

You know, we use so many excuses to justify forgetting the Lord.

"Lord, I'm working hard. Lord, my health, my money, my bank account, my wife, my kids…"

We obscure the clarity of God's instructions to us by putting so many things in front of it. But this is one thing that is not negotiable. It's not grey. It's very clear. It's black and white.

Do not forget the Lord your God! As you're lavished in this world and all that God has given you in this life, don't forget who gave you the gift of your life. When it all comes down to it, there is not one thing you can do to make sure you have another breath or control over when your heart stops beating. That is a gift from God to you, and one primary purpose of life is to know for sure that you're going to heaven when your time on earth is up.

Another primary purpose is bringing others to know of God's love. This starts by seeing them through God's eyes.

I had a friend whose mother died. He was a guy about fifty years old. His mother's last words—to her four adult sons gathered around her death bed—were, "Be tolerant of people. Accept people. Be tolerant of people's differences and opinions and ideas." She had been a Christian her whole life, yet with her four sons gathered around her, these last words were so important to her.

With everything she'd learned in her life, she said to them, "Be tolerant of people."

If we truly loved people and valued them as God does, we would be more tolerant of them. We would see how beautiful every single one of them is through the eyes of God, created by Him for a special purpose.

The Truest Test

Bill and Theresa are friends of mine. They are older than me and they adopted their four grandchildren as their own children. Theresa was diagnosed with cancer, and the cancer was moving fast. Bill didn't know what he would do if Theresa passed away, and we were praying for a miracle. Here's the email she sent me as this was happening:

> I met with my oncologist today to review the test results. It was not the news we hoped for. The Nexavar didn't stop or shrink the tumors. In fact, there's been some growth, and they can see additional tumors. Also, my cough and the fluid build-up around my lungs are being caused by the cancer, so the cough will not go away, and we'll have to watch carefully for any more fluid. Apparently, I have a very rare and aggressive form of thyroid cancer. It is not going to give up easily. My oncologist, endocrinologist, and pulmonary doctor have been consulting and contacting others around the country concerning my case. There isn't much known to do, but there are a couple of options to try. There's a clinical trial

1: Going All In

at the Mayo Clinic in Jacksonville. The endocrinologist knows one of the doctors involved. They're going to try to get me in one day next week for a consult.

I have to admit that Bill and I were quite disappointed when we heard the news, and yesterday was a good cry day for both of us. But, I just kept going back to the fact that I know in my heart that God has a good plan in all of this. This may not make any sense right now, but I just know it. I also know that the enemy is tough, but nothing is tougher than my God, so don't count me out yet. We continue to pray that He will work a mighty miracle of healing and, in the meantime, give us the grace, courage, strength, peace, and faith to walk this journey. I pray too that you will not become discouraged with this news. Thank you for walking this path with us. I cherish you more than you know.

Blessings,
Theresa

Man, that's the test of faith, and here is someone who passed it. No matter what happens, she's giving glory to God and has faith in God. That's what God wants to see in our lives. We shouldn't wait for an "I'm dying" situation but instead we should show our faith in God in every situation! Certainly, if we were dying, we should be very happy that we're going to be seeing Jesus and we should be very grateful for the life that we've lived, this abundant life that we've got.

It's still definitely a challenge to face the possibility of death with full faith and trust in God. But anything we go

(Commitment In The Christian Life)

through—whether we're out of work, whether we're having problems with our kids, whether it's marital, financial, physical, spiritual, anything we're going through—we should have an attitude of faith. Why? Because the world is watching, and they're depending on us to shine as lights and be examples of Christianity in their life. That's what we need to do.

In Matthew 4:7, Jesus says, "Do not put the Lord your God to the test." Don't test God. Do we do that sometimes? Do we test God?

I think we're sometimes like, "Lord, if you give me this, I'll give you that. Lord, if you do this for me, I'll do that. Lord, if you let my baby live, if you let my husband come back. Lord, if you let this deal go through, then I'll do these mighty things for you."

You know what? Your baby may or may not live. Your husband may or may not come back and that deal might or might not go through. That's God's providence; He will have His perfect way. We shouldn't respond by testing God. "God, if I don't get what I want then you're not God anymore. I don't trust you." Regardless of what happens, our response should be like that of my friends Theresa and Bill, we need to give God glory.

Theresa did eventually succumb to cancer and went home to be with the Lord but not before being an amazing witness to her family, children and friends. Her faith and her life shined brightly for Jesus and her light still burns brightly today in the lives of all those she touched. I was one of them. What a blessing!

St. Louis Blues

Matthew 28:16-20 says:

Then the eleven disciples went to Galilee, to the mountain where Jesus had told them to go. When they saw him, they worshiped him; but some doubted. Then Jesus came to them and said, 'All authority in heaven and on earth has been given to me. Therefore go and make disciples of all nations, baptizing them in the name of the Father and of the Son and of the Holy Spirit, and teaching them to obey everything I have commanded you. And surely I am with you always, to the very end of the age.'

Jesus says, "Teach them to obey everything I have commanded you."

It was 2011, I'd been saved for nineteen years then, and I was as usual minding my own business. God said "That's the problem. You're minding your own business, not my business. You need to be about my business, Jack, not your business."

And God spoke to my spirit in a way so strong, I don't know that I felt anything like it since I first felt the salvation call of God in my heart in 1991.

(Commitment In The Christian Life)

I said, "Well, all right God, I get that. So what's going on here? What do you want from me?" In May of 2010, I went to my nephew's college graduation in St. Louis. I did not like St. Louis. It was like a slum and I don't mean that disrespectfully. It was dark, dreary, and depressing—the opposite of Florida. I remember leaving St. Louis that weekend and saying with relief, "I'll never be back here again."

Come July, two months later, God put on my heart, "No, Jack, you need to go back to St. Louis and you need to do mission work there."

I was like, "God, are you kidding? I'm not going to St. Louis."

He said, "Yes, you are going. Do you want to be obedient or not?"

So, with visions of being swallowed by a whale running through my head, I said yes. We went back in October, and then again in December for five days of street ministry culminating in a revival night service in a theater we had rented.

It was awesome!

We saw God's power at work in lives of people as we ministered each day on the streets and in the Thursday night service. I never would have seen any of that if I hadn't obeyed. I would not have experienced His power to transform the hearts of those people if I hadn't followed God's bidding.

God has shown me His power, like never before, because of my obedience to Him. A great lesson for all of us. The more obedient we are to God, the more we enable Him to bless us!

On the Field

If you asked Jesus Christ into your heart and you know Him as your personal Lord and Savior, you're not condemned by the law and you're not judged by the law. First Timothy 1:8-9 says: "We know that the law is good if one uses it properly. We also know that the law is made not for the righteous but for lawbreakers."

We are already considered righteous. The righteous, according to God, are those who believe in Jesus Christ. You were made righteous, not by what you did but by what Jesus did for you on the cross. By accepting Jesus, God now sees you clothed in the righteousness of Jesus, holy, blameless, and above reproach. A great deal for us!

The Scripture above states that the law is good if it's used properly. How do I use it properly? I use it properly as a mirror. I use it properly to show me what sin is. I use it as a score card to see how I'm doing.

The law is there to show us our sin but not to condemn us for it.

Romans 8:1 tells us, "There is no condemnation for those in Jesus Christ." None. Zero. No condemnation. We know

(Commitment In The Christian Life)

what zero means. I think we can all relate to having "zero" money in our bank account. It's not fun, but we've probably all been there at some point.

There is no condemnation for those in Jesus Christ. That means no matter what you do, you're not condemned. God has forgiven you. So, we're to look at the law as a mirror of, "This is what I'm supposed to do, but I'm not judged by it. I do the best I can." We're not judged by the law, but we are rewarded for our obedience to God.

Baseball great Babe Ruth was a notorious drunk and womanizer. Everybody knew it. Another baseball legend Ty Cobb was a known bigot and a racist. Are some of today's modern heroes like that? Yes! Are Tiger Woods and Alex Rodriguez any better, morally speaking? Of course not. Sad to say, they're spiritually bankrupt. Hopefully they get it right with God and turn that around. Yet, when we look at them, if we were to judge them based on their accomplishments on the field, they'd all be in the Hall of Fame. Every single one of them. They're amazing. They're great ball players.

So, when you look at the law, just so you know, you're not being condemned. When God looks at your Christian life, He's looking at your accomplishments on the field, not your sin! You know, the good works He speaks about in Ephesians 2:10, the one's He's prepared in advance for you to do. He knows you have sin in your heart. The Word of God says that the heart is deceitful above all things. (Jeremiah 17:9) He already paid the price for the sin in your heart. And He wants you to go give your best effort out on the field.

The field we're called to is the one Jesus spoke of when He was on earth. He said, "Lift up your eyes and look at the fields,

1: Going All In

for they are already ripe for harvest." (John 4:35) We are given the task of reaping the harvest of lost souls, bringing them into the Kingdom while there is still time. "For the night is coming when no one can work." (John 9:4) All God asks is that we do our best. The time to do it is now!

Every Step

The apostle Paul says: "Even though I was once a blasphemer and a persecutor and a violent man, I was shown mercy because I acted in ignorance and unbelief." (1 Timothy 1:13)

Paul was a blasphemer. He was a violent man, but God showed him mercy. Why? Because he acted in ignorance and unbelief. He didn't yet know that Jesus was Lord. When Jesus appeared to Paul on the road to Damascus, then he knew, and he got down on his feet and said, "What do you want me to do, Lord?" and from that moment on, he listened and lived his life following Jesus every step of the way.

How many of us have followed Jesus every step of the way since we were first introduced to Him? I think that's what God wants from us. He wants our undivided love and attention in our lives and everything we do. Paul says, "The grace of the Lord is poured out on me abundantly along with faith and love that are in Christ Jesus." (1 Timothy 1:14)

So, let me get this right. Not only do I get the grace of the Lord poured out on me, but I also get the faith and love of Christ Jesus abundantly when I turn to God? Yes! And that's

1: Going All In

what you should be experiencing right now in your life. God wants you to have this!

Which one of you, as a parent, wouldn't want his kid experiencing abundant grace, peace, mercy, and love? Which one of you, as a parent, wouldn't want his kid to be happy and joyful and living up to the talent that God gave them—whether it's music, academics, business, sports, just being a great guy, a teacher, what's the difference? All we wish for our kids is that they live up to their potential, that they're happy and joyful, and that they don't waste their lives because that would really stink.

Don't be a bum for God. Don't make Him say of you, "Yeah, I really love him/her, but they're not doing very much with the life I've given them." God has given us too much. God wants to bless us. We have so much potential. Don't limit what God wants to give you.

We get the grace, love, and faith of Jesus poured out to us abundantly. God is pouring it out.

How much do you want? How big is your cup? How much of God's grace, faith, and love do you want? Because that's how much you will get. Personally I hope I get so much that I am swimming in it!

Popcorn Life

Do you like popcorn? I grew up with Orville Redenbacher popping corn. We used to put pans on the old electric stove and make the popcorn. I used to love watching the kernels pop like crazy—the hotter the fire got the faster they popped. Listen to what the Bible says in 2 Timothy 1:6, "For this reason I remind you to fan into flame the gift of God, which is in you."

When you fan a flame, the fire grows bigger. It grows hotter. God is saying, "Fan into flame the gift you've got."

Picture a jar of popping corn. If it stays in the jar, all it will ever be is kernels. Worthless. Bird food. But when we put the kernels in the pan with some oil and we put them on the flame, they turn into something great that we all love to eat when we're sitting around watching a movie. We say, "Yay! Popcorn!"

That's what God says with our lives. When you're willing to take your gift of life from God and fan it into the flame, He says, "Yea! A Christian! Look at him blossom! This is so great! My son is blossoming! You're fanning into flame the gift I've given you."

1: Going All In

Leave it in the jar, and it's worthless—birdseed, and not even useful as birdseed if it always stays in the jar. Man, are we going to be birdseed or are we going to be popcorn?

Are we going to take hold of this life that we've been given and do something with it, or are we just going to waste it? We need to bring the truth of the Gospel to those who need it most.

Who needs it most? It is those to whom God has led you. It doesn't need to be the Umbutu tribe in the deepest tropical jungles. It can be your next door neighbor, your sullen co-worker, or your great-aunt Erma. It is the people God has placed in your path and whispered to your heart, "I need you to bring them the Gospel." All you have to do is reach out and touch someone's life with the love of Christ.

The field is ripe, all ready to harvest, and it is waiting for reapers before it's too late to gather it in. God desires to take hold of your life and do something wonderful with it.

That's what God wants for you.

Every Single Day

If you have ever been on a ministry trip or a mission trip, you know that you put the things of your life off to the side, and you become Mr. or Mrs. Ministry. You're out there and all that matters at that time are the people you are witnessing to, bringing them to the Lord. You do this by sharing with them His great love for them. His sacrifice on the cross for them and His unending mercy to them.

When I went to St. Louis for a week of ministry, we were pulling people over in the streets night and day, 24/7. We were living for the Lord. We were focused and purposed for a week, and then we came back and returned to living our same old lives.

God didn't tell me, "Oh, Jack, you've got to do that every single day of your life. You've got to be this madman for Jesus." But He did say, "I want your heart, every single day of your life, to be like it was when you went on that St. Louis mission trip. I want you thinking about other people. I want your life focused on other people."

There's a movie out called Bully. It's about these kids who have been bullied; there are four different kids whose stories are profiled in the movie.

1: Going All In

One of them was a fifteen-year-old boy who had hung himself. His father said, "This movie had to be made. This movie has to be seen by everybody. Everybody needs to understand what a tragedy bullying is. We can save lives."

Here this poor parent had lost a child and obviously this issue, building awareness about bullying, had become a passion of his life. I thought to myself, Man, I don't want there to have to be a tragedy in my life for me to live a life that matters for God. I'm sure you feel the same way.

Foot Bath

I know someone who is a radical Christian, an on-fire guy for Jesus. About eleven years ago, he sold his landscaping business. Since then, all he has done is minister for the Lord to homeless people in places like Toronto, California, New York, Florida and anywhere else the Lord leads him. He's all about God and he has nothing to call his own but his backpack and clothes.

He's extremely radical for Jesus. He's so radical that he has no place or patience for the church with its politics and denominational differences. We disagree on that and a few things, (his attitude towards the church being the one I find most bothersome), but he definitely lives a totally sold out life for God.

When I look at this guy's life, I have one problem. The problem I have is that he lives his life as if Jesus Christ is coming back tomorrow, and I don't. And he's right about that 100%. Whether his theology is right or wrong, as I said I don't agree with all of it. But one thing I do know for sure is this man is sold out and he has sacrificed his life for Jesus Christ. I admire that. I think that's something that all of God's children need to take a hold of.

But what do we do? How do we get there? How do we make sure that we live a life that matters for God? The key principle is tied into what God was trying to show me when He said that my thoughts and prayers, my focus had been about myself rather than about others. A life that matters for God is a life lived for others.

So important is the principle of loving each other more than ourselves—serving each other and living sacrificially—that Jesus shared with His disciples exactly how we're supposed to do that. Jesus wanted to make sure that there was no confusion in the disciples' hearts, or in our hearts today. If you are a follower of the teachings of Christ, you are a disciple because that's what a disciple is—a follower of a teaching.

Jesus shared this particular principle by washing His disciples' feet. They were at the last supper, and Jesus knew that Judas was soon going to betray Him. Jesus started to wash some of the disciples' feet. That was the worst job that could possibly be had at that time in history. Think of it as cleaning out a septic tank. In those days, people walked barefoot or with dusty sandals. Feet were dirty and they were the worst, smelliest part of the body you could imagine. It was a job always done by servants, and not just any servants—the lowest in the chain of command.

Jesus definitely made a statement by washing the disciples' feet. He went up to Peter who asked, "Lord, are you going to wash my feet?" Jesus replied, "You do not realize now what I am doing, but later you will understand." "No," said Peter, "you shall never wash my feet." (John 13:6-8)

(Commitment In The Christian Life)

Peter was probably thinking, "I should be washing your feet. I know you're the Lord and Savior. This is ridiculous. We can't have the Lord washing people's feet."

Jesus answered and said, "Unless I wash you, you'll have no part of me." Peter, realizing that Jesus was serious said, "Well, in that case, Lord, wash all of me."

Can you imagine Peter hearing Jesus say that and thinking, well if I'm not going to have any part of you unless you wash me, then here. Here are my feet. Wash them both. Wash all of me. Wash my head and hands too. Jesus answered, "Those who have had a bath need only to wash their feet; their whole body is clean." When he had finished washing their feet, he put on his clothes and returned to his place. "Do you understand what I have done for you?" he asked them. "You call me 'Teacher' and 'Lord,' and rightly so, for that is what I am. Now that I, your Lord and Teacher, have washed your feet, you also should wash one another's feet. I have set you an example that you should do as I have done for you." (John 13:10-15)

That's Jesus talking. Jesus, who sacrificed His life for us on the cross so that we could live. Jesus, who said, "Love one another." Jesus, who washed the disciples' feet, was in essence saying, "Don't ever come and stand before me, before the throne of God and say that God didn't tell you what to do…not after the example I set. You can't say that anymore. You know how you are supposed to treat other people—just the way that I did, by taking the humble seat, by doing the humblest and lowliest jobs." In addition, we believers today have no excuse, because we now have God's Word and His

1: Going All In

Holy Spirit telling us specifically that we are to love others and live a life of sacrifice.

Jesus came and told us exactly what to do, how to live a life that truly matters. Go and wash people's feet. Go and do likewise and you'll be blessed.

He says that's how you invest in the kingdom of God. He'll reward you thirty, sixty, a hundredfold. Do we believe that God will pay off on His promises? If we did, we should be and would be living like it.

I Know A Real Apostle

My radical, sold out, modern-day apostle acquaintance wrote me a letter a few years ago, and his words inspired me. Here's a portion of the letter:

The only way to fully overcome the flesh is to get such a tremendous revelation of God that we are changed by the revelation. This is saying that holiness comes not by way of our trying to be holy but by our coming to know the holy one Himself. This is why it's so important we get our eyes off of ourselves, off of our sin, our sickness, or whatever and fix them on God. The light of the Glory of God is seen in the face of Jesus Christ, and this is most often revealed to us in the midst of our greatest trials, yes even our greatest failures. Sometimes we have a preoccupation with trying to get free from the things that beset rather than just resting in what God has already accomplished for us in Christ. A lot of people are missing it. They are missing Him.

My personal experience these days is that every circumstance I find myself in, whether good or bad,

1: Going All In

from a natural perspective, seems to be orchestrated by God that I might see God in it and thereby get to know Him better. Yes, it's all designed as part of the eternal plan, God's plan, for me to see the face of Jesus Christ, which is about getting to know God's character and His nature, even about getting to know His ways and purposes.

Oh, that we might soon come to know Him in the power of His resurrection life by overcoming our carnal perspective on things. Whatever it is that you and I are now going through, we must see it all as an opportunity to get to know God better. He simply wants to meet with us in the midst of what we are going through, whatever that may be. He wants us to see His face in it. I hope that what I have shared on this inspires you to look up that you might see God in all your trials and tests, tribulations and temptations. Beloved, we're given an opportunity to advance in our knowing of God in all of these things. It's all intended for us to see Him and in that way fall deeper and deeper in love with Him and in that way come to know true freedom.

Man, I'm motivated by that! I've watched this guy live his life for Christ—sell everything and go share God wherever the Holy Spirit led him. He's got the courage to do something I haven't done. Chuck it all and follow Jesus.

Jesus said, "Whoever wants to be my disciple must deny themselves and take up their cross and follow me." (Matthew 16:24)

(Commitment In The Christian Life)

He has done that with his life. He's sold out to the Lord 100%. I often look at him and say, "God, I'm falling short." Oh, I can use the excuse, "Well, Lord, you've wired me this way. You've given me business talents, and this talent, and that talent, so I'll just keep one foot in the world and one foot with you, Lord, and that's okay, right?"

Well, it seems to be okay most of the time...until I look at someone who's 100% sold out for Christ, who has truly forsaken all to follow the Lord. Then I see how far short I fall from what God wants of me. I'm reminded that my righteousness is but filthy rags before the Lord, and it makes me even more grateful for the saving grace of Jesus Christ and His righteousness in which I am fully clothed.

Jesus said, "Be holy because I am holy." (1 Peter 1:16) We are to imitate Jesus, to just try as hard as we can to walk and live our lives fashioned after Jesus. It's not about perfection. It's about progress.

Doing Good

Jesus died to purify us so that we would be His people, eager to do what is good. What's good in God's eyes?

Remember, "For we are God's handiwork, created in Christ Jesus to do good works, which God prepared in advance for us to do." (Ephesians 2:10)

Jesus said he came to serve and we should do likewise. Doing good and sharing with others, according to God's word, is a sacrifice pleasing to God (Hebrews 13:16).

"This is a trustworthy saying. And I want you to stress these things, so that those who have trusted in God may be careful to devote themselves to doing what is good. These things are excellent and profitable for everyone." (Titus 3:8)

Those who trust in God must be careful to devote themselves to doing what is good; if you're not careful, you won't devote yourself to doing what is good. You'll devote yourself to living selfishly for the things that you want, that you think are important, and you'll miss the full blessing of Jesus Christ. It's so easy to live for the things that we see and feel around us and then wake up one day realizing that our life has been wasted in pursuit of material things to the neglect of the things that last forever.

(Commitment In The Christian Life)

Don't let that happen to you. Be careful to devote yourself to following Jesus and doing what is good—making your life a living sacrifice, or you'll miss it. And that's not what God wants. God's word couldn't be any clearer than Philippians 2:3-8:

> *Do nothing out of selfish ambition or vain conceit. Rather, in humility value others above yourselves, not looking to your own interests but each of you to the interests of the others. In your relationships with one another, have the same mindset as Christ Jesus: Who, being in very nature God, did not consider equality with God something to be used to His own advantage; rather, He made himself nothing by taking the very nature of a servant, being made in human likeness. And being found in appearance as a man, He humbled himself by becoming obedient to death—even death on a cross.*

Could God be any clearer? I don't think so!

Ephesians 3:18-21 reads,

> *May we have power, together with all the Lord's holy people, to grasp how wide and long and high and deep is the love of Christ, and to know this love that surpasses knowledge—that you may be filled to the measure of all the fullness of God. Now to Him who is able to do immeasurably more than all we ask or imagine, according to his power that is at work within us, to Him be glory in the church and in Christ Jesus throughout all generations, for ever and ever.*

1: Going All In

It's God's power at work within us—His power. We can't do it on our own, but God has promised us today that He will work through us and enable us to do what He has called us to do: "But the Lord is faithful, and He will strengthen you and protect you from the evil one." (2 Thessalonians 3:3)

And my prayer to God is that of 2 Thessalonians 2:16

> *May our Lord Jesus Christ himself and God our Father, who loved us and by his grace gave us eternal encouragement and good hope, encourage your hearts and strengthen you in every good deed and word.*

Just offer your life over to God. Let Him have full control; only then will you understand that His grace alone is sufficient. Only He can enable you to do good.

Return on Investment

When we make an investment, we expect to get something back in return. When we put our money in the bank, we expect to get a certain amount of interest. When we invest in a stock or a business, we hope to get a return on the initial investment. The unknown variable in the stock market or in a business is usually how much that return will be, but if we have invested, we obviously thought it was a good investment at the time or we would not have bothered.

On that same train of thought, I think about God; when Jesus died on the cross, He invested everything He had in you and me. And God must be looking at it and saying, "Okay, I hope I get a good return on my investment." He would have done it anyway. He died for that thief on the cross as much as He died for someone who lives his entire life for Him, but I'm sure He loves to see the return on the investment He has made. That concept goes hand in hand with the parable of the talents. (Matthew 25:14-30)

God has been encouraging me to take a look at my own life and see what I can do to give not just a better return on

1: Going All In

His investment, but on mine as well. It's a spiritual law, a real parallel that the more we bless God with our obedience, the more God blesses us.

When we invest our life in God, we get an abundant return on our investment—thirty, sixty, or a hundredfold—as the Word of God tells us. We can expect a major return in this life and infinitely more in the life to come.

You've got to run the race to win the prize. And the prize is awesome—abundant joy and purpose here and now and an eternity of things so wonderful. God's Word says, "Eye has not seen, nor has ear heard, neither has it entered into the hearts of men, the things God has prepared for those who love Him." (1 Corinthians 2:9) So amazing we can't even imagine it. It's beyond our comprehension.

"...for those who love Him." We must love Him, and if we love Him we will follow Him, serve Him, and obey Him. The return you get on that comparatively small investment is an eternity of joy and peace and wonders in heaven. If you let Him get the best return on the investment He has made in you, He will make sure the return you get is greater than anything you could ask or hope for.

How can you know for sure? There's only one way to find out. Run the race to win the prize.

Encouragement from a Renegade

I sold my TV production business in 2002. Before I made that final decision to sell my company, I met a guy that my pastor wanted to introduce me to—a friend of his from Laurel, Mississippi. I liked him right away. He's just one of those guys where you see the love of God in his heart. He and his wife came in and he told me his story.

Richard had a big sign business in Mississippi, and he was bought out; he had sold his business to go into ministry. He had been a wild drug addict, a renegade pilot raiding foreign countries' treasures, a motorcycle guy and a man with no concern for others or life. However, God got ahold of him one day as he was plunging his plane straight down to commit suicide, and God said, "I'm not done with you yet." Richard's life changed that day as he came to personally know God and God's love for him. He has been sold out to Jesus ever since. If you want to read more about Richard's changed life, Google Richard Headrick and read some of his books! They will inspire you!

At the end of our conversation that day in my office, Richard

1: Going All In

said to me, "Jack, God has your life in the palm of His hand." He showed me the palm of his hand where he had written my name, Jack, before he came into the office.

I think I have only seen Richard three times. That day, another time he visited my wife and me in our home, and I think I've seen him one other time in the eight years since I met him. Yet he's had such an impact on my life. When he came in that day, I made the decision to go into ministry, and I sold the business. I've never told him the impact he had on my life that particular day. If I talk to him once every two years, it's a lot. And yet, how's that for impact? A guy I've met a couple of times who's closer to me as a kindred spirit in the Lord than many people I see all the time. It's a deep connection.

I got a letter in the mail from him recently. It included a DVD of a speech he gave in Kansas City to theological seminary students. I watched the DVD, and I started crying because through his speech, God made me realize that we forget the impact that we have on people. This is an excerpt from his speech:

> *Man, do something for Jesus. Get out there and make business for him...Stand firm. Defend your faith. Never compromise it. Never quit. Ephesians 6:19 says that the freedom of speech may be given to me that I may open my mouth boldly and make known the mystery of the gospel. That is the purpose. Our mission—our mission—is to preach the gospel of Jesus Christ from the pulpit, on the streets, and in our homes...*

(Commitment In The Christian Life)

I have a friend who lives in Boca Raton, Florida. His name is Jack Levine. Jack Levine had a very successful TV production company. He was making lots of money. One day, he got a phone call from God. He said, "Yeah God, what do you want?"

[God] said, "I want you to quit and become a preacher boy." "Alright, what do I do next?"

He said, "Sell your business and start preaching."

Jack said, "Done deal."

Jack is now preaching. One of the happiest men I know is Jack Levine. If you'd like to have a born again Jew really turn your people on, get Jack. You think I'm excited? That boy's excited about Jesus.

But then years and years ago when I was not a Christian I had dealings in and out with the mafia down in New Orleans, Louisiana, and one morning I had to meet a guy at a warehouse in New Orleans east. I got there a little bit early, and I got in that warehouse looking at all these "toys." He had Mercedes, and he had the Bentleys, and he had all these cars that rich men buy to satisfy that inner longing in their heart. I had been there a little while, and Bob came in, and he opened that door, and I said, "Bob, you've got to be the happiest person on planet earth."

The boy's countenance just fell, and he said, "No, Richard. I'm probably the most miserable person you know."

1: Going All In

I said, "Bob, what's the deal?"

He said, "When I was a young, man, God called me to be a preacher boy."

And he said, "I was so excited about it, I could hardly wait to leave my school and go over to my fiancée's house and tell her that I was going to get to be a preacher, and she was going to get to be a preacher's wife. I got there, I walked in, I said, 'Sally, I'm going to be a preacher boy, and you're going to get to be a preacher's wife.'"

He said, "Richard, her countenance changed, and she said, 'Let me tell you something, Bob. I'm not going to be a preacher's wife because I don't want to be poor all my life. I want to wear nice clothes. I want to have a nice car. I want to have money. I want to have a nice house. I want to go places. I want to do things. I want to be somebody. Let me tell you something. You can either have me, or you can have that God of yours, but you can't have both.'"

The next day, Bob went on back to school, and some of his friends there said, "Well Bob, what's Sally think about being a preacher's wife?"

He said, "Well, we kind of talked about it, and I'm going to stay in my studies here, and I'm going to go ahead and make a lot of money, and I'm going to buy Sally a nice car. I'm going to buy her a nice house. I'm going to buy her fine clothes. We're going to go places and do things, and we're going to be somebody."

(Commitment In The Christian Life)

He said, "Richard, I did just that, and I've been miserable ever since."

Don't you ever let anyone take the privilege of what God has called you to do for him away from you. You hear me? Don't you ever let anyone take the privilege of what God has called you to do for him away from you.

The point is, what does it profit a man to gain the whole world if he forfeits his soul?

We don't know the impact we have on people, and here's Richard speaking to however many thousands of students, sharing a story I didn't know he was going to tell, and that's just a wonderful thing. I cried when I heard that because I had been selling God short a little bit. I had been discouraged because of my perceived "batting average" of what, if anything, I had been accomplishing for God.

God is using you and sometimes you get a glimpse of it. You may never get a glimpse of it until you get to heaven, and then you will get not just a glimpse but a total panoramic view of it. Whether you're a pilot, a preacher, a fireman, a teacher, a principal, a student, a wife, a worker, it doesn't matter. God is using you wherever you are, and the impact that you have on people can be phenomenal. Don't get discouraged.

Don't Miss It

My home church recently bid farewell to a dear member who went on to his home in heaven and I am certain an awesome reward—Mel Stewart. Mel was a common man by the world's standards, but he was an uncommon man by God's standards. Mel truly lived a sold out life for Jesus Christ. There's not one doubt in the minds of any who knew him that when Mel Stewart got to heaven, he heard, "Well done, good and faithful servant. Come and share your master's happiness."

It should be common for every single believer to live a life just like Mel did. Sold out to Jesus in every way, talking about Jesus, sharing Jesus, living Jesus, loving Jesus.

Due to an illness later in life, Mel walked with crutches and he always said that they were a blessing to him. Because of his crutches people would talk to him more readily. That allowed him to talk to more people about Jesus. He said that's the uncommon life that God wants us to live, and that's where the blessings and the true treasure in Jesus lay. Those of us who knew Mel saw it in his life and in his face, and everybody should be able to see it in us. That's what we need to aspire to, that kind of love and compassion for Jesus.

(Commitment In The Christian Life)

Paul says in Hebrews 2:1, "We must pay the most careful attention, therefore, to what we have heard, so that we do not drift away." Your enemy the devil is out prowling around like a lion seeking to devour you. He's seeking to sift you like wheat. He's seeking to destroy your life, your marriage, your family, everything he can just by distracting you. He wants to take your focus off of God and put it back on the world so you miss the blessings that God has in store for your life.

Mel Stewart didn't miss it. I don't want to miss it, and I hope and pray that your desire is not to want to miss it today. So when God says we must pay the most careful attention to what we've heard so we do not drift away, pay attention. If the bridge is out and the sign says the bridge is out, it would be a good idea to pay attention to that sign so we don't crash and die. Let's listen to God.

Pouring Out Perfume

Not long before Jesus was crucified, he journeyed to Bethany. He was eating dinner at the house of Simon the leper, and a woman came in with an alabaster jar of perfume. She bent down at Jesus' feet and started to anoint His feet with this oil, this expensive perfume.

The people who were having dinner at the house immediately started to grumble. They said, "Oh, this isn't good. This perfume should be sold and the money given to the poor. This woman is wasting it. This is ridiculous. She's taking this valuable perfume, and putting it on Jesus' feet. This is crazy." Jesus' response knocks all their lofty, self-righteous thoughts to the ground, as He says in Mark 14:6-8, "Leave her alone. Why are you bothering her? She has done a beautiful thing to me. The poor you will always have with you, and you can help them any time you want. But you will not always have me. She did what she could."

Jesus goes on to say later in the verse, "She poured perfume on my body beforehand to prepare for my burial. Truly I tell you, wherever the gospel is preached throughout the world, what she has done will also be told, in memory of her." (Mark 14:8-9)

(Commitment In The Christian Life)

That woman's heart, her mind, her spirit, her soul, her body, every ounce of her was focused on what she could do for Jesus Christ. She took all she had, everything of value, and she laid it on Jesus' feet. Everything she had, she laid on Jesus' feet. She did what she could for Jesus.

I'm telling you, we better be able to say that same thing to God when we get to heaven on judgment day. If we want to hear, "Well done, good and faithful servant. Come and share your master's happiness," (Matthew 25:21) we need to be able to look God in the eye and say, "I did what I could."

Again, it's the parable of the talents. We want to answer, when He returns to ask what we did with what He gave us, "Whatever you gave me I did the best I could—wherever you put me."

We talk glowingly about Alexander Graham Bell, Albert Einstein, The Wright Brothers, John F. Kennedy, Babe Ruth, and a host of other people who have died, who we know for their accomplishments. Their accomplishments are living on long after they've gone away. Jesus said about the woman who poured perfume on His feet, that what she did through her faith and love, wherever the gospel is preached her story will be told and will live on.

I believe that God wants to say the same thing to you and me, just like Hebrews 11, the Hall of Fame of Faith. God is writing our record books now, and if we're obedient and faithful, we'll have that same thing said about us. "They did what they could." Wherever the gospel is preached you can rest assured Jesus is going to be proud of you for the faith and love you showed Him, the trust and the confidence that, "Yes,

1: Going All In

Jesus you are God. I believe in you although I haven't seen you," I'm going to live that way because I love you and trust you.

Eye on the Prize

The Bible says that He must increase and we must decrease. We're to die to ourselves and live for Christ. It's easier said than done. But the blessing, the crown, the reward from God is for that. That's what it takes. There is a prize to be won, and not everybody is going to get that prize. The apostle Paul tells us to live our lives as if we're running the race for Jesus Christ.

I ran into a buddy of mine recently. He has a drinking problem. He's had it for a while so I said, "You should go into rehab, man. You'll learn why you drink, and you'll learn about yourself, and it will be a great thing." Before this time, he had a good run, about six months of being clean but he was back drinking again. He got angry at me for bringing up rehab and said, "You're not going to sell me rehab! Just stop talking. I don't want to hear about it. You're not going to sell me on that."

I said, "Good luck. I love you no matter what you do. We've been friends for a while, but here's the thing that's going to help you (rehab), and you're resisting it."

His logic was, "You know how many people don't succeed in rehab?"

1: Going All In

I said, "Well yeah, probably at least a third. I know I've sent fifteen guys there and only ten of them made it and the other five haven't."

And he replied, "See, see? Thirty percent don't make it."

I said, "Yeah, but you just need one guy to make it. You just need you to make it."

He didn't want any part of the one thing that could help him.

Not everybody will get the prize. Not everyone is serious enough about it to run for it. But if you want the prize, then don't fool around. Be serious about it. Keep your eyes upon the goal and the prize as you run, and you will win. You will live a life that matters for God!

2

THE FATHER AND HIS CHILDREN
(How God Relates To Us As A Father)

The Empty Home

Back in 2011 I was feeling sorry for God. That might sound like a crazy statement. You have to wonder, how could I feel sorry God? He's the creator of the world. He has everything He could want. He created everything.

Well, at first I was feeling sorry for myself. And then I began to feel sorry for God.

My wife and kids had gone away for a week. Normally that's not a bad thing. I would typically enjoy some quiet time and make the most of it—spend some quality time with God, study, and work. But this particular week, I don't know why, I missed them very, very much. It's not uncommon for my wife to go visit her mother up in Syracuse for a week and take the kids. But, man, I couldn't put my finger on what the problem was. I just know I was feeling sad, lonely, depressed, and upset, and I missed them immensely from the day they left.

And I thought, wow, this is how God must feel about his children who are far from Him! I know how much I love my family and how much I just want to be around them and be with them.

It's not that we spend every moment together dancing in the moonlight and having fun, but we're a family. We're there.

2: The Father And His Children

We're together. Honestly, that week, I realized what it was like when people get depressed. I'm a very happy guy overall, but I was sitting there and could totally understand the concept of how somebody could just get depressed and bummed out and how life could seem not worthwhile, not worth living. I was definitely not suicidal, mind you. I was just sitting there going, "You know what? This stinks. This is terrible."

I was thinking how my life without them would be terrible. It would just be empty and lacking so much joy. God gave me that little glimpse for those few days. And now that it's over, I'm glad for that time.

I knew they were coming back. That's what I believed, and fortunately they did, and I was very grateful for that. But while they were gone, I just sat there and thought, "Man, this feels so empty." I began to imagine how God must feel when we're far from Him and separated from Him.

I believe that God's greatest joy is a relationship with His children—with us. That's what God wants. It shouldn't take a special day to draw near to Him. It shouldn't take Easter or Christmas or Thanksgiving for us to "get in the spirit or to give thanks to God for or blessings." It should be each and every single day of our lives. I think sometimes we take for granted this wonderful gift of life that we've been given.

The Face in the Crowd

One summer, my wife and I put our two younger kids in Vacation Bible School (VBS) camp. They had their presentation one Thursday night and it was great. It was called Saddle Ranch and had a cowboy theme. About 150 kids were up there on the stage singing these Saddle Ranch songs. And, just like what happens at little league games—I only saw my kids, Jackson and Talia. Those were the only two faces I was watching.

I was watching them and totally loving it, seeing their huge smiles up on stage. I was so happy, thinking, "This is so great," when all of a sudden, God really put it on my heart that, wait a minute, I need to look at the other kids at least once.

So, I did. I specifically made it a point to look at the faces of those beautiful children. It just came to me how much their mothers and fathers love them—as much as I love my own children—and how beautiful and special each child was in the eyes of his parents.

Even more so, I started thinking how much each child is beautiful in the eyes of God. That night, God took me one step further. He said, "Now, I want you to look around at the adults. Take a look at the crowd."

2: The Father And His Children

There were men and woman, black people and white people, big and small, fat and skinny people, some guys with a lot of hair and some with no hair, guys with bellies and guys with no bellies. I'm looking around and suddenly I'm seeing the beauty in God's eye of every single person there.

I began to see how important it is that when we look at people, we see how beautiful they are to God. We cannot just look at our own kids who we love so much, but also we need to see how the people we come into contact with are so beautiful to God. That's why Jesus died on the cross. We need to focus on people as individuals, each one beloved of God, and created for a unique purpose by Him.

What's the Problem?

The psalmist David said, in Psalm 9:10, "...for you, Lord, have never forsaken those who seek you."

Never. Not once in a while, not even when you've done something wrong. God has never forsaken you. Never. He will never forsake those who seek Him.

Let me ask you a question. If that's the case, if God has promised that He'll never forsake those who seek Him, and we seek Him and we believe Him, then what problem could we possibly have? God said He's never going to forsake us.

We know the Lord. We know who He is. We trust in Him. So where is the problem? To me, it would seem like hallelujah time. I've felt that way since 1991 when I came to know Jesus Christ. It's hallelujah time. It's the most amazing thing ever. It's better than winning the lotto, it's the jackpot. It's a homerun. It's winning the World Series. It's the greatest thing that I could ever want. It should be the greatest thing for you.

We should trust in God always—not just when it's convenient, not just when things go our way. If we made the decision to trust the Lord, we know that He is never going to leave or forsake us. He is with us always! So what's the problem?

2: The Father And His Children

In Isaiah 52:10 we read, "The Lord will lay bare his holy arm in the sight of all the nations, and all the ends of the earth will see the salvation of our God." God will reveal Himself. Everybody will see the salvation of our God. The difference for us today is that we get to see a glimpse of it now. We have the salvation of God through the sacrifice of His Son. So we get to walk through our earthly lives with God's Holy Spirit living inside of us. So what's our problem? What are we complaining about? Holy cow, what an unbelievable promise, and that's what all our hope is in.

Isaiah 53:5 says,

> *But he was pierced for our transgressions, he was crushed for our iniquities; the punishment that brought us peace was upon him, and by his wounds we are healed.*

We're healed, man.

If you were to go into a hospital and tell all the people who are suffering, sick, and dying that they are all healed, they would parade with joy New Orleans style dancing and singing, "When the saints come marching in!" They'd be the happiest people in the world. And they wouldn't stop dancing in a half hour. No, they'd be happy for the rest of their lives. "It's a miracle! We've been saved!"

What about us? We should be happy each and every moment because the punishment that brought us peace was upon Him. We should have taken the punishment, but instead, we have peace. That's what God brought us. Shouldn't we show and reflect that peace a little more often in our lives?

(How God Relates To Us As A Father)

That's why Jesus died on the cross. He crushed Satan's head. We have victory over death. We have the peace of God inside of us. By His wounds we are healed.

Isaiah 53:11 says, "By his knowledge my righteous servant will justify many, and he will bear their iniquities."

Do you have knowledge of God? Jesus has borne our iniquities—mine and yours. He has taken our sin on the cross. The guilt of sin should no longer be in the believer of Jesus Christ. You're free. "All whom the Son sets free are free." (John 8:36) Why would we be living like we're prisoners?

I asked myself a question, and I believe God wants to ask you this same question. I asked, "Jack, is God bearing my iniquities?"

The answer is yes, of course. So I said to myself, "Then what's my problem?" Man, I have no problems! God is bearing my iniquities.

Hosea 6:3 says, "Let us acknowledge the Lord; let us press on to acknowledge him..."

How do you acknowledge the Lord? When the Queen of England comes, I'll bet everybody here knows how to acknowledge her. You would bow or curtsy for the queen. When the president of the United States comes, we know how to acknowledge him. We play "Hail to the Chief" and salute. When Bruce Springsteen comes on stage, his fans know how to acknowledge him. We all yell, "Bruuuuuuuuuuuce!" When the Miami Dolphins play defense, we scream, "Defense!"

But we don't know how to acknowledge our God. Man, we should be cheering and screaming for Jesus, and we should be living a life that acknowledges Him. The rest of the verse reads:

2: The Father And His Children

"As surely as the sun rises, he will appear; he will come to us like the winter rains, like the spring rains that water the earth."

God goes on to say in verse 6: "For I desire mercy, not sacrifice, and acknowledgment of God rather than burnt offerings." Mercy, not sacrifice. He desires acknowledgment of God rather than burnt offerings. He wants a relationship with you.

Acknowledgment to God is, "God, you're my Father." That's the acknowledgment He wants. "God, you died on the cross for my sins." That's the acknowledgment He wants. "God, I love you." That's the acknowledgment He wants and a life that reflects that gratitude of what He's done. That's how you acknowledge God. It's not a secret.

Hosea 6:7, says, "Like Adam, they have broken the covenant—they were unfaithful to me there."

Have you broken that covenant with God? Have you been unfaithful in that regard? God has asked you to acknowledge Him. As a believer, have you been unfaithful to God in that way?

"Woe to them, because they have strayed from me! Destruction to them, because they have rebelled against me! I long to redeem them but they speak lies against me." (Hosea 7:13)

If you have not acknowledged God, if you're not where you need to be with God, hear what He says. God says, "I long to redeem them." It's the desire of God's heart to bring you right back to the forefront of your father/son relationship with Him, just like the prodigal son.

Here is His sad accusation to Israel. Is it His accusation to us as well? "They do not cry out to me from their hearts but

(How God Relates To Us As A Father)

wail upon their beds. They gather together for grain and new wine but turn away from me." (Hosea 7:14)

Two things: cry out to God from your heart and turn towards Him.

You want God to bring you right back to where you want to be? You want to be repositioned and returned to your right inheritance in God? You want to be sitting there as God's kid and feel the love and electricity flow between you and God again like it did when you first got saved?

Just cry out from your heart and turn towards God.

Interrupted Blessings

When my oldest son, who I love with all my heart, was twenty-two years old he did some stupid stuff. I tell you this with his permission. He said to me, "Dad, if there's anything you can do to help somebody else, share my story." Here's a brief version of that story.

In a drug and alcohol-induced binge, he put a shopping cart through a store window at 2 o'clock in the morning. The cops caught him right away, threw him in jail for thirty days, gave him three years drug-offender probation, and confiscated his car—which was a $14,000 Hyundai that his mother and I had given him on his twenty-first birthday.

So, he went from living in his own apartment, with his own car, and having a great job in restaurant management, to being in jail, having his car confiscated, losing his job and his apartment. A year after that, he's at a halfway house and he's doing great. I think part of that is because he had to; he was on probation. I hope it's also because he wanted to.

But you know what I thinking? The last thing I would do at that time was give him a nickel. That changed down the road, but at that time that was how I felt and I wasn't budging. I loved him so much, but I wouldn't even consider buying him a scooter. He walked to work or rode a bicycle.

Everything he made at work, he had to give to the halfway house so that he could live there. He got by, but he didn't have an extra nickel. And I'm glad about that. I'm thinking, "Every day of your life, buddy boy, I hope you remember what you had and what it was like when you lost everything. So next time, when you get your freedom, when you're off probation, and you're sitting there thinking about whether you should do drugs or not, drink or not, I hope you remember this."

I love him so much, believe me, I'd love to buy him a scooter. I'd love to buy him another car, but I didn't then because I knew it's was not in his best interest, until he got his life together for real. He had interrupted the blessings that his mother and I had for him. The only way I could bless him then was to give him some food to take home with him, but we wouldn't do much more than that.

I had a lot more blessings I wanted to give him, but by his disobedience and actions, he interrupted those. He never interrupted my love for him. I loved him then as much as I ever did. He could murder someone, and I'd still love him. There's nothing he could do to remove that love, and that's the great news for you. There's nothing you can do to remove God's love from you, but you can interrupt the blessings by being disobedient.

Jump!

In the summertime, there's one place every kid wants to be—at the pool. The cool water, the games, the splashing around; it's just so much fun. Parents love it too because their kids use up a good amount of their seemingly endless energy in the water rather than running circles in the living room wearing out the carpet.

It's adorable to watch small children jumping into the water, holding tightly to their daddy's hands as their feet leave the pavement and hit the water. For some children, that's their favorite part of swimming. They'll grab Daddy's hand, as he stands in the water, jump in, get right back out and do it all over again. Not every kid. I remember sitting by the pool side, watching my own kids splash around in the water, and then seeing a father try to persuade his little boy to jump in the water.

"Come on, son. It's so much fun! I'll catch you. Just hold on to my hands and jump." The boy was not easily convinced. I don't know if it was fear of the water, or fear of jumping, but he refused to trust that if his daddy said it was okay, he'd be safe and everything would turn out alright.

(How God Relates To Us As A Father)

That little boy's fears kept him from enjoying what otherwise could have been a wonderful, joyous time. Do we allow our fears, our lack of trust in God, to keep us from all that He has for us?

Wrong Turn

Solomon was king of Israel—David's son, the king. He was a great king, very smart and wise. He had a lot of money and did a lot of good, but at the end he did something that God had specifically warned him not to. He had many different wives from many different places. As a matter of fact, in 1 Kings 11:2 God said of some of these places, "You must not intermarry with them, because they will surely turn your hearts after their gods."

But what did he do? The rest of the verse tells us, "Nevertheless, Solomon held fast to them in love."

The Bible says in 1 Kings 11:6, "So Solomon did evil in the eyes of the Lord; he did not follow the Lord completely, as David his father had done."

Already, God is a little aggravated that Solomon didn't follow Him completely.

God is saying, "Look, it's not okay to just follow me a little bit of the way. You have to follow me completely. You have to follow all the directions."

If I give you directions to my house and you follow all of them perfectly except one, you're not going to get to my house.

(How God Relates To Us As A Father)

If my directions were to take a left out of the driveway and head west, and instead you take a right out of the driveway and head east, even if you follow the directions perfectly after that, you're still lost. You take one wrong turn and you're lost. You need to follow directions completely.

God became angry with Solomon, and in 1 Kings 11:11-12,

> *The Lord said to Solomon, "Since this is your attitude and you have not kept my covenant and my decrees, which I commanded you, I will most certainly tear the kingdom away from you and give it to one of your subordinates. Nevertheless, for the sake of David your father, I will not do it during your lifetime."*

In the Old Testament days before Jesus, God would speak to people through prophets. They heard the word of God and they would speak to people directly.

In 1 Kings 11:31 God speaking through Ahijah the prophet says He is going to tear the kingdom away from Solomon and give Jeroboam ten of it's tribes.

God continues on saying:

"But for the sake of my servant David and the city of Jerusalem, which I have chosen out of all the tribes of Israel, he will have one tribe. I will do this because they have forsaken me and worshiped Ashtoreth the goddess of the Sidonians, Chemosh the god of the Moabites, and Molech the god of the Ammonites, and have not walked in my ways, nor done what is right in my eyes, nor kept my statutes and laws as David, Solomon's father, did." (1 Kings 11:32-33)

2: The Father And His Children

I want you to understand this about the effect we can have on our kids and the generations to come and the blessings they do or do not have.

God says in verse 34:

> *But I will not take the whole kingdom out of Solomon's hand; I have made him ruler all the days of his life for the sake of David my servant, whom I chose and who observed my commands and statutes.*

God was going to take everything from Solomon, but He said, "You know what? Because of what David did I'm not going to take it all."

Our actions have an effect on generations to come. Our obedience—or lack of it—affects our kids and their kids, and we need to factor that into the decisions we make.

Now, yeah, they can blow their own blessings or earn their own blessings, absolutely. But think about it. Solomon had all the blessings from David. He was David's son, and he had all the blessings. But he didn't obey, and God had to take some of them away. It was God's intent, however, to bless David's family based on David's obedience.

It's God's intent to bless us and our families based on our obedience as well.

Ask for Directions

God is speaking directly through the prophet Ahijah to Jeroboam, promising him the kingdom of Israel in 1 Kings 11:37-38:

As for you, I will take you, and you will rule over all that your heart desires; you will be king over Israel. If you do whatever I command you and walk in my ways and do what is right in my eyes by keeping my statutes and commands, as David my servant did, I will be with you. I will build you a dynasty as enduring as the one I built for David and will give Israel to you.

I believe that God promises the same thing to each and every believer today. God promises that if we will walk in His ways, if we will obey His command, if we will hear His voice, if we will seek His heart, we will get to heaven and we will hear, "Well done, good and faithful servant. Come and share in your master's happiness."

I also believe that if we don't do that, if we're disobedient to God, then we will still be welcomed into heaven based on

2: The Father And His Children

our acceptance of God and our salvation. We're saved, after all. But am I going to be welcomed in like Solomon—who disobeyed God in the latter part of his life on earth—or am I going to be welcomed in like David—who stayed true to the end of his life?

I believe that's a choice that you and I can make of how we're going to live and what we're going to do, whether or not we are going to live a life that matters for God.

Jeroboam obtains ten of the tribes of Israel when he becomes king after Solomon, according to God's promise. You would think he'd be happy. "Hey, I just got these ten tribes. One day I had none. Now, I have ten. I was a servant exiled. Now I'm king. This is a great deal."

But instead, he's scared.

What is he scared about? He is scared that the people would rather follow Solomon's son, Rehoboam, than him. He thinks to himself in 1 Kings 12:27:

> *If these people go up to offer sacrifices at the temple of the Lord in Jerusalem, they will again give their allegiance to their lord, Rehoboam king of Judah. They will kill me and return to King Rehoboam.*

He's scared. You might have faced this sometime in your life, where there are some people who like you and some people who don't. One of your buddies happens to have a friendship with the people who don't like you, and your concern is, "Oh man, they're going to say bad stuff about me. My buddy is going to get polluted by them. I have to keep my buddy away from them."

(How God Relates To Us As A Father)

That's exactly what's happening. King Jeroboam thought, "Look, I can't let the people go back to worship even though that is what God is telling them to do, so here's what I'm going to do. I'm going to set up a worship for them right here, right by me, so they don't have to go too far. And just to make sure it's safe I'm going to set one up on the north end of the city and one up on the south end of the city. So, either way they want to go, they'll have a place to worship, and that will be great." That's what he does, and he tells the people, "Here's your new place of worship."

Jeroboam was paranoid. He didn't trust God. Here God—through the prophet—had told him, "You're going to be king over these ten tribes." It came true. He was. And now he doesn't trust God?

Do we do that in our life? Does God deliver us, or come through on something in our life and go, "Wow, this is awesome! You're amazing! This is terrific!" and then we don't trust Him with the very next thing? It's almost like we're saying, "Well God, you must've used all your power on this one, so I better take control and do everything else." God probably looks at us in disbelief.

Sometimes we look at our kids and think, "How stupid can you be? What part of 'I love you and I'm doing everything for you and I'm not lying to you and I have your best interest at heart' don't you understand?" And they just look at you defiantly and then go do what they want to do.

That's what was happening in this passage. We need to make sure that we see into our own life because it definitely happens to us is well.

2: The Father And His Children

First Kings 12:28-29 says:

> *After seeking advice, the king made two golden calves. He said to the people, "It is too much for you to go up to Jerusalem. Here are your gods, O Israel, who brought you up out of Egypt." One he set up in Bethel, and the other in Dan.*

Who did Jeroboam seek advice from? Whoever it was gave him bad advice. It certainly wasn't God. Who are you listening to in your life? Who is giving you advice? We need to be listening to God. God will give you all the advice you want if you just ask Him and talk to Him.

Jeroboam took it upon himself to change God's word and instruction for his own good—for his own means, his own gain, his own pride, his own kingdom. And God can never honor that. God can never bless that. We take the word of God and we pollute it and pervert it and change it for our own justification and means, and we think, "It's okay. God loves me." You're right, God does love you. And there's nothing you could do to make God love you any less, but you know what? God wants to bless you.

Is there something in your life that you know you're not doing right with God? You know it. It's not even a question mark. It's not gray. You know. And God is trying to show you, "Look, that doesn't fly." He wants to give you that opportunity to turn it around.

The Reptile Store

God wants you to be blessed because you're His child. I know that because I have children and the desire of my heart and my wife's heart is to bless our children.

One day my wife, Beth, had gone out of her way to make a very special day for my son Jackson who was ten at the time. My daughter Talia, who was eight, and I had a father-daughter day planned and we were off to lunch and a movie. So Beth took Jackson to the reptile store. Jackson loves reptiles. He loves lizards and snakes and everything. For him it's a dream come true. She spent two hours with him in the reptile store, and she made sure the staff let him hold every animal and every reptile. She went out of her way to make sure that he would have such a great day.

They came home that night and I asked Jackson, "So how was it? How did you enjoy yourself?"

He said, "Oh, I thought it would be better."

Here's this ten-year-old kid: so ungrateful, not recognizing the sacrifice and effort his mother had made on his behalf to make sure he would have a great time and be excited and enjoy something. He just took her efforts for granted.

2: The Father And His Children

We do that with God sometimes.

My wife came to me crying. She said, "I can't believe it. I spent this whole day for him so he would be joyful and he says, 'I thought it would be better.'"

What to do? It was a ten-year-old boy's comment. It was just a thoughtless comment that came out of his mouth too quickly. When I asked him again about it later, of course he said how great the day was. We look at God the same way sometimes. We take God for granted. We forget to thank Him and to be grateful. We act as if we're entitled to this wonderful life, as if we're entitled to these blessings. We don't realize that they came with a price, the price of Jesus' death on the cross. And we don't realize that God did this because he wants a love relationship with us. He wants to walk with us and talk to us, and every once in a while He'd like to hear, "Hey, Dad—hey, Father—thank you so much for giving me this life. Thank you that my eyes are open, that I can see, that I can speak, that you are listening. Thank You, Lord, that I'm alive."

We take so much for granted. We think that life owes us something. When we don't get what we want, we're so miserable. And when we get what we want, we want more, or we say, "It could be better," or, "It's not good enough." You know what? We're just selfish brats, and it's the truth. I pray that our lives reflect an attitude of gratefulness to God for all that He has done. And I pray that my son, as he gets older, develops an attitude of gratefulness to people for all that they do for him and especially to God for what He has done.

Pizza Detours

God hears our prayers. He loves it when we come before Him with our issues and problems, like we as parents are happy when our children come to us for answers. We prefer that they ask us how to do something rather than hiding a problem from us and things wind up a big mess. We can even influence and change God's mind about an issue through prayer. It is our appeal to our Father.

Sometimes we'll be driving along and my kids will want to go to Pasquale's, their favorite pizza place. They love it there. There's a TV in the back. They love the mozzarella sticks and pizza. They go, "Daddy! Daddy! Please take us to Pasquale's."

And I respond, "No, we're on the other end of town. We can go to a different pizza place. We'll go to Pasquale's over the weekend or something."

They keep insisting, "Please, Daddy! Please!"

You know what? Sometimes I give in. I just want those little faces to be happy and have joy, even though it's another thirty minutes for me to drive or I might have other things I needed to do. I just want them to be happy. They're so pleased their pleading can change my mind even though I had my mind made up. They can change it because I so love my children and want them to be happy. I believe God does the same thing with you and me. Our prayers can change the mind of God.

In Job 42:8, God says to Job's friends:

> *"Take seven bulls and seven rams and go to my servant Job and sacrifice a burnt offering for yourselves. My servant Job will pray for you, and I will accept his prayer and not deal with you according to your folly. You have not spoken the truth about me, as my servant Job has."*

Job's friends were telling Job he must have neglected to confess sin in his life. They were wrong, and after God spoke to Job and worked a few things out with him, He tells these guys, "Find Job and have him pray for you. I will accept his prayer and not deal with you according to your folly." God will only accept their prayer if Job prays for them, because Job—His servant—was righteous. The prayer of a righteous man is effective and because Job prayed for these men, God promised not to judge them based on their foolishness.

Does that sound familiar? Because Jesus prayed for us, and He was righteous (and sinless), God will not judge us according to our folly, according to our sin, according to our weakness, according to our flesh. God will judge us based on our faith in Jesus Christ. He'll judge us based on our spiritual birth, on our rebirth in Jesus Christ. He'll judge us based on Jesus' death on the cross and He will see us holy, blameless, and above reproach, clothed in the righteousness of Jesus Christ because we have accepted Christ as Lord and Savior.

(How God Relates To Us As A Father)

God is willing to accept the prayer of Job, yet not of the other men. "You have not spoken the truth about me as my servant Job has." I pray that's an example to you and me, and to every believer, that we would be found to be righteous in God's sight, man after God's own heart. I pray that we will be the ones who have spoken the truth about the Lord as Job did. Clearly, if we do that, God will hear our prayers, and He will act on our prayers and answer them.

The Kidnapper

I have kids, and if you have kids too, you understand a parent's worst nightmare. My worst nightmare would be that my kids get kidnapped, and that something horrible happens to them.

You know what? That's God's worst nightmare too for us, because we're His children. In 1 John 2:26, he says: "I am writing these things to you about those who are trying to lead you astray."

Doesn't that sound familiar? "Those who are trying to lead you astray." We caution our little kids; we teach them that they shouldn't take candy from strangers or talk to someone they don't know. Why can't they take the candy from the strangers? Because the stranger is the bad guy? Not always, but he could be. He's could be trying to lure them in with the free candy or a ride at the amusement park, so he can steal them away and do something terrible.

That's exactly what Satan wants to do to us. He wants to lead us astray from the word of God. He wants to lure you in with the "candy" of the world—with sex, drugs, rock and roll, money, power, greed, lots of girlfriends (or boyfriends), —

(How God Relates To Us As A Father)

with the mindset of, "Do anything you want. It's okay. God will still love you."

Satan told Adam and Eve, "You can eat from the tree." Is that what God said? No, no, no! It was a blatant lie.

It was a trick, and Satan does the same thing to us today. God is saying, "Listen, I'm writing these things to you about those who are trying to lead you astray." The next verse says:

> *As for you, the anointing you received from him remains in you, and you do not need anyone to teach you. But as his anointing teaches you about all things and as that anointing is real, not counterfeit—just as it has taught you, remain in him.*

You've been taught. You know what to do, now do it. Just remain in Him. Don't be led astray.

After all, God has so much more to offer us than that! In 1 John 3:1, the Word of God says, "How great is the love the Father has lavished on us, that we should be called children of God!"

That is what we are! Let's live like children of God, then we can be certain we will be living a life that matters for God.

The Car Keys

As parents, we try to guide our children based on our own life experiences, based on the road that we have walked down, knowing they have not yet walked down that road. Sometimes it's hard for them to believe us and follow our guidance because they don't realize or refuse to believe we've already been down that road.

When Ricky was in his early twenties, he would sometimes come to me and ask to borrow my car. Now, during the times when he's was being wonderfully obedient and doing the right stuff, my response was, "No problem! Here, man, take the keys. You know what? Here's an extra fifty bucks. Go have a good time."

I would do that. I would bless him abundantly when he's doing the right stuff. I would love to bless him more than he could ask or imagine, and not just financially. I would go out of my way to give him anything he wanted—within reason—and more.

This is exactly how God, our Father, works with us. If we just live our lives according to the word of God, He is free to bless us immensely. He'll not only give you what you ask for, he'll give you more.

(How God Relates To Us As A Father)

Now, imagine that same analogy, but now our son, is just ignoring his curfew consistently and literally blowing us off by deciding he doesn't need to do what his mother and I ask him to do, so he's not being responsible in any way. Then he comes up and says, "Dad, can I have the keys to the car?"

"No. Absolutely not."

"Why not?"

"Well, because I can't trust you with the keys to the car, man. I love you, but I'm certainly not going to give you my car keys. You're not listening to anything I say. What makes me possibly think that you're going to drive safely and do the right thing and be responsible with the car? No keys for you."

I think God does the same thing with us. God says he who is faithful with little will be faithful with much. He who is not faithful with little, even what he has will be taken away.

Tell Daddy the Truth

Matthew 5:17 says, "Do not think that I've come to abolish the law or the prophets. I have not come to abolish them but to fulfill them."

Jesus has come to fulfill the prophecies of old from Isaiah through to the New Testament. He came to fulfill all of them. You probably know Matthew 5:21: "Do not murder. Anyone who murders will be subject to judgment." Matthew 5:36 says, "Do not swear by your head for you cannot make even one hair white or black."

"Do not murder" seems like an easy one. If I murder, that's pretty bad. That's like the top of the sin level, so I'm probably going to be in a lot of trouble.

But then God says do not swear, not even by the hair on your head. God says, "Let your yes be your yes and your no be your no." Why can't you swear? Because you're swearing to God. Don't swear to God. Just say yes or no. Truth should always come out of you. You shouldn't need to swear for us to know you are telling the truth.

God says we know a tree by its fruit. A good tree bears good fruit, a bad tree bears bad fruit. If you claim to be a Christian

(How God Relates To Us As A Father)

man or woman, shouldn't you speak the truth? And if you don't, shouldn't you feel remorseful immediately as the Holy Spirit of God convicts you to confess the truth right away?

My friend Rene's five year old daughter came to him the other night and was convicted because she lied to him about being asleep in the car. She came in crying and said, "Daddy, I'm sorry. I lied to you." Her heart, her pure, little, childlike heart, was convicted right away when she told a lie. Here's this little girl whose heart is breaking, and she confesses to her father. Jesus says we're to be like that, like little children and accept the kingdom of God, we're to believe and trust in what He says.

Are we like that? Do we confess to our Father? I daily confess to God what I think I've done wrong because I can't stand the thought of having something standing between God and me. God is daily reaffirming me and blessing me. He tells me to press on and tells me that He understands—that's my human flesh. He understands the weakness of my flesh, how crappy and cruddy I am, and that's why He had to die for me on the cross. I understand that and it gets me so excited and joyful and happy. It's just the best thing ever. I'm not saying this from a prideful standpoint. I'm saying it from a God-giving-me-joy standpoint.

Don't Be Troubled

I love John 14:1, during Jesus' last supper with His disciples, when Jesus said, "Do not let your hearts be troubled. Trust in God. Trust also in me." What could be clearer than that?

Is your heart troubled? It is not God's desire that your heart be troubled. As a matter of fact, He has been most careful to tell you those exact words, "Don't let your heart be troubled."

It's pretty easy these days for us to be troubled. Look at all the horrible stuff going on in the world. There's war. There's famine. There are earthquakes. There's disease. There are bad guys killing everybody. There are drug epidemics wiping out our kids. How could I not be troubled?

Yet God says, "Look, I'm in control. I have everything under control. I have a perfect plan for your life. When you die, you're with me forever. You have nothing to worry about. Do not be troubled."

What happens if you are troubled? Well, you live your life troubled, upset, aggravated, and anxious. You miss out on the joy that God intended for you to have. Not good.

Can you imagine—and those of you who are parents can—how miserable I would be if my children were unhappy all the

(How God Relates To Us As A Father)

time? My three wonderful, precious joys of my life, my children unhappy all the time...That would be a disaster, a nightmare! If you are a parent, you know that you get a glimpse of how much God loves you when you see how much you love your kid. If my children were unhappy and miserable, my heart would break. I would be miserable, and I bet God looks at us the same way. I bet when we're unhappy, God says, "Why would you be unhappy? I've given you everything. You already have the keys to the kingdom. Why would you be unhappy?"

Do not let your heart be troubled.

Bad Company

First Corinthians 15:33 says, "Do not be misled. Bad company corrupts good character." Don't be fooled. You hang out with bad people, you're going to get corrupted.

Don't be misled. You think you can hang out with drug addicts and not do drugs? You think you can hang out with people drinking and not drink? You think you can hang out with thieves and not steal? No. Bad character will corrupt you. Do not be misled.

Here's another "do not" clause: "Do not be yoked together with unbelievers. For what do righteousness and wickedness have in common, or what fellowship can light have with darkness?" (2 Corinthians 6:14)

This is talking about marriage or a business partnership. It doesn't say you can't work for an unbeliever, or that you can't have a contract with an unbeliever or minister to one. You can do those things; you can and should even love them. It says don't marry them, and don't be joined at the hip with them in a partnership in business. Do not be yoked together with unbelievers.

God is giving you these various instructions, not as rules to punish you or to hurt you, but as guidelines because He loves

(How God Relates To Us As A Father)

you and wants to help you. When I tell my young children Jackson and Talia, "Don't go in the middle of the road when cars are coming," it's not because I'm mad at him and don't like him. It's because I don't want him to get run over and killed. It's because I love him.

So, when God says "Do not do these things," it's not because He's mad at you and doesn't like you. It's because He doesn't want you to get hurt or killed. It's because He loves you. He wants you to be happy and joyful.

A Father's Discipline

"Do not let anyone who delights in false humility and the worship of angels disqualify you for the prize." (Colossians 2:18) Your prize is your place in heaven. That's your prize with God. God is saying don't let anybody who worships another god tell you about another doctrine and confuse you and make you think that you've lost your place in heaven. There is nothing that can take away your place in heaven.

If you are a parent, you clearly know that there is nothing that can separate you from your love for your child. Nothing. Their disobedience can interrupt your blessings on their life, without a doubt, but it cannot separate them from your love. Nothing can do that, and nothing can separate you from the love of God. God is saying don't be fooled by anybody who says differently.

Paul says in Hebrews 12:5, "Do not make light of the Lord's discipline, and do not lose heart when He rebukes you."

What's that? You're going to get rebuked by God?

Absolutely.

When you screw up, God is going to whack you. First, He's going to tap you nicely and say, "Hey, don't do that." He does

(How God Relates To Us As A Father)

this to me in my spirit as often as is needed: "Hey, Jack, don't do that. That's a sin. You don't want to go down that road."

"Well, Lord, I think I'm going down that road anyway. I know you love me. I just need to take a little look. I'll be back. Don't worry about a thing."

Then He goes ahead and whacks me. He'll discipline me. He'll say, "Hey, you don't want to do that. I love you too much to just tell you, 'That's okay, go find yourself.' No, son, you need to find me."

When you've found God, you've found everything that you could ever want to live for. That's why God says don't lose heart when He disciplines you. You should be happy that He loves you so much to care about you.

I have some friends whose parents didn't care about them at all, and it's evident by their behavior. They look at the parents who did discipline their kids, and they wish that they had parents that loved them enough to discipline them. We're so lucky to have a God who loves us so much that He is willing to discipline us.

April Fools

Recently I was a victim of a practical joke. When I arrived at church I realized that the pants and jacket I usually place in the car before leaving the house were not there. I could just see my kids laughing on the other end of the phone. Then I heard, "April Fools, daddy! How are you going to preach in your underwear Daddy?" But they didn't know that daddy had resources that they're not aware of, and that daddy can make things happen that their minds can't comprehend.

So I called my parents in Boynton Beach. "Mom and dad, could you bring over one of Dad's suits before 10:00?" And they did.

The moral of the story is that Daddy had plans that my kids didn't think of. Daddy has resources they don't know about, and Daddy can make things happen that they can't imagine in their minds. And thank God that our God has plans we don't know about, resources we can't even imagine and He can make things happen beyond our wildest dreams.

Does God Know What He's Doing?

Here are the highlights of a couple articles I've read, the kind of stories that bring a different perspective to our lives than the day-to-day cares that usually consume our thoughts:

A woman is dying of cancer at twenty-seven years old. She has two sons, a five-year-old and a four-year-old, and she says, "If cancer has taught me anything, it's that big houses aren't important. Being rich isn't important. It's my sons who are important. It's being alive that's important." She realized as she was facing death what mattered.

Then there's the story of Patrick Knight. This one goes back a few years. He was sitting at Thanksgiving dinner with his family, and a relative came in and shot everybody. Killed his wife and kids, and he survived miraculously after being in a coma for years. The article said, "When the killer had vanished, he left four dead, including Knight's wife Lisa, her twin sister, their aunt, and their cousins, and their six-year-old daughter."

2: The Father And His Children

Patrick Knight said, "You get to decide how you want to carry it for the rest of your life because you can't get rid of it. You can't make it go away, but you get to choose how to carry it." Now today he has a different story to tell. He says it's not about being a victim but about being a survivor. It's about focusing on the blessings and not on misfortunes.

What a great reminder that people can take what seem to be tragedies in their lives and turn them into blessings by simply focusing on their blessings and not on their misfortune; by simply trusting that God has a greater purpose, that God knows what He's doing even when we don't think He does, even when we think God is making a mistake.

Do we truly believe that God knows what He's doing?

This is one more thing. It was sent to me in an email from a pastor I know up in New Hampshire. It's about someone on her prayer list, and she says, "A huge day Thursday for Suzanne. Please uplift her before the Lord, for the Lord has brought hope where there seemed to have been none. This second cancer in her liver looks like a very rare but totally unrelated one to the cervical cancer. The prognosis could mean she has more time than the six to nine months they gave her. To a mother with three children under four years old and one only eight months, that's massive. She wants her baby to remember her."

Man, and we think about the stuff that we spend most our time thinking about and sometimes fail to realize how truly valuable life is. Here's a mother who knows that her time on earth is short, and all she wants is a little more time, not for herself but so that she can impart wisdom and love into her

(How God Relates To Us As A Father)

children so when they grow up without their mother, they'll know that their mother loved them. They'll know that their mother cared and is with them in heart and soul and spirit.

Isn't that a marvelous example of trust and faith? God is with us, right now, in heart and soul and spirit. And He has a perfect plan for us in everything that He allows in our lives.

Dirty Diapers

Do you know how much God loves you and rescues you in your life? Those of you who have a baby know when go into their room, you can't wait to get in there. You just can't wait for those little precious arms to reach out and to hear "mama" or "dada." That little, beautiful, sweet child just wants you so much and depends on you and has so much love in them and wants to give you all this love, and you want to give it all back. It's the greatest feeling in the world, and you can't wait for it.

However, some mornings you come into the room with that exact attitude, but there is this little smell because the baby has done business in his diaper prior to you getting in there. And you know what? That's how we are with God. We stink before God. But just like us as parents, when we come in and detect an offensive odor coming from the baby, we don't say to that kid, "How dare you! I can't deal with you. Go clean yourself up. Get yourself straightened up. Come back all clean and then I will give you my love." No, quite the opposite. We clean the baby up. We clean him up, no matter how much he stinks, because we love that child so much.

(How God Relates To Us As A Father)

That's how God is with us in our lives. God doesn't want you to run away from Him when you think that you've failed or disappointed Him because you have not lived up to the bar that you set for yourself. Hey, the only bar that God has is, "Love me with all your heart and soul." That's all God expects of you.

We're human beings, not human doings. We think we have this list of accomplishments we need to do to be right with God. God says, "No, you don't. The only thing you need to do to be right with me is accept me, which you've done upon salvation, and believe in me with all your heart and soul. I'll take care of everything else."

That's how we are. We're the babies who just need to reach out and say, "Daddy!" God loves us and will never turn us away.

Refusing a Gift?

A child is told what to do. His steps are ordered for him. Matthew 18:3 says, "Truly I tell you, unless you change and become like little children, you will never enter the kingdom of heaven."

A Godly father will order his child's steps. He will take care of his child and prepare him by feeding his child and helping him and doing what's best for him. The child may not want to do what daddy tells him to do, but oh how he's cared for, and oh how he's loved.

That is how God cares for you and me. Oh, how God loves us. And all God wants us to do is respond accordingly to Him— to do what He's called us to do, to follow the steps He's ordered us to take so He can bless us. The steps that He has ordered are for us to proclaim the kingdom of God to everyone.

His kingdom is open to all, even to sinners, it's open 24/7. "Jesus said to them, 'Truly I tell you, the tax collectors and the prostitutes are entering the kingdom of God ahead of you.'" (Matthew 21:31)

The tax collectors and the prostitutes are entering the kingdom of God because they believed. That's the only require-

(How God Relates To Us As A Father)

ment. Because they believed, they're entering the kingdom of God. Anybody is welcome into the kingdom of God. There is nothing you could do that can separate you from the love of Jesus Christ. It's been demonstrated on the cross. Now, you can refuse it. You can let Satan get into your head and say you don't deserve it. That's right, you don't deserve it. It's a gift from your father. A gift for you!

Tell me how many gifts you've returned to your wife or your parents or friends and said, "Oh, I couldn't possibly take this because I'm a terrible friend. I'm not a deserving husband, and I'm a rotten father. I refuse the gift." None, Zero. I doubt you could tell me you ever refused a gift in your life.

And yet God's gift? "Oh, I'm not worthy." What a load of garbage, what a stupid excuse. Man, come on. That's right, you're not worthy. You don't deserve it, but God loves you so much He wants you to have it. Just like the daddy loves his child so much, that he's preparing and ordering his steps and doing everything he can so that when that child grows up, he has the best opportunity in life, so that he can be blessed more than he could ever imagine.

Do you think that any young child has any idea in his little head of what's in store for him in his life, of how much his parents love him and how much they're providing for him and what they're doing to ensure that he has a great life? No.

We're the same with God. We just don't get it. Our job is just to love God and respond accordingly. That's how you live a life that matters for God.

Not Just One Pitch

If you have kids, you know that sometimes your kids do right and sometimes they do wrong. It doesn't mean you don't love your kids when they're not doing the right thing. Of course, you wish they'd get their hands out of the cookie jar, or stop hitting their little sister, but it doesn't mean you don't love them.

This is important. When God looks at us, it's kind of like a baseball manager looks at his player. A manager doesn't judge a baseball player by one bad pitch and say, "Oh, you stink. I'm taking you out of the game. You just threw a ball and it was awful!" A manager doesn't look at a batter who swings and gets one strike and say, "You're the worst hitter ever. You can't play anymore." No. He doesn't look at one at bat or even one game. He looks at a season or a series of seasons; he follows the player's performance over time.

God is tracking our journey over time. You're allowed not to be perfect. God didn't create us perfect. Jesus is perfect. Jesus was the only one who was perfect. He was the perfect sacrifice for our sins. God created us as we are. He knew we would sin and from time to time succumb to the desires of our flesh over that of our spirit. He knew it would happen, but God has provided for us all along the way.

In the story of Abraham, God tells him: "I will bless Sarah. I will bless her and will surely give you a son by her. I will bless her so that she will be the mother of nations; kings of peoples will come from her." (Genesis 17:16)

In the very next verse, Genesis 17:17, Abraham fell face-down laughing and said to himself, "Will a son be born to a man a hundred years old? Will Sarah bear a child at the age of ninety?"

He doesn't believe it. So he goes on to say something else to God in the next verse: "If only Ishmael might live under your blessing."

Hold on a minute. Not only does he not believe God, but then he tries to get God to buy into his way. "Oh, listen God, my other son Ishmael (who he had not by his wife Sarah, but by a slave woman) if only you take Ishmael and give him the blessing, everything would be perfect," according to the plan of Abraham. But God had the plan of God, not the plan of Abraham.

So here's Abraham, who just five chapters ago was Mr. Righteousness, Mr. Friend of God, and now he's mocking God and questioning God.

God asks a question to Abraham. "Is anything too hard for the Lord?"

He goes on to state His promise: "I will return to you at the appointed time next year, and Sarah will have a son." (Genesis 18:14)

I believe God asks you and me that same question today. Is anything too hard for the Lord? Is any marriage too broken?

2: The Father And His Children

Is any child, prodigal son, too far gone? Is there any health issue that God can't cure? Is there any financial situation that God can't turn around?

God asks if there is anything too hard for Him. I think sometimes like Abraham we say, "Yup, I think this one is a bit out of your range of power." No, God is making a point, a point that He would love to make in our lives as well.

There is nothing too hard for God.

The Refrigerator

If you are a parent of young children, you most likely have a cluttered refrigerator. Not the inside, but the outside. Little children love drawing pictures for their parents—suns and stars, or trees and apples, or rainbows and hearts. Every picture is a masterpiece, perfect in the eyes of the child and even more perfect in the eyes of his parents. It is placed proudly upon the refrigerator for all to see.

The lives that we live for God are the masterpieces we're creating. And one day soon He's going to portray them for all the world to see. What is the picture of your life, your "masterpiece" going to tell the world? I pray your masterpiece would be a picture of your love for God.

A Child's Prayer

A friend of mine, a mother of three rambunctious young kids, told me about an evening when she had a bad headache. She put a video on for her kids and then disappeared to her room to lie down. Of course, it wasn't long before she was discovered by her youngest. The three-year-old came bounding in and stated, "It's not time to sleep."

"I'm not feeling so well so I am just lying down for a minute," the mother responded.

Well that little boy climbed up on her bed, folded his hands, squeezed his eyes shut and said, "Jesus, take away the pain. Help mommy feel better. Amen."

It didn't matter that a moment later he was asking her to get up and get him something from the fridge. During that moment, he was doing the best thing he knew how to help the situation. He asked God for help! We should do the same.

God's Kid

A buddy of mine—a music guy, a ministry guy—was upset and depressed that he wasn't able to use his musical talents for the kingdom of God as much as he wanted. He felt like he was letting God down. It was Satan lying to him, a fiery dart thrown by the evil one looking to defeat this child of God and separate him from the love of his Father. This man said to me, "God reminded me that He still loves me because I'm His kid, whether I use my talents or not." He knew God still loved him no matter what.

Of course, we should use our talents and gifts for God and we want to and we will. But God loves you because you're His kid, not because of the wonderful things you do. The things we do for God should come as a result of our gratitude for the love God has for us. And because of that love, we should always do what we can. If we hear it said of us, "He has done what he could," wouldn't that be enough for you? I think it would be plenty for me.

A Better Plan

In First Corinthians 13:9, 12 God's word says: "For we know in part and we prophesy in part, but when completeness comes, what is in part disappears. For now we see only a reflection as in a mirror; then we shall see face to face. Now I know in part; then I shall know fully, even as I am fully known."

God has created a perfect plan for our lives. He knows what He's doing, just as He did on Palm Sunday. When Jesus came in on that Sunday, on a donkey, the people bowed before Him. They cried, "Hosanna! Hosanna! The king is here! Praise! Rejoice!" They were so excited because their plan was going to be fulfilled. Their plan, their hope—that an earthly king would come, that an earthly king would save them. Here He was, this man of miracles. He could turn water into wine. He could heal lepers. He could raise the dead. Surely, this was the earthly king. So the people applauded, and they were so happy. They were psyched.

Just five days later, on that Friday, it looked like things weren't going according to their plan. God had a bigger plan, a heavenly plan that would last for all eternity, a plan that

(How God Relates To Us As A Father)

involved us living with Him forever—but they couldn't see it then. All they could see was their plan, what they wanted.

So when they didn't get what they wanted, they shouted, "Crucify him!" just five days after shouting, "Hosanna," it was, "Crucify Him."

We need to remember and trust that God knows what He's doing even when it's not what we want. When we don't think we're in the position we want to be in, or we don't think we have the mate we want to have, the body we want to have, the life we want to have, when we say, "Lord, no, this isn't what we want," God says, "Exactly! It's not what you want. It's what I want! You need to trust me because I have a better plan. I am your Father. I have riches you know not of. I have heaven. I have prepared a place for you that you may go to where I'm going."

You know the way, and that way is Jesus Christ. He is holding His hands out to you, saying, "Walk with me. I'll keep you safe and I'll bring you into an awesome place where you'll be with me for eternity."

Isn't that worth sharing with someone else today?

Fishing Trip

A pastor buddy of mine told a story. He and his family went to their country house in Alabama, and he looked forward to spending time with the kids and fishing and relaxing. One day they were going fishing and he asked his kids a question before they got on the boat. He asked, "Kids, where do you think the best fish are? Do you think there are more fish out in the open in the middle of the lake, or do you think there are more along the sides, on the edges of the lake under the trees?"

They said, "Well, Daddy, probably under the trees where there is shade."

He said, "Right," and he took them under the trees to start to fish. It was a powerboat, and he had to hold the boat in position at the perfect angle to get it at the edge of the lake so that the kids could catch fish. He sat there, and his hand was hurting because he was holding the boat in place and he kept having to adjust it and keep it in the right position so the kids could fish. He did that for a couple of hours.

The kids caught some fish and they came back to shore where my friend's wife asked, "How many fish did you catch?"

(How God Relates To Us As A Father)

The first kid said six fish and the second kid said eight fish. The wife said, "That's great," and she asked my friend Keith, "Well, how many did you catch?"

He replied, "None. I was holding the boat motor and keeping the boat positioned so the kids could catch the fish." My buddy shared with me that God spoke to him and said, "That's exactly what I do in your life."

We're God's kids and God is there always positioning us to get the best out of life. God is working things for us. He is there, angling the boat of our lives perfectly so that we have the best opportunity to catch the most fish possible, so that we have the best opportunity to receive the most blessings possible. This comes as a gift from God; because He loves us so much, He's willing to sacrifice for us.

God doesn't need to catch any fish. God loves you so much He sacrificed Jesus on the cross. God wants you to catch the fish. God says, "I'm well pleased with you." I took that story to heart in my life. It was a perfect time for me to hear it, and I hope you take it to heart as well. God is always with us, and He has a perfect plan. He is angling the boat of our lives just right to enable an awesome "catch."

Scared of the Ball

My son Jackson played little league baseball. He was a little guy, about 9 years old then and I was thinking, what if I said to him, "Sit down, man. Listen for a minute. I get it. You're scared, man. You might get hit by one of those pitches, and that would hurt. Why take that risk? If you got hit, it would hurt. Why don't you just sit down and don't play the rest of your life. I'll let you do that, son. You'll have no suffering. You'll never have to worry. I'll protect you and coddle you so that nothing difficult or rough will ever happen to you."

Imagine if that's how we interacted with our children. Imagine if that's how we looked at life. We'd never try a new food. We'd never learn anything new. We'd never experience our first kiss. None of us knew everything from the beginning. Then we learned. And wasn't it wonderful? Wasn't it worth the trying, worth the hassle?

You may have trials and tribulations here on this earth, as God told us we would. James Chapter 1 points out that God is going to use those trials and tribulations. He told us to not just accept grudgingly the difficult things we go through; but he said:

(How God Relates To Us As A Father)

> *"Consider it pure joy, my brother, when you fall in trials and tribulations of many kinds. They're meant to build up your faith, your strength, your perseverance so you may be mature and complete and lacking nothing." (James 1:2-4)*

God wants you to have everything. So when He says, "Listen, I want you to suffer and share in my suffering in this life," don't pass up that offer. It might not sound like much of one to you now, but again, it all depends on your focus. Focus on God and on His many wonderful promises for you, and you will see just how wonderful an offer like that can be.

He has promised in 2 Timothy 2:12, "If we suffer with Him, we will also reign with Him." And in Romans 8:18, "The sufferings of this present time are not worth to be compared with the glory that shall be revealed in us."

God isn't going to let us miss the blessings of all He has in store for us. He knows that the greatest and most enduring blessings lie on the path of difficulty and trial. The apostle Paul said:

"We glory in our sufferings, because we know that suffering produces perseverance; perseverance, character; and character, hope. And hope does not put us to shame, because God's love has been poured out into our hearts through the Holy Spirit, who has been given to us." (Romans 5:3-5)

Having the right focus, keeping our eyes on God, brings us the right perspective—suffering brings perseverance, character, and hope. It helps us to see the Holy Spirit working in our lives and bringing us into even greater things.

There is nothing too small for God, and there is nothing too big for Him either. All we have to do is keep focused on

Him, and then there will be nothing too big for us to face, because, as God's Word tells us in Jeremiah 32:17, "Nothing is too hard for the Lord."

Consider it Joy

Sometimes we can look at our trials and say, "Hey, I sinned. Maybe God is trying to teach me something." But sometimes deep trials come and it seems they have no reason!

Job was doing the right thing in the midst of his trials. But still, Satan wasn't done with trying to prove his point. In Job 2:3 we read:

> *Then the Lord said to Satan, "Have you considered my servant Job? There is no one on earth like him; he is blameless and upright, a man who fears God and shuns evil. And he still maintains his integrity, though you incited me against him to ruin him without any reason."*

And Job still says, "I trust you, Lord. I love you. I don't know why. I don't understand, but I trust you, and I love you."

God is impressed. Satan isn't. He replies in verses 4-5:

"Skin for skin! A man will give all he has for his own life. But stretch out your hand and strike his flesh and bones, and he will surely curse you to your face."

2: The Father And His Children

Satan said, "Oh yeah, you took everything, his stuff, even his family, but you didn't hit him. Hit him, and then let's see how much he loves you, Lord."

"So Satan went out from the presence of the Lord and afflicted Job with painful sores from the soles of his feet to the top of his head." (Job 2:7)

I mean, really, a tough day for Job. Job's wife says to him—in today's version, "Are you an idiot? It doesn't look like following God was a good idea. Don't you think this guy is not the guy you should be betting on anymore? You're crazy." What she said in the Bible was, "Are you still holding on to your integrity? Curse God and die." That was his wife's opinion.

Job replies in verse 10, "You are talking like a foolish woman. Shall we accept good from God, and not trouble?' In all this, Job did not sin in what he said."

Look at Job's attitude. Job was standing on James 1:2-4 the same verse we just talked about in the last chapter:

> *Consider it pure joy, my brother, when you fall in trials and tribulations of many kinds. They're meant to build up your faith, your strength, your perseverance so you may be mature and complete and lacking nothing.*

Job was standing on it before it was even written. He knew it.

Job said, "Shall we accept good from God and not trouble?" Meaning "God is God and whatever God gives, I still love You and trust you, God. I will follow You God no matter what."

That should be the attitude of our heart. Job says in Job 10:12, "You granted me life and favor, and your care has preserved my spirit."

(How God Relates To Us As A Father)

What a great acknowledgment of God's power and love and sovereignty from Job. How about us? What's our acknowledgment to God of His power and love and sovereignty?

3

PLUGGING IN
(Accessing The Power Of God)

Power Flow

I told you about my mission trip to St. Louis. It was a great trip and I clearly saw God's healing power at work. I had seen it at work mightily before I left for St. Louis with a few people I knew—a baby, an older lady, and a young man who needed heart surgery.

After I saw the miracles at home and in St. Louis I said, "Okay, God, I get it. I get it. There is nothing too hard for you, Lord. You can heal, you can save, you can do anything, God."

I believe the Spirit of God was telling me, "You know, Jack, I didn't show you My power so that you could just go back to your life and to your little world and just use it once in a while—maybe from time to time when somebody comes up to you and they're sick and you lay hands on them and try to heal them." I heard the Spirit of the Lord telling me, "My power is not for a once-in-a-while thing. It's an all the time thing"

I know that God is pruning me to make me better, so I can be more effective for the kingdom. As well I know—like Jesus being tempted in the desert for forty days—Satan desires the exact opposite. Satan doesn't want me to get closer to God.

3: Plugging In

Satan doesn't want me to access the power of God. Satan doesn't want me to share and tell people about the healing power of God. Satan wants me on the sidelines focused on the things of the world, focused on selfish things, focused on things that I care about.

So imagine how shocked I was, when I got back from St. Louis, God said to me in the Spirit, "Jack, I've called you to a closer walk with me and a greater purpose but I can't use you as you are."

And I was like, "Lord, excuse me? What do you mean you can't use me as I am? I just got back from St. Louis. Satan tried to stop us from going but we plowed through and did the job. It was an amazing mission trip. We did all these great things. What are you talking about can't use me as I am?"

God replied, "Jack. It's a good thing that you know the things of God, and it's a good thing that you can implement and execute the things of God from time to time. But I need more than that from you. If you really want to know my power and live a life that glorifies Me, I need my Spirit to envelop you completely in every aspect of your life, in everything you do. I need it to be a part of everything you do so you reek of it like you would reek of garlic when you come out of an Italian restaurant, that it's just flowing through you, that it encompasses every single part of you."

What do you say to something like that? So I said, "Yes, Lord. Yes. Please let me do that."

Ravi Zacharias said in one of his books, "Your faith in Christ will carry you. If not, you will have to carry your faith. It will become quite exhausting." It's an exhausting life that

(Accessing The Power Of God)

continues to try and work for the love of God and to equate works and benefits with the love of God. That's not what it's about. It's about allowing the love of God to flow through you by faith. God does it, not you. And we need to stop fighting that desire to keep earning points for God. We just have to love God with all our hearts. That's how we access his full power and that's how we allow him to bless us abundantly and exceedingly more than we can ask or imagine.

Power Now

I wonder sometimes if God is testing me, like an "Abraham offering up Isaac" moment. You know, "Lay your son down. I want to see if you'll do it or not." Or maybe He is seriously asking me to sacrifice my own will for His.

I can tell you that His call is clear and He will make known to me exactly what I am supposed to do. My response needs to be and I pray it always is, "Yes, God."

What do you want your response to be? What has it been so far? Is it, "Ask someone else?" Is it, "Maybe later," or, "No way"? Or is it "Yes, God. Not my will but Thine be done."

My friend Charles Carrin is an evangelist, preacher, pastor and writer; I know him to be a great man of God. He has told me that he believes that God's instruction is teaching us to obey what He has commanded us. Of course I agree with that and I am sure you do too. Charles went on to describe a big problem for many Christians today in his book *The Edge of Glory*,

> *Modern Christianity (and I say this respectfully) has convinced itself that Jesus has provided two different gospels and two different faiths—one for the first century church and the other for those who followed*

after it. The first century church was miraculously empowered. The second one was not. The first had the baptismal gift of the Holy Spirit. The second was merely given a book telling what the Holy Spirit had achieved in the past. I'm here to tell you that Jesus has provided everyone—past, present, and future— with a faith that is true, strong, and powerful. Jesus said, 'I am the same yesterday, today, and forever.' If that's the case—if Jesus isn't lying and He's the same yesterday, today, and forever—then we have to look at what God wants to do in our lives.

So which team are you on? Those who live in the past believing God's power was only available to our past Bible heroes. Or with those who live in the present, trusting in the word of God that His power is alive and real and it working you and I today.

You're on God's team, right? So why don't we go out and try to hit some home runs or score some points for the Lord? Why don't we live our lives and play the best game that we can for the Lord and do the best we can while we're alive. In order to do that it would be a good idea to take full advantage of all the tools you've been given. If you're a baseball player it's a good idea to go to home plate with a bat, a carpenter should have his hammer and screwdriver and a Christian should access the full power of God so he can be as effective as possible. God says the same power that raised Jesus Christ from the dead is the same power that's alive in you today. God is not a liar. Access His power, live in it and with it and then you can rest assured you will live a life that matters for God.

Rooted and Established

You want more of the power of God? Then believe God. What does God have to say about His power? In Ephesians 3:14-16, the apostle Paul is praying for the church at Ephesus (and for you and me today). He says: "For this reason I kneel before the Father...I pray that out of his glorious riches he may strengthen you with power through His Spirit in your inner being."

Paul is praying that the church will get strengthened with the power of God. How do you do that, Paul? Well, you get strengthened through the power of God, with God's spirit in your inner being. You need the spirit of God inside you.

You can't accomplish anything without the spirit of God inside of you. So here's Paul praying for you and me, that God strengthens us with His power. He goes on to say in the next two verses, "And I pray that you, being rooted and established in love, may have power, together with all the Lord's holy people, to grasp how wide and long and high and deep is the love of Christ."

Paul is saying, "You've got to get it. Oh, you have the ability to get it. I'm praying you take it and use it." Why? Well, in those days they were seeing a lot of Christians in the church who weren't using the power of God. They didn't accomplish their purpose, so Paul was upset. So he's praying that they would have the power of God. And then he says in verses 20 and 21, "Now to Him who is able to do immeasurably more than all we ask or imagine, according to His power that is at work within us, to Him be glory…"

It's according to God's power that's at work in us. That's how you do these things. It's got to be God's power. It's not us.

God wants us to have His power today. Second Timothy 1:7 tells us, "For God did not give us a spirit of timidity, but a spirit of power, love and self-discipline." That's God Himself saying He gave you a spirit of power!

Getting the Keys Now

I have compassion for kids I don't know, and I feel sorry for them when I hear on the news about bad things that happened to some of them. I am horrified by the thought that any adult could abuse a child—physically, emotionally, in any way. I just can't even get my mind around it, and I have great sympathy for any child who had to suffer those atrocities. And I am talking about people I don't know as I haven't experienced this first hand.

If we are talking about my own kids the truth is, I've got a lot more concern and sympathy for them than I do for children I don't know. I believe God says the same to us. In essence saying, "Look, I'm very concerned about you guys, my own kids, not missing the blessings I have in store for you." Jesus tells us in Luke 12:32, "Do not be afraid, little flock, for your Father has been pleased to give you the kingdom."

It is God's joy to bring His kingdom from heaven down into your very life and touch you and bless you with a blessing that can only come from Him. You have the keys to the kingdom right now—you don't have to wait until heaven, God and his blessings are accessible now...not later—now. You can experience God's kingdom in the midst of your life and through all of your life and here's how.

Here are God's instructions to you and me about how we can maximize the kingdom of God in our life, they are found in Romans 14:17-18, "For the kingdom of God is not a matter of eating and drinking, but of righteousness, peace and joy in the Holy Spirit, because anyone who serves Christ in this way is pleasing to God and receives human approval."

What's that, God? The kingdom of God is not a matter of eating and drinking? It's not a matter of eating this food and not eating that food or drinking this and not drinking that. It's not a matter of rules and regulations. That was Old Testament. Now it's a matter of righteousness, peace, and joy in the Holy Spirit. Anyone who serves Christ this way is pleasing to God and also receives human approval, wow a double blessing! What a great deal.

If I live righteously I can know I am walking in God's will and thus I can expect I will have the peace of God upon me and within me. Then I can also expect I will have God's joy overflowing in me and through me. This deal just keeps getting better!

So whatever you do, don't say you didn't know what to do to be pleasing to God. You do and if you follow God's instructions on this matter you can rest assured you will live a life that matters for God.

The Power

In 1 Corinthians 4:20, the apostle Paul says, "For the kingdom of God is not a matter of talk but of power."

God's power. When you live the righteous life of God and you have the Holy Spirit inside of you, you have an abundance of peace and joy and righteousness coming from you—not because you have to feel that way, but because you're so grateful to God for the gift you've received. You're so overwhelmed that God loves you so much—you, a stinking, rotten sinner—that God has given you this grace, this salvation, this mercy, this place in heaven, this abundant life. You're so overwhelmed that out of you flows nothing but gratitude towards God. So when God says, "Live this way," you gladly live that righteous, peaceful life and you are filled with the joy of the Lord.

The kingdom of God is a matter of power. It's not a matter of talk. The power of God comes through you.

It's the Word of God that speaks, that brings Spirit and life. It's the Word of God that's alive—not my word, but God's word, not my power but God's power working in us and through us to accomplish the will of God (the good works

(Accessing The Power Of God)

that God prepared in advance for me to do, Ephesians 2:10). It's the power of God that super charges the Word spiritually in your heart and draws you to the Holy Spirit and excites you in the Holy Spirit. It's the power of God in us and in our life that equips us to do great things. It's the power of God and its alive and working in your life today through the Holy Spirit of God deposited in your heart at salvation.

God has the power to forgive. God has the power to heal. God has the power to love. God has the power to restore. God has the power to magnify. God has the power to enlarge. It's supernatural power. It's the same power that when people had nothing to eat, Jesus used to break two loaves and some fish and fed five thousand people with it. It's the same power that allowed Jesus to turn water into wine. It's the same power that Jesus used to raise Lazarus from the dead. It's the same power that raised Jesus from the grave. It's that same power that comes into every believer of Jesus Christ. But you've got to take it and more importantly you've got to use it.

Yet sometimes we doubt God. We ask Him, "God, prove to me that you have the power." He doesn't have to do that. God says there's not going to be another sign and we know we are not to test God. The sign was and is Jesus on the cross. The proof is the Holy Spirit in your heart confirming everything that God has said. You already have the sign from God because you already have the Holy Spirit. The kingdom of God is within you.

We're already there. We're already there in the kingdom of God today. God has brought us into the kingdom of the Son He loves. And we need to love like it, laugh like it and we need to live like it. Every Christian should be living in that certainty, confidence and fulfilled space that comes from knowing for sure that we're already in the kingdom of God, that we have the kingdom of God at work in our life now and for all eternity.

We should be laughing with joy because we're untouchable by the world's standards. We can do anything. We're kingdom kids. "Therefore, since we are receiving a kingdom that cannot be shaken, let us be thankful, and so worship God acceptably with reverence and awe." (Hebrews 12:28)

We have been promised a heavenly kingdom, one that cannot be shaken or changed. Your bank account can be shaken. Your real estate portfolio can be shaken. Your health can be shaken. Your marriage can be shaken. Your relationship with your kid can be shaken. The world will shake the crap out of you. The kingdom of God cannot be shaken. That is the one thing you can depend on no matter what.

Look at what Revelation 1:5-6 says: "To Him who loves us and has freed us from our sins by His blood, and has made us to be a kingdom and priests to serve His God and Father." It's important you understand that's our purpose: to serve our God and Father. We are His priests here on earth and created to declare His glorious light, created for His pleasure to serve Him and love Him and to be loved by Him, created to bear fruit and fruit that was to last, created to do good works which He prepared advance for us to do, created to be with God forever and ever. What a great deal!

Staring Contest

People ask, "How do I make sure I can live a life that counts for God?"

You'll find the answer in 2 Peter 1:10-11, "Therefore, my brothers and sisters, make every effort to confirm your calling and election. For if you do these things, you will never stumble, and you will receive a rich welcome into the eternal kingdom of our Lord and Savior Jesus Christ."

If I told you to stare at my face and never take your eyes off me, do you think you could ever forget what I look like—remember you were continually staring at my face and never took your eyes off me? No, of course you wouldn't forget what I look like. God says we're to stare at His face to keep focused on Him. We're to stare at the face of Jesus, never taking our eyes off God, and we'll never forget what He looks like, and we'll never forget what we're supposed to look like. Then we won't stumble.

The kingdom of heaven is upon us. All you need to do is confirm your calling and claim what is already yours. Claim that eternal ticket, the greatest gift ever, and share it with others. Proclaim the kingdom to all. It is His good pleasure

3: Plugging In

to give you the kingdom. Don't miss the calling on your life from God; it's not too late to do the right thing for God. If you want to make sure the bank balance in your bank account was correct, you would call the bank or check online and confirm it. If you want to make sure a flight was leaving on time, you call the airline or check online and confirm it. If you want to make sure what your kid was watching on TV, you would get up, go to the TV and see what they were watching. There is an action required on your part. God is telling you to make sure of your calling and election to confirm it by and with the actions of your life. Remember God's word tells us, "Faith without works is dead." Let's make sure we are men and women of action for God. Then we can be sure we are living a life that matters for God.

God wants to reveal His power to you, and He's told you how to do it. He's told you how to get it. He wants to see you living in righteousness and having peace and joy. He wants you to have the kingdom and take it and embrace it. God wants to do mighty things for you, and He will. Just ask, believe, and follow.

Just Shut Up

With Jesus' death and resurrection, every believer has God's Holy Spirit inside of him—that still, small voice of God that speaks to our hearts, minds and souls.

There are two things you've got to do to hear God.

One, you have to shut up; if you're talking, you can't be listening.

How many times have you just wanted to tell someone to shut up? "Shut up. You just don't know what you're talking about." Many, many years I dealt with my own drug addiction; I've dealt with my son's drug addiction. I know how a drug addict or alcoholic can tend to be in denial. That's the kind of person to whom you just want to say, "Shut up. Stop talking. Start learning."

The second thing you need to do to hear God is to shut out the world. Don't go away from the world. Unless you're an astronaut, that would be an impossible feat. Don't go out of the world, but definitely learn how to shut it out when necessary.

When I was growing up, there were two great baseball pitchers: Bob Gibson and Steve Carlton. There were a lot of

3: Plugging In

really good baseball pitchers, but those two guys were known for their intensity and focus. You couldn't talk to them the day of the game. They were mean to their own teammates because they were so focused on their purpose and job. They were so focused they wouldn't let you distract them.

Al Pacino, when he was making some of his now famous movies, took his roles very seriously. Before he did Scarface—not that that's a movie you want to glorify—he took that role home for two months. Could you imagine being his wife and getting the Tony Montana treatment? He was Tony Montana at home. That's how serious he was about his profession, and that's how serious we should be about our God.

If you shut up and shut out the world, God will speak to you very clearly. If you dare to go spend time with God, He will show up. He will speak. You will hear His still, small voice. I am certain if you do, you will never come back to me and say "Hey, God didn't show up. God didn't speak to me."

Do the things that God says are important. Spend time with Him. If you do that, you'll have time to do everything else in your life, and you won't feel pressured or rushed. If you feel anxious, depressed, upset, like you can never get enough stuff done, like the world's always crashing in on you, like you're running on that hamster wheel, guess what? God's not your first priority. Because if God was your first priority and you were walking right with God, you'd still have the same amount of stuff to do, but you'd feel a lot differently about it. You would have the peace and joy of the Lord. You would be leaping and rejoicing as you went through this life. That's definitely the way God wants you to go and it's definitely the best way to go!

Pit Stop

Be like a NASCAR driver. I don't know if you're a NASCAR fan. I'm not a huge one, but I like and understand the sport. I know that sometime during the race (often more than once) they have to pull the car in for a pit stop. What's the purpose of that? Well they may need more gas. They won't be able to finish the race if they don't have enough gas. There may be carburetor problems and it's slowing down the speed of the car. There may be engine problems. There may be tire issues. There might not be enough tread on the tire to gain traction to go fast or too little air pressure. A variety of different reasons that you would come in for a pit stop so that you can run more efficiently. Why? So you can win the race.

If you're a parent—especially of a boy—you might have seen the kids' movie Cars. It's about a racecar named Lightning McQueen. The movie begins with him starting a race. He's without a doubt the fastest car on the track, but he is so cocky and sure of himself that he doesn't want to take time for a pit stop, and so a tire blows out and he doesn't win the race. We all need those pit stops in life to refuel, to make sure

3: Plugging In

we're in the right gear and have what we need to make it the next leg of the race, and to finish strong. We need to make time for those pit stops with God.

The apostle Paul told us we're to run the race so as to get the prize. We're to run hard and fast and efficient so that we can win and get the prize. We do that by living the life that God has called us to. We're to live up to this calling we've obtained—the calling to be sons and daughters of God. So this particular chapter is meant to be a pit stop for you. It's for the purpose of seeing what we're doing right…and seeing what we're doing wrong. When we come in for a pit stop, we fix what's wrong and go back out and continue the race. Remember…we fix what's wrong! Whatever time we have on earth is a gift from God. It's wonderful. We should want to live it fully. Even better we can determine and control certain aspects of eternity, specifically our rewards, which last for all of eternity. How? By the way we live today. By whether or not we choose to get on the track and run the race for God. Start your engines…it's race time!

The One Percent Army

There is a spiritual warfare going on in life. Beyond the boundaries of what we can see and feel with our five senses, there is an entire world of the spirit. And in that world, there is a war for the hearts and souls of men.

In 2 Chronicles 20:15, God says to King Jehoshaphat, "Listen, King Jehoshaphat and all who live in Judah and Jerusalem! This is what the Lord says to you: 'Do not be afraid or discouraged because of this vast army. For the battle is not yours, but God's.'"

There was a vast army coming against Jehoshaphat. He could've easily been terrified, but God said, "Don't be afraid of this vast army. The battle is not yours. It's God's."

We sometimes look at the overwhelming circumstances in our life, and we are so scared. We're sometimes paralyzed with fear. God says, "Don't be afraid. This isn't your battle. It's mine."

It's God's battle. We just have to be faithful, like Gideon when God whittled down the army down from thirty thousand to three hundred so that Gideon couldn't claim the victory as his own. But instead would give the credit and

3: Plugging In

glory where it belonged, to God! The people couldn't claim the victory. Only God could claim the victory. There would be no doubt it was God who moved and acted.

That's the kind of faith that will glorify God and lift us up, individually and corporately. There is a spiritual warfare. The battle is being fought in heaven and all around us…but the battle is already won. God has already told us what the outcome will be. The battle is already won. The result is in. Jesus crushed Satan at the cross.

Proof

Which is better, growing up homeless, or being brought up by loving parents? That's a no brainer, isn't it? Can you imagine if you were brought up homeless and without a family? Nobody to love you, nobody to care for you, nobody to feed you, nobody to teach you, nobody to watch over you, nobody to guide you, nobody to love you. Man, that sounds like a hard life to me. Now, imagine being brought up with loving parents. You're loved, you're nurtured, you're fed, you're schooled, you're taught, you're trained, you're groomed, you're cared for, you're taken care of. Which would be better? It's obvious what your answer would be.

A life without Jesus Christ is like being the homeless guy. A relationship with Jesus Christ is like knowing the Father and having that loving and caring family and being part of it.

I recently had a conversation with a buddy of mine—a smart guy—and he said, "Jack, I have a scientific mind. I need proof of Jesus." I said okay, and then I started to describe my personal relationship with Jesus Christ since 1991, from the day I got saved until today. I told him about the love and the peace and the joy and the one-on-one individual relationship that I have with God and how much I love God. I told him how much I know God loves me and how I know God's with me every step of the way. He'll never leave me or forsake me. He's got a perfect plan for my life. His plans are to prosper me and not to harm me. And that's all in the word of God. That's God telling me all this, and I believe God. I believe His word.

My friend looked at me with these sad puppy dog eyes and he said, "What you're talking about, that's what I've wanted all my life." And I'm like, of course that's what you wanted all your life. You want that relationship with your Father. You want to be loved and know that you're loved and cared for.

Listen, if you were in the hospital dying, you wouldn't say to the doctors, "Prove to me the medicine works before you give it to me." No. You'd say, "Give me the medicine, and I'm hoping it does what you say it does because I'd like to live."

How do you get the medicine from God? It's in John 3:3: "Jesus replied, 'Very truly I tell you, no one can see the kingdom of God unless they are born again.'"

In the natural world we want to see to believe. But when we know Jesus Christ, we believe to see. That was the whole issue with "doubting" Thomas after Jesus had risen. He refused to believe Jesus had been raised from the dead and was alive after seeing him crucified on the cross, and his words were pretty direct to anyone who tried to convince him otherwise. He said in John 20:25, "Unless I see in His hands the print of the nails and put my finger into the print of the nails and put my hand into His side, I will not believe."

In the very next verse, we find that Jesus did appear to him and said to Thomas, "Reach your finger here and look at my

(Accessing The Power Of God)

hands, and reach your hand here, and put it into my side. Do not be unbelieving, but believing."

Needless to say, Thomas believed from that point forward. Jesus' admonition to him, in verse 29, speaks to us today: "Thomas, because you have seen me, you have believed. Blessed are those who have not seen and yet have believed."

We might not see everything today, but we are called to believe. That's the key to living a life that matters for God.

A Face from the Past

Over the last few weeks during my quiet time, God has been speaking to my heart. I felt God, through the Holy Spirit, saying, "Jack, I think you've been selling me short lately. I think you've been underestimating my power and what I can do in your life."

He brought this statement to life through something amazing that happened to me. A couple of weeks back, God reminded me of a guy I haven't seen in twelve years. This guy's girlfriend used to work for me, one of two hundred employees, when I owned a TV production company. She came in one day and said her boyfriend was having a drug problem. I said, "Well, bring him in. I'll talk to him."

I talked to the guy and decided to put him through drug rehab. We paid for it—it was expensive, but money was flowing at that time, and he was very grateful. I would say that over eight or nine years, we put probably fifteen people through rehab. Drug abuse is a problem I could recognize right away, you couldn't fool me because I had the same problem myself. So we tried to help where we could.

I remembered how grateful this particular guy was, and a few weeks ago out of the blue I was thinking, "Man, I wonder whatever happened to that guy after all these years. He was so grateful. I hope his life turned out alright." I mentioned it to my wife as well because I hadn't thought about the guy once in over ten years. I said, "Hey, remember that guy, Tom, whose girlfriend worked for us? It's been like twelve years since we helped him through rehab. I wonder where he is now, how he's doing."

Well, the following week my wife Beth and I went to the ball field to take my son Jackson to T-ball. It was the first day of practice for him. I heard somebody say, "Jack?" I looked over and he said, "It's me. Tom" There he was. And at that very moment I thought, this must be like what Zachariah felt when an angel came to him and told him that he would have a son and Zachariah didn't believe him. And God just shut him up because of his unbelief.

God just looked at me—I believe, spiritually—and He said, "Is there anything too hard for me? Is there anything else you need to see? Any other proof you need?"

That moment, for me, was personal and poignant. The Holy Spirit works personally within each of our lives. And I understood what God meant when He had been whispering to my heart, "You have been selling me short. There is nothing too hard for me. You just need to plug in to my power and feel it and use it because you have it. You have access to it."

I'm not the only one who has that access, by the way. You have it too. "For the message of the cross is foolishness to those who are perishing, but to us who are being saved it is the power of God." (1 Corinthians 1:18)

This "message"—the message of the cross—is the power of God. It's the power of God in your life and in my life. We have that power and God wants us to use it. When we give power to politicians and policemen and firemen, they use it. When we give power to surgeons and doctors in the hospital, they use it. Why wouldn't we use the power that God has given us? I hope you take that question as a challenge because God's power is available to you today. There is nothing too hard for Him.

I don't want to betray Jesus any longer by refusing to access His power, by living my life pretending that it doesn't exist. It would be like living my life without the modern conveniences that electricity brings just because I was too lazy to flip the switch and turn it on. God wants us to turn on His power in our lives, and to use it for His glory.

One on One

The message of the cross is the power of God. Is that power showing forth in your life? Is your life filled with peace, joy and happiness? Those things come from God. If you don't have those things, God tells you how you can get them. The apostle Paul says, "We have not stopped praying for you and asking God to fill you with the knowledge of his will through all spiritual wisdom and understanding." (Colossians 1:9)

You get the knowledge of God's will for your life through wisdom and spiritual understanding. You want to know what God wants? It's not difficult to find out. You can find out very easily. Get wisdom and spiritual understanding. If I wanted knowledge about economics or philosophy or psychology or biology, I'd go to college and take the classes they offered or sit at the feet of an expert to learn from them. If I sat there and learned, I'd have a lot of knowledge. Remember knowledge is the beginning of the road to wisdom, so the more I learned the smarter I'd get.

God says the same thing. Are you showing up for class? Each and every day, He's there, ready to teach you and fill you

3: Plugging In

and make you the smartest, wisest, and fullest-of-His-Spirit Christian in the world. The more wisdom you get, the more joy you'll get and the more blessings you'll get because you'll know more. You'll understand what God is thinking and how he wants to bless you. How amazing would that be? How incredible?

So, we get knowledge of God's will through spiritual wisdom. If you're out living in the world, and most of the time you are doing your job or playing golf or some other sport, cooking, or shopping, where is your time with God to get spiritual wisdom?

"Well, I go to church."

Well yes, that's good, but that's just a start. Sermons are great, and of course God can and will speak to you through them. He speaks to me a lot like that, when I hear people preach, or teach, or talk about God—wherever it is—I love it. It doesn't have to be at church. It could be anywhere—just people talking about Him. But the times when God takes my heart and really knits it with His are when He and I are alone—one on one. It only happens when I am sitting there saying, "Teach me." I'm showing up for the "classes." And I don't understand everything, so I get to ask questions. "Hey God, I don't understand. Can you explain this to me? Can you show me this?" And sure enough, God shows me, just like He will show you. He is faithful, and He is more than happy to fill you with His wisdom by the guidance of His Spirit.

All-Access

The word of God says, "He died for us so that, whether we are awake or asleep, we may live together with him." (1 Thessalonians 5:10) Jesus bled, died, suffered and sacrificed on the cross so that whether we're awake or asleep—that means alive or dead—we may live in Him. That explains the abundant life in heaven that we'll have when we are with God forever and ever. But God wants us to live with Him right now. Think about your best friend, spouse, or child. I'll bet you know them pretty well. I'll bet you know what they do, where they're going, what their lives are like, what they're like. And I'll bet they know you really well, too.

How well do you know God? Let me tell you, God knows you really well. And God would love nothing more than for you to know Him really well, too. There is nothing to be scared of. There is only excitement and joy to be gained and this greatest life ever as you come closer to God. And as you learn more of Him, you will grow in faith. "Faith comes from hearing and hearing by the Word of God." (Romans 10:17)

Ephesians 2:14 says, "He Himself is our peace." God Himself is our peace. It goes on to say in verse 18, "For through Him

3: Plugging In

we have access to the Father by one Spirit."

God is our peace. We have access to Him. Whether we choose to use that access or not is up to us. It's up to us whether we choose to draw near to Him. But you'll never be able to look God in the face and say, "I didn't know you. I didn't know how to have access. I didn't know how to get it." No, through Jesus Christ we have access to Him.

As a father, all I want to do is give my kids access to my knowledge and my wisdom, and blessings, whatever I can give them. I want to bless them. If I could just take a chip out of my brain and put it in theirs and they could know all the good stuff and not the bad, how happy that would make me. I want them to have access to everything I know for their benefit, for their blessing, not for mine, because that's the joy of my life—to see them blessed.

It's the joy of God's life to see you blessed. God wants you to have access to Him and take advantage of that individual relationship. Don't underestimate His power, His ability to work in your life. You have instant access to it right now. The message of the cross is the power of God, and that message is love, light and hope for all the people of the world. It's for you and me, and it's also for the lost. "Go therefore and teach the nations," we are told in Matthew 28:19, so that we can bring them also to the excellence of the knowledge of the power of God. God has a calling for you and He is more than willing to give you the knowledge and spiritual understanding you need to discover His will for your life.

Don't betray Him by neglecting to access His power. There is enough betrayal in the world around us every day and you

(Accessing The Power Of God)

can see it in the news every night and in the world around you every day. The saddest betrayal is a life that fails to receive the reward and blessings of God, the fails to fulfill the highest calling of all: "The prize of the high calling of God." (Philippians 3:14) What a prize! Get in the race and start to run! I can assure you of this—in running the race to the best of your ability, not only will you win, but you can be certain that you will live a life that matters for God.

4

LIGHT ON THE PATH
(The Importance Of The Bible)

Which Stage?

I believe there are three stages for people in life.

One is that stage in life when people say, "I want God." Maybe they do, but they're not willing to do anything to get Him. They want Him, but they're not willing to put forth any effort to find Him.

Another stage is when they say, "I need God." Oh, they need God. They know they need God, but they're not willing to give up the things of this world—addiction, sin, possessions, power, pride, things of the world—to get God. They're simply not willing to do it.

The third stage is when people say, "I can't make it without God." Those are the ones who succeed, because they will do whatever it takes to find God. They have to have him! What about you? Where are you in your life today? What stage are you at? Are you at the point where you're saying, "I can't make it without God?"

God says, "You will find me when you seek me with all your heart." That's Jeremiah 29:13. If you hunger and thirst for God, you will be satisfied. If you don't hunger and thirst for God and you hunger and thirst for the things of this world,

4: Light On The Path

then it's no surprise that you're not satisfied. It's no surprise that you're angry, depressed, upset, anxious, frustrated, mad, envious, jealous, and that you don't have any peace. That's what happens when your eyes focus on the world.

God wants to give you clear direction so that you will have a path to walk down, and God promises that his path will lead you to peace and joy and happiness.

What's For Dinner?

Listen to Jeremiah 15:16 and I pray God uses it to speak to your heart. Jeremiah says: "When your words came, I ate them; they were my joy and my heart's delight, for I bear your name, O Lord God Almighty."

What are you eating these days? Whose word are you eating? Are you eating the word of Satan or the word of God, the word of the spirit or the word of the flesh? What is the joy and delight of your heart? Is it the things of God or is it the things of the world?

The more of Jesus I have in me, the more of Jesus I get. He must increase, we must decrease. The first three verses of Psalm 49 say:

> *Hear this, all you peoples; listen, all who live in this world, both low and high, rich and poor alike: My mouth will speak words of wisdom; the utterance from my heart will give understanding.*

Could God be any clearer? You need to hear the word of God to get understanding. You want understanding of God? You want to get closer to God and walk closer to God? Go

4: Light On The Path

and meditate on His word. That's how you get understanding. Now, listen to God's warning in Psalm 49:13-14:

> *This is the fate of those who trust in themselves, and of their followers, who approve their sayings. They are like sheep and are destined to die. Death will be their shepherd.*

So, the Bible is saying, "Listen, you don't want to go God's way? You don't want to meditate on the word of God? You don't want to get closer to God? You don't want to walk with God? You don't want to be blessed by God? Okay, no problem. Let me just tell you the fate of what happens if you don't. You will die and spend eternity separated from God!"

There is no other way out. It's not a joke when you're going to jail. It's not a joke when, if you don't accept Jesus, you're going to hell. It's not a joke when, if you're a Christian, it's judgment day and you get your eternal reward. God said it is based on what you did with the gifts He gave you.

It's the parable of the talents. Here is your life. Here are your gifts. Go use them for the kingdom, and you'll be rewarded accordingly. If you don't, that will be a problem.

God has spoken this next verse to my heart, and I know He's saying it to your heart as well. Psalm 49:15 is for every believer: "But God will redeem my life from the grave; he will surely take me to himself."

God will redeem me. It's hallelujah time! What a great promise from the Lord that salvation is assured because of God's great promises to us. We have nothing to worry about. God will redeem us from the grave, and He'll receive us. It's the greatest news of all time. And if this next passage doesn't get you dancing and cheering, then nothing will. Hebrews 9:27-28 says: "Just as man is destined to die once, and after that to face judgment, so Christ was sacrificed once to take away the sins of many people; and he will appear a second time, not to bear sin, but to bring salvation to those who are waiting for him."

That's the word of God. Your place in heaven is assured. Jesus has promised it. Of course, we should be leaping and rejoicing in this life. God wants to give you this great gift.

I have it. God gave it to me. I just did what God said, and you can do the same thing.

Love and Statutes

Jesus died to make peace between man and God. Adam and Eve sinned in the Garden of Eden. They broke the peace by disobeying God and sinning. So now we're all born sinners because we're descendants of Adam and Eve, as we have Adam and Eve's blood in our bodies. We're born with that sin. So, now we can't get to heaven. Why not? Heaven is perfect and pure. God can only have perfect and pure stuff in heaven.

But God loved us so much that He said, "I'm going to fix this. There is a debt for your sins. The penalty of sin is death. Somebody has got to pay it. There's a consequence. I'm going to give Jesus Christ, my son, the one I love most to pay off your debt and the debt of every man." God is saying to me, "You think you love your kids, Jack? You think you love Ricky, Jackson, and Talia? You have no clue. I love you so much I'm giving my son on the cross so that the gap is bridged and you and I can be together again, for all eternity. My Holy Spirit will come to live inside of you now. You can have my abundant life now and you'll be with me in heaven forever and ever."

We who believe in him have the keys to the kingdom of heaven.

(The Importance Of The Bible)

Jesus knows your pain and suffering here on earth. He understands exactly what you go through. Hebrews 4:15-16 says:

> *For we do not have a high priest who is unable to sympathize with our weaknesses, but we have one who has been tempted in every way, just as we are—yet is without sin. Let us then approach the throne of grace with confidence, so that we may receive mercy and find grace to help us in our time of need.*

We are to draw near the throne with confidence. That's the right of every single child of Jesus Christ. You can go to your Father with confidence. He loves you. You can receive mercy and find grace, and then you have God's peace. There it is. Thank you, Jesus.

If you don't have that confidence today, if you're not there yet, you need to grab it. You need to get your peace with God. When you got your driver's license, you were probably sixteen or seventeen. Do you remember how excited you were? Holy cow, man, the world had just opened up to you. "Wow! I can drive now! I can go here or there. I can do all these amazing things! My whole life just got so much better. This is the greatest ever!"

That's exactly what will happen to you spiritually in your Christian walk if you grab hold of the peace of God. And the peace of God is not something you should just have once in a while. It's not something you get and you lose. It's something you should have all the time.

Have a Peace

Let's see what God has to say about His peace. Colossians 3:15: "Let the peace of Christ rule in your hearts, since as members of one body you were called to peace."

In order for the peace of Christ to rule in your heart, you first need to have it. Then you need to let it rule in your heart. Philippians 4:6-7 tells us:

> *Do not be anxious about anything, but in everything, by prayer and petition, with thanksgiving, present your requests to God. And the peace of God, which transcends all understanding, will guard your hearts and your minds in Christ Jesus.*

That's how you get the peace of God. You present your requests through prayer and petition in every situation to God. If you will do that, you will have the peace of God which transcends all understanding. It will guard your minds and hearts. If you don't do that, you won't have the peace of God that transcends all understanding and guides your mind. It's pretty simple. What part of God's word is unclear? You want the peace that transcends all understanding, you present to God your wishes with your prayer and petition.

(The Importance Of The Bible)

But there's one more piece to that. You need to trust God with the outcome. You need to trust God even when God's answer isn't what you want to hear. In every situation—whether it's a health, money, relationships, physical, work —it doesn't matter. God is God. We need to trust Him. Romans 8:5-6 give us the clearest instructions you will ever hear from God:

> *Those who live according to the sinful nature have their minds set on what that nature desires; but those who live in accordance with the Spirit have their minds set on what the Spirit desires. The mind of sinful man is death, but the mind controlled by the Spirit is life and peace.*

Which one do you choose? God said the mind governed by the flesh is death. The mind governed by the spirit is life and peace. You want the peace of God? Let God govern your life and you'll have it. And if you don't have the peace of God, it means you're not letting God govern your life. You don't have it because you're doing it wrong.

God didn't say you would like the outcome to everything. He said you'll have peace through it—peace that transcends all understanding. He also said you'll have rivers of joy flowing through you and that your cup will overflow. I love how it is put in Psalm 4:8, "In peace I will lie down and sleep. For you alone, Lord, make me dwell in safety."

In 2008 I was able to go to sleep. How? Markets were crashing. House values were tumbling. All over the nation, people are asking, "Is America going to survive? Is our dollar going to be worth anything?"

Today I sleep very well even though there are earthquakes, tsunamis, nations fighting against nations. End times signs

4: Light On The Path

for sure. I see the signs. I get it. I don't know if it's going to be today or a ten thousand years from now. No one can predict that. Only God knows the hour and the day.

But I can sleep because I have the peace of God. You should be sleeping too. Some people tell me I'm the happiest guy they know. I probably am, which is sad for anyone who says that. Why? Because they can have the same happiness and joy. My happiness and joy come from my relationship with Jesus Christ and every single child of God should have the same thing.

Psalm 85:8 says, "I will listen to what God the Lord will say; he promises peace to his people, his saints—but let them not return to folly."

He promises peace to his people, his faithful servants. We can have that same peace, and we should. But there's a warning from God in that line: "…but let them not turn to folly."

What's folly? Anything that comes between you and God is folly. Sin, money, a relationship, pride, sports team, golf game—anything in the world that's come between you and God. You need to keep your eyes focused on the author of your faith, Jesus Christ, and you will have no problem. You will have the peace of God. But God warns you, do not turn to folly. Psalm 119:165 says, "Great peace have they who love your law, and nothing can make them stumble."

I mean, is that line like the greatest insurance policy of all time? Great peace have those who love God's law. Nothing can make them stumble, and your premiums have been paid in full forever. God has paid for your insurance premium with the death of His son, Jesus Christ, on the cross. Every believer has that great promise from God.

Encouragement from Joel

The book of Joel says:

Declare a holy fast; call a sacred assembly. Summon the elders and all who live in the land to the house of the Lord your God, and cry out to the Lord. Alas for that day! For the day of the Lord is near; it will come like destruction from the Almighty. (Joel 1:14-15)

When was the last time you fasted for God? When was the last time you sought God with all your heart and fasted? God has told you how to seek Him. You do it with all your heart! While it's not always about fasting, fasting is a good idea. The Lord tells us, in Joel 2:12, "'Even now,' declares the Lord, 'return to me with all your heart, with fasting and weeping and mourning.'"

Could God be any more specific? Not later, not yesterday. "'Even now,' declares the Lord."

All we have to do is say, "Hey, God, I'm sorry. I'm sorry I blew it. I'm sorry I wasn't living the right way. I want to live the right way. I want to overcome whatever needs to be overcome. Lord you've created me to be an overcomer. I have victory in you. I'm sorry. I really mean it. I have godly repen-

4: Light On The Path

tance and sorrow and I'm going to do it right from now on. I'm coming back home." And obviously, it doesn't need to be those exact words. Just a prayer from your heart, and the actions that follow.

God says in Joel 2:13:

> *Rend your heart and not your garments. Return to the Lord your God, for he is gracious and compassionate, slow to anger and abounding in love, and he relents from sending calamity.*

God wants your heart, not just your actions. He is gracious and compassionate. You don't need to fear for what you've done, or be concerned that you're going to get punished and whacked in the head, or that God is going to send you to Africa if you don't want to go. It's not about any of that.

It's about this wonderful hug from God in this crazy world we live in. God is our life coach reminding us how to live. His words wrap around you with a warm hug, rescuing us from the hurt and the pain that is in the world.

When you get up in the morning, you might have a little peace; but you walk out the door and the waves of the world come crashing in on you and you're fighting and just trying to tread water and keep your head up and not go under. God reaches out to you and says, "I have this big hug for you. I love you. You're mine. Don't worry. I'm with you. It's a journey. Relax. Refocus."

Joel 2:19 says, "The Lord will reply to them: 'I am sending you grain, new wine and oil, enough to satisfy you fully; never again will I make you an object of scorn to the nations."

(The Importance Of The Bible)

God was speaking to Israel, but I believe He is speaking to us as well. Verse 21 says, "Be not afraid; be glad and rejoice. Surely the Lord has done great things."

The greatest thing he's done for you was up on the cross where He gave His son's life for you so we would have life abundant and eternal. What a gift.

He goes on to promise in verse 30 and 32, "I will show wonders in the heavens and on the earth…And everyone who calls on the name of the Lord will be saved."

That's it. You just have to call on God's name. Then He saves you and He gives you this new life and He comes to live inside of you. You need to stay (on a daily basis is a good idea) filled with the Holy Spirit of God. We do that by continuing to access God and by spending time with him. We can have as much of God as we want. He is always available to us, as His Holy Spirt lives inside our hearts. The question is do we make time for him, or are we busy with ourselves?

More of God's Holy Spirit is something you should want, not something God should have to track you down like bounty hunter and grab you when you're down, begging you and pleading with you to access and be blessed by His Holy Spirit. God asks, "Don't you want more of my Holy Spirit? You can't like living like this, feeling separated and apart from me."

No, we should be running to God, "Lord, please fill me with your Spirit because I love the joy. I love the feeling of your fullness. I don't want the world. I want you."

The Gift of "Do Not"

God has given us a list of simple instructions and regulations to help us live this better life. They're not meant to be rules but instructions, just like the ones I would give my kids. When I say to my young son Jackson, "Don't put your hand in the fire," it's because I don't want him to burn his hand. Sometimes I even have to raise my voice to tell him things because he's young and inexperienced. Don't you wish that only applied to seven-year-olds? But nope...it applies to all of us! Well, God has laid it out for us clearly.

I know the truth of God; I've sat down and studied it. If other preachers only give half the gospel or leave something out or pollute it or change it, I know it. You should never depend on any one preacher or teacher; you should always depend on your own study of the word of Jesus Christ to confirm or deny what is truth or not.

As Christians, we spend a lot of time talking about what God tells us to do. But what does God tell us not to do? Sometimes getting it straight about what we're not supposed to do clarifies in our hearts those things we are supposed to do.

(The Importance Of The Bible)

We're happy when there are laws in place about what people can and cannot do. We're happy to see that there's a speed limit on the highway so cars aren't crashing into us all over the place. We're happy that guys can't legally take their guns out and shoot us at sporting events or concerts. There are laws against those kinds of things. There are laws that say, "Do not." Do not drive recklessly or you might crash into me and kill my family. Do not take out your gun and shoot me. There are laws against those things, and there is punishment for people who don't obey the law.

God has His own list of "Do nots." Thankfully, for those who believe in Jesus, there is no punishment. There is only grace, mercy, and salvation. We should accept those things as gifts from the Lord, and we should do our best to follow His "Do nots" just as much as we want to follow His "Dos."

In Genesis 15:1, God says, "Do not be afraid. I am your shield, your very great reward." Do not be afraid. You have nothing to fear.

Philippians 4:6 piggybacks on the previous verse: "Do not be anxious about anything, but in everything by prayer and petition with thanksgiving present your requests to God."

We shouldn't be living in this world as fearful human beings. We should be living joyfully—leaping and rejoicing through our life each and every day, and that's what the world should see in Christian believers, in us.

When I Doubt

In Matthew 21:21 Jesus makes this point: "If you have faith and do not doubt you can do what was done to the fig tree." (Jesus cursed the fig tree so it would never bear fruit again). Jesus went on to say, "You can say to this mountain, 'Go throw yourself into the sea,' and it will be done." Now to me these are verses of great reassurance—creating confidence in me—not instruction to hurt me but rather to help me and bless me so I don't miss out on God's best for me.

What? My faith can move mountains if I what? If I do not doubt. Do we doubt God? Hey, if we don't doubt God, then we have all the faith that we need.

I know it says don't doubt God, but what should I do if I doubt God? I know that I've doubted God in my past. Well, for starters, you need to go to God and say, "God, I doubt you."

One thing I never do is lie to God. I go to God and say, "God, I doubt you. Can you renew my mind Lord? Can you increase my faith? Can I have more of you, Lord, so that this doubt is gone? Can you show me, Lord, and teach me so that this doubt is gone? The desire of my heart is that the doubt would be gone, but it's here."

(The Importance Of The Bible)

You need to express that to God and get one on one with God. Tell Him the issue, but then open your heart and let God teach you. When you ask God for something, let Him give it to you. When you ask God for knowledge, and wisdom, and insight into His word, don't run the other way and go to the movies and or go out to eat. Spend time in God's word and let Him give you the answer because He will. That's His promise. God will give you the answer. God says, "The Holy Spirit… will teach you all things." (John 14:26)

Don't Be Stupid

One great verse is Ephesians 5:17: "Do not be foolish but understand what the Lord's will is." God basically says, "Don't be stupid." Understand the Lord's will because if you understand His will and you do it, you're going to get amazing blessings on earth now and in heaven later. If you're foolish and you don't understand the Lord's will, how would you know what to do?

If you have ever worked for somebody, you know that the boss tells you what to do. If you go to the boss and ask him, "Boss, what's my job?" you won't hear him say, "Well, I can't tell you. Do what you want, and I'll decide how you did." No, of course not. He says, "Here's your job. Go and dig some holes."

"Okay, I dug holes. I did good, right?"

"Right. You did exactly what I told you. Great."

When you have a boss, you should know what to do. He should tell you. God says the same thing. You are to know His will so you know what to do. That's your responsibility. If you're not sure what you need to do, open up your Bible and start reading in the New Testament—read the Old Testa-

(The Importance Of The Bible)

ment as well, but start in the New Testament—and God will clearly reveal His will for you. God says in Jeremiah 29:11, "'I know the plans I have for you,' declares the Lord, 'plans to prosper you and not to harm you, plans to give you hope and a future.'" How's that for God's awesome will for you! Now that's should make you happy and excited!

Words Have Meaning

I was watching a comedy television show the other night where a father goes to school with his son to do something, and the teacher says, "Oh, by the way, since you're here, would you lead us in The Pledge of Allegiance?" And he couldn't remember the words.

But it's not just the words, it's what they mean. In this day and age, there are people who are trying to change The Pledge of Allegiance. They're trying to take out the words "one nation, under God" as if that's not what the intent was by our founding fathers. I hope and pray that never happens. We know clearly what the intent was—for our nation to stand united under God. It's important that those words have meaning to us in our life, and that we're grateful for this country we live in.

It's even more important that we understand what God has done for us, and we have gratitude to God for what He has done for us each and every day. We don't want to forget John 3:16, "For God so loved the world that He gave His only begotten son, that whoever should believe in Him shall never perish but shall have eternal life." It shouldn't just become a

(The Importance Of The Bible)

slogan in our lives—like a car slogan or an advertising slogan, but the words should have meaning in our lives each and every day and we shouldn't let other people's opinions or lies change what God's word truly means.

A Work of Art

I think God likes to get personal with us. Ephesians 2:1-2 says, "As for you, you were dead in your transgressions and sins, in which you used to live…" When He says, "As for you," it's pretty clear that God wants to get personal with you.

God's word goes on to say to us:

…because of his great love for us, God, who is rich in mercy, made us alive with Christ even when we were dead in transgressions—it is by grace you have been saved. And God raised us (that's you and me) up with Christ and seated us with him in the heavenly realms in Christ Jesus, in order that in the coming ages he might show the incomparable riches of his grace. (Ephesians 2:4-7)

As for you, God saved you. He raised us with Christ and seated us up with Him in the heavenly realms. God did that for us. Man, that's amazing. You have been raised up with Christ in the heavenly realms.

You say, "Then Jack, what am I still doing here on earth?" Well, God has a perfect plan for your life here on earth. A purpose for every believer. He has come to live inside of you. He has given you grace. He has blessed you abundantly and

(The Importance Of The Bible)

exceedingly—more than you could ask or imagine. When your time on earth is up, you'll get to be with Him forever and ever, reigning in heaven.

He says the kingdom of heaven is inside of you.

Consequently, you are no longer foreigners and aliens, but fellow citizens with God's people and members of God's household. And in him you too are being built together to become a dwelling in which God lives by his Spirit. (Ephesians 2:19, 22)

You are no longer foreigners. You're citizens with God's people and members of His household. Of course you're a member of His household. You're God's kid. You're God's child, and He loves you. He says, "You know what? Here's what I want to do. I want to build you up so you're a dwelling in which I live by my spirit."

I live in south Florida. Sometimes I drive by a construction site and see a foundation for a building. It looks like cement with some pipes sticking out. It doesn't look very pretty. But when it's finished, it's a beautiful building. It could be a new office building, hotel, condominium, stadium or the Taj Mahal.

When a little baby girl is born, she's not a beauty queen. She hasn't hit eighteen, nineteen, or twenty. She hasn't attained that look that would make her a beauty queen. When an artist takes his paintbrush and puts his first splotch of paint on a canvas, it's not a masterpiece. And when an author writes one word or one sentence or even a chapter, he hasn't completed his great novel yet. He only just started it. But, when he completes it, it's a masterpiece. It's amazing.

4: Light On The Path

God is building you up to be His masterpiece, and you can take that to the bank, each and every one of you—as individual as a snowflake, with a fingerprint that is un-replicated by anyone in the world, with a mind that belongs especially to you, and a body, spirit, and heart that are yours individually. Each one of you is a masterpiece of the Creator, of God Himself. And God wants you to live that way.

It's His hand and His signature on your life. All God's works are masterpieces—all of them. It might take time, the molding and making process, but He's the potter. God says, "I am the potter. You are the clay." If we are willing to be clay, the word of God will shape us and mold us and make us into exactly who God meant us and created us to be.

The Devil's Plan

Franklin Delano Roosevelt, when he was president, used to hand out a Bible to every soldier. Each Bible had the following inscription:

The White House
January 25, 1941
To the Armed Forces,

As Commander in Chief, I take pleasure in commending the reading of the Bible to all who serve in the Armed Forces of the United States. Throughout the centuries, men of many faiths and diverse origins have found in the sacred book words of wisdom, counsel, and inspiration. It is a fountain of strength, and now, as always, an aid in attaining the highest aspirations of the human soul.

Very Sincerely Yours,
Franklin D. Roosevelt

Man, he had it right back then. I recently read something that struck me as ironic. In a fair number of prisons in the United States, prisoners are encouraged to read Bibles.

4: Light On The Path

Teachers, on the other hand, are not allowed to bring Bibles to school and read them to students. Is it any wonder why prisons are now overflowing? Encouraging Bible reading once someone is in prison is like building a hospital at the bottom of a cliff rather than building a fence at the top.

We need to catch them before they fall. We've got to get the Bible back in our servicemen's arms, back in our schools, and back in our hearts where it belongs. There's a contrary side to that. There's Satan's side, and you may have heard this, but this is one version of what Satan would like to accomplish. It says:

> *If I were the devil, I would gain control of the most powerful nation in the world. I would delude their minds into thinking that they had come from man's effort instead of God's blessings.*
>
> *I would promote an attitude of loving things and using people instead of the other way around.*
>
> *I would convince people that character is not an issue when it comes to leadership.*
>
> *I would make it legal to take the lives of unborn babies.*
>
> *I would make it socially acceptable to take one's own life, and I'd invent machines to make it convenient. I would cheapen human life as much as possible so that the lives of animals are valued more than human beings.*
>
> *I would come up with drugs that sedate the mind*

(The Importance Of The Bible)

and target the young, and I would get sports heroes to advertise them.

I would get control of the media so that every night I could pollute the mind of every family member for my agenda, and I would attack the family, the backbone of any nation. I would make divorce acceptable and easy, even fashionable, because if the family crumbles so does the nation.

I would compel people to express their most depraved fantasies on canvas and movie screens, and I would call it art.

I would convince the world that people are born homosexuals and that their lifestyle should be accepted and admired.

I would take God out of the schools where even the mention of his name would be grounds for a lawsuit.

I would convince people that right and wrong are to be determined by a few who call themselves authority and refer to their agenda as 'politically correct.'

I would persuade people that the church is irrelevant and that the Bible is for the naïve, and I would dull the minds of Christians and make them believe that prayer is not important and that faithfulness and obedience are optional.

I guess I would leave things pretty much the way they are.

4: Light On The Path

That's Satan's view and by the looks of it, he must be pretty happy with the way things are going right now. In a nation that once proudly claimed to be "under God," today many people are striving to remove the one thing that brought it into being and kept it together so far—God. That's both sad and fatal.

Great Reward

How should we live our lives? According to God in Psalm 19 it should be by the laws, statutes, precepts, commands, fear, and ordinances of God. Essentially, the Word of God. The answer is shown in Psalm 19:11: "By them your servant is warned; in keeping them there is great reward."

The Psalmist tells us, "By them your servant is warned." Here is your warning.

Hey, if I'm driving and there is no more road and the bridge is out, I would like a warning. "Jack! Bridge is out! Stop!" If there is a fire burning in my house and I'm going to burn and die with my family, I would love it if you would tell me, "Fire! Get up!" Ring the bell. Sound the alarm. That would be the biggest favor you could ever do me in my life. If you ever see me walking and I have a piece of toilet paper hanging from my butt, please tell me. Okay? You won't insult me. If I ever have anything hanging from my nose, please tell me. I will personally be very grateful, as I'm sure you would be.

We want these warnings. We would heed them, wouldn't we? God doesn't stop there. The second part of Psalm 19:11

4: Light On The Path

is, "In keeping them there is great reward." God is telling us if we keep His decrees and His word, there is a great reward in store for us. This message from God couldn't be any clearer. The decrees of the Lord are firm. All of them are righteous; not some of them, all of them. By them your servant is warned; in keeping them there is great reward. The best way, the only way, to live our lives—to complete our journey—is by following His way.

The next verses, 12-14, go on to state: "But who can discern their own errors? Forgive my hidden faults. Keep your servant also from willful sins; may they not rule over me. Then I will be blameless, innocent of great transgression."

That is the psalmist's prayer. He's asking, "Look, who can figure out their own errors? Lord, please keep me from willful sins. I don't want to sin willfully. Keep me from that. Then I'll be blameless." He's praying to God for help. He realizes, "Look, I can't figure out my own problems sometimes. I can't be objective about myself."

Ask me anything about my life, and I'll tell you I'm right. I mean, do you go around thinking of stuff and say, "Oh, let me tell you my opinion because I know I'm wrong?" No. Of course you think you're right. We all think we're right or we wouldn't say something. We believe we're right.

The first thing we need to do is look at our lives and make sure that we are not giving into willful sins—that they're not ruling over us.

If something is holding you captive, if you're in bondage or enslaved to a sin, addiction or a problem or something—that is an issue. Any issue that has "victory" over you is a problem.

(The Importance Of The Bible)

God says, "A man is a slave to whatever he hasn't mastered." (2 Peter 2:19).

As you are praying to God, let this be the prayer of your heart today, that you will be blameless and innocent of great transgression before the Lord. God has told us how to do this. Believe God, keep the faith, and do what He has told you. He's teaching you out of love and joy because He wants you to have the great reward.

"Hey Lord, keep me from my own errors. Forgive my hidden faults. Keep your servant from willful sins." I pray that this is the prayer of your heart and my heart.

Lifting the Veil

I believe that God wants to change your heart. I believe He wants to change the very focus of your life. If you're a little off focus, God wants to get you right back on focus, right now.

I had the privilege of praying for my friend's mom the other day. She's about ninety, and we were praying with her for some physical healing. She said the most amazing words to me. This is a sold-out Christian woman who, in the midst of her pain and suffering and asking God for physical healing, said, "Jack, I can't see beyond the love of Jesus." This woman loves Jesus so much, and is so focused on Jesus that she's looking at the world and still she says, "I can't see beyond the love of Jesus. There are other things to look at, but I don't see them. I just see the love of Jesus." You can see the love of Jesus flowing from her life.

I want to be like that. I want to be at the place in my life where I can't see past the love of Jesus Christ. Where the love of Jesus is all I see.

I hope and pray that's where you want to be, and I believe God wants to bring us there. In the New Testament, Paul is talking to the church at Corinth, and he's reminding them that there's a veil of spiritual darkness, of spiritual blindness, that prevents people from seeing the truth of God. That veil still exists today—a blindness that prevents people from seeing Jesus Christ. God gives us the answer through Paul of how we can take away that blindness and remove that veil. We find it in 2 Corinthians 3:15-16: "Even to this day when Moses is read, a veil covers their hearts. But whenever anyone turns to the Lord, the veil is taken away."

Whenever anyone turns to the Lord, the veil is taken away. That's your answer. It's like a man in the desert who is dying of thirst. He sees a sign that reads, "Water. This way." Where would you go? If I was dying in the desert I'd follow the sign that says there is water. God says if you want that veil taken away, you need to turn to the Lord. That's how you do it. Is there any one of us to whom God is not saying, "Turn to Me"? I don't think so. The word of God goes on to say, in the very next verse: "Now the Lord is the Spirit, and where the Spirit of the Lord is, there is freedom."

Do you want slavery or freedom? Do you want freedom from worries, anxieties, stress, and strain? From the physical, emotional, spiritual, relational, and financial problems in your life? Do you want freedom? God didn't say you wouldn't have those problems. He said you'll have freedom so they won't overrun your life and ruin it. You can have the freedom of God in your life today—all of it.

There is victory in Christ, and the most important thing you'll have freedom from is death. You and I, as believers in Jesus Christ, know what's going to happen when our time on earth is over. We're going to live with Jesus forever and ever. That's the certainty, the blessed assurance that enables us to live our lives not being able to see past the love of Jesus because we're so grateful for what Jesus has done for us.

Qualifying

My kids—the young ones, Jackson and Talia—don't know the things they're going to know five years from now. They're going to get a lot smarter as they go. So are you and I. God is going to teach us. We're going to get a lot smarter as we go. But if we don't go—to Him in prayer and seek more knowledge of Him—we won't get any smarter. The apostle Paul says, "We continually ask God to fill you with the knowledge of his will… so that you may live a life worthy of the Lord and please him in every way." (Colossians 1:9-10)

Isn't that what you want to do? Isn't that the purpose of your life? To live a life worthy of the Lord and to please Him in every way. Wow! It surely is the purpose of mine.

If that's what you really want, God's Word tells you how to do it. There are four ways:

Bearing fruit in every good work, growing in the knowledge of God, being strengthened with all power according to His glorious might so that you may have great endurance and patience, and joyfully giving thanks to the Father, who has qualified you to share in the inheritance of the saints in the kingdom of light. (Colossians 1:10-12)

4: Light On The Path

Bearing fruit in every good work.

Growing in the knowledge of God.

Being strengthened with all power according to His glorious might.

Joyfully giving thanks to the Father.

First though, what does it mean, "God qualified us?" That means He made it happen. If you ever went for a mortgage and the mortgage broker qualified you, he made sure your application was in order so you could get the mortgage. God qualified you to get to heaven. You didn't do it yourself. You didn't get to heaven based on what you earned. It wasn't because of your credit rating. God qualified you based on the perfect credit score of Jesus, and His blood shed for you. You're in. When His blood was spilled, that was your ticket, your pre-qualification.

So, back to the four things Paul mentioned. If you want to please God, the first one is bearing fruit in every good work. Jesus says it again in John 15:16: "bear fruit – fruit that will last." That's why you were created.

Second, grow in the knowledge of God. It's not me saying it. It's God's instruction to you. You want to live a life that's worthy of God? Grow in the knowledge of God.

Third, be strengthened with all power. The power of God is within you. It's there already, waiting for you to just say yes, to believe and receive. You can have as much of it is you can stand. As believers every one of us has God's power within us. Why? So that we may have great endurance and patience. Obviously, those are two things we need—endurance and patience. Man, try living life without it. Try living life frustrated, unable to endure.

(The Importance Of The Bible)

The apostle Paul says we're to run our race with our eyes on the prize. The prize for us is heaven. We're to endure. It's a long race. It's not a sprint. It's a marathon. That's the Christian life. But God's power gives us the ability to endure with patience and to receive the prize.

Lastly, giving thanks to the Father who has qualified us to share in the wonderful riches of heaven. 1 Thessalonians 5:16-18 says, "Be joyful always; pray continually; give thanks in all circumstances, for this is God's will for you in Christ Jesus." Do this and you can be sure you will live a life that matters for God.

5

GENEROUS GOD
(God's Overflowing Kindness Towards Us)

Help Me Choose

It was Patrick Morley who said that it's not one bad choice that ruins your life. The thought is, if you smoke one joint, you're not a pothead. You eat one burger and you're not going to clog your arteries up and die of a heart attack. It's the series of bad choices that will ruin you. It's continuously smoking pot that will cause a loss of brain cells and lack of motivation. If you keep on eating those burgers and fries, you'll eventually have to deal with the ramifications of that.

It's a series of bad choices. And you have a choice before you now. Ask yourself: How have I been looking at the world and the things going on around me? Is it possible for one instance to happen and completely change my view of the world? Or am I so anchored in the solid rock of God that no matter what happens—when my body fails me, when my relatives die, when I lose my money, when people don't like me, when people criticize me—I have the joy of the Lord and that's all I see? Am I focused on Him, the Rock of my salvation? Is that what's most important to me?

Psalm 32:8-9 says:

5: Generous God

I will instruct you and teach you in the way you should go; I will counsel you and watch over you. Do not be like the horse or the mule, which have no understanding but must be controlled by bit and bridle or they will not come to you.

Here is God saying that He'll instruct you and teach you in the way you should go. He'll counsel you and look over you. He will, but you have to be there for God's teaching and instruction. Don't be like the horse or the mule without understanding. He shouldn't have to grab you by the hair to get you to listen and teach you these things. You should be receptive. You should want to learn these things.

I have some land up in north Florida, and I was trying to save our investment in the land by turning it into a solar farm. Back then I knew nothing about the solar business. Through a friend of mine, I met a high ranking executive at Progress Energy in Florida and he said to me, "Listen, I'll guide you through every step of the way. I'll take you through the process."

My response was, "Whoa, you've got to be like the greatest guy in the world. Thank you so much."

I was so grateful, so happy to get this guidance and knowledge and wisdom in an area that I don't understand because I don't want to mess up.

Why don't we have that exact feeling towards God? God says he'll guide us every step of the way. Why aren't we so happy and joyful to get guidance and wisdom from God? He's promised it to us. We should be grateful.

Fill Up

God wants us to be filled completely with His spirit. How does that work, though? Some people say, "I got all the Holy Spirit I'll ever need the day I got saved." Other people say, "Oh, I'm a leaky vessel. I have the Holy Spirit, but it leaks out of me, and I need to be filled up again and again."

God says that if you ask, you'll receive. God says, "What makes you think that I wouldn't bless you with all you need if you ask?" If you want more of God's Holy Spirit, all you have to do is ask God for more. Look at God confirming words in Matthew 7:9-11 says "Or what man is there among you who, when his son asks for a loaf, will give him a stone? Or if he asks for a fish, he will not give him a snake, will he? If you then, being evil, know how to give good gifts to your children, how much more will your Father who is in heaven give what is good to those who ask Him!"

You are filled with the Holy Spirit of God. When you accepted him as your Lord and Savior, His Holy Spirit came to live inside of your heart. You have the Holy Spirit of God inside of your heart. You've got it. Now, the question is: Are

5: Generous God

you going to use it? Are you going to fill your heart and life with the things of the spirit, or are you going to instead fill your heart and life with the things of the world and drown out the power of the Holy Spirit? Are you going to feed the Spirit, or are you going to feed the flesh? One of them is going to get stronger and one of them is going to get weaker.

If you think you're a leaky vessel, fill yourself up. If you had a tire, and there was air leaking out of it, would you just let all the air leak out and never drive your car again? No, that's not what you would do. You would keep filling the tire up, or you would replace it with a new one, but you wouldn't stop driving. I've had slow leaks. I've had to fill them up every three or four days. That's what I do. I fill it up so I can keep driving.

That's the spiritual equivalent of what we do in our lives. So, why wouldn't you fill yourself up with the Holy Spirit of God? God is available. God is here. All you have to do is ask. Say, "God, I want more of you. Lord, fill me with your spirit."

And understand it's not a feeling of, "Oh, I've got the spirit," or, "Oh, I don't feel like I have it." It is a faith that says, "God, I asked you for something. You said if I ask in your name according to your will, I'll receive. Certainly, it's in your will that I be filled up with Your Holy Spirit so I can glorify you in every single thing I do. So, fill me with your spirit. I will trust that I've asked and you've answered, whether I feel it or not. I've got it, and I'm going to go live that way."

That's what God wants. God wants us to be filled with His Holy Spirit. Have you asked for it? He will give you as much as you want. So ask for a lot!

For Your Enjoyment

God is so good. God is so faithful. God is so...God. Here's a message of great hope that I am inspired to share with you. It starts with 1 Timothy 6:17: "Command those who are rich in this present world not to be arrogant nor to put their hope in wealth..."

The first place not to put your hope is in wealth, in money, in stuff. Why? Why shouldn't I put my hope in wealth, Lord? What's wrong with that? He goes on to say that it's so uncertain. He says: "Command those who are rich in this present world not to be arrogant nor to put their hope in wealth, which is so uncertain..."

Well, then what should I do, Lord? He goes on to say: "...but [tell them] to put their hope in God, who richly provides us with everything for our enjoyment."

You want to know where to put your hope? Here's what God tells you. Put your hope in God. He says if you do that, He'll provide you with everything—not some things, not a few things, not most things, everything. For what? For our enjoyment.

God wants you to be happy. God wants you to love being alive. God wants every day to be an adventure—this great

5: Generous God

journey that you're taking with Him through life with the certainty that you know where you're going to wind up.

And you say, "Well, wait a minute, Jack. That verse doesn't apply to me. You see, I'm not rich. Very clearly it said in the verse 'command those who are rich in this world.' But I'm not rich. I don't have a million dollars in the bank. I sometimes don't even have a thousand. It doesn't apply to me."

Really? By the world's standards, you are probably one of the wealthiest people in the world. Oh, you may not be the wealthiest person in some parts of the United States. I get that. But by the world's standards, percentage wise, comparing to all the people who live in the world, you are probably amongst the top one to two percent of the richest people on Earth—based not only on how much you have in the bank, but on the stuff you have, on the way you live, on the luxuries that we take for granted like electricity and fresh food and air conditioning. We have so many things that other people don't have. Trust me. You're rich in this world.

God says put your hope in God—that's the answer—who richly provides for us everything for our enjoyment. If you want to enjoy life and you want to be happy, you need to put your hope in God. It's all there, right in 1 Timothy 6:17:

> *Command those who are rich in this present world not to be arrogant nor to put their hope in wealth.*

Rich people can easily be fooled into thinking they have something of value because the world values money. The world says that's a good thing.

God says that's nothing. "For what does it profit a man to gain the whole world if he forfeits his soul?" Money means

(God's Overflowing Kindness Towards Us)

nothing. Spiritual riches mean everything. God says, "If you put your hope in me, I'll give you everything for your enjoyment."

Healing

Let's say I was teaching at Florida Atlantic University (which I'm not), and you came to my class and you said, "Professor, I'm here but I have no notebook and I can't study. Can you just sum up your whole class for me? Or just give me one key idea you want me to take away and remember from this class."

Well, I thought about it like that and here's what I believe God would want you to take away from His "class." It's a parable. It's Matthew 8, and the story starts in verse 5. It is titled "The Faith of the Centurion" in the New International Version of the Bible.

"When Jesus had entered Capernaum, a centurion came to him, asking for help. 'Lord,' he said, 'my servant lies at home paralyzed and in terrible suffering.' Jesus said to him, 'I will go and heal him.'"

Take note right there that Jesus was willing to go and heal that guy's servant; Jesus is also willing to heal you.

Jesus is always willing. For example, when I was struggling with my drug addiction, Jesus was always willing to take my addiction from me, but He waited until I was ready to respond

(God's Overflowing Kindness Towards Us)

and open my heart and life to Him completely. He was always willing to fill me with more of His Holy Spirit. He was always willing to love me. He was always willing to bless me. He was always willing to give me a life that would give me everything I could ever dream of spiritually.

He is always willing.

It was always me who wasn't willing to give it to Jesus. My life, my addiction, my pride, my future, are just some of the things I previously held back from God. It was always me who wasn't willing to plow the field. It was always me who wasn't willing to cry out to God with all my heart. It was always me who wasn't willing to seek God with all my heart, soul, and mind.

Jesus is willing now, this very moment, to heal you and free you. The story continues in verse eight: "The centurion replied, 'Lord, I do not deserve to have you come under my roof. But just say the word, and my servant will be healed.'"

"I'm not worthy of you." The centurion was saying.

Is anyone in this world worthy of the love that we're freely given from Jesus Christ? Nobody. Not me. I'm the least worthy of everybody I know. None of us are worthy. We all know that. But look at the centurion. He said, "I'm not worthy. Lord, you don't even have to come to the house. Just say the word and he'll be healed."

What a great demonstration of faith. And yet, we question God on every single decision regarding everything that happens in our life, like we're the board of directors of God Inc. and we have to evaluate His performance to make sure He's doing His job so we can get the dividends we want. That's

5: Generous God

not the way it works. You didn't pay a nickel for your life. God paid it all. It's free. He gave it to you. It's a trust account in your name. It's all for you. And the benefit and dividends you receive is all of the kingdom of heaven. Everything you could ever want. Abundant life now and eternal life forever. Seriously, what more could we ever want?

True Riches

The centurion we just talked about in our last chapter says in Matthew 8, "For I myself am a man under authority, with soldiers under me. I tell this one, "Go," and he goes; and that one, "Come," and he comes. I say to my servant, "Do this," and he does it.' When Jesus heard this, he was astonished."

I love that line. That's actually how it reads in the Bible. Can you imagine Jesus being astonished like, "Holy cow, I can't believe this!" Jesus amazed? Jesus shocked?

Jesus was astonished at the centurion's faith and He said, "Such faith like this I haven't even seen in Israel." When God looks at us, that's what He's looking for. Trust. Faith. He wants us to say, "Lord, You said it and I believe it. Lord, I trust you. I love you."

Jesus said, "I tell you the truth, I have not found anyone in Israel with such great faith. I say to you that many will come from the east and the west, and will take their places at the feast with Abraham, Isaac and Jacob in the kingdom of heaven."

I love that. There it is in "God and white." It says many will come from the east and the west, and will take their places at the feast with Abraham, Isaac and Jacob in the kingdom

5: Generous God

of heaven. There's a feast? Yes! There's a feast, and you have a place at the table. You, personally, and every believer of Jesus Christ will be at that feast with Abraham, Isaac, and Jacob, and Jesus, and God the Father and other believers.

So what's your problem? What's my problem? With a promise like that, what more could we ask for?

But listen to this warning: "But the subjects of the kingdom will be thrown outside, into the darkness, where there will be weeping and gnashing of teeth."

That line in Matthew 8:12 specifically applies to the Pharisees who claim to be clean on the outside but were dirty on the inside, who followed religious tradition, but their hearts were far from God. It also applies to all people who call themselves Christians, yet don't believe God in their hearts. It doesn't matter what you call yourself. It matters who you are. You can go out and say, "I'm a pastor of Victory United Church" Even if you're not. While you can call yourself that all day long; it doesn't change the fact that you are not the pastor of Victory United Church. You can walk into K-Mart and introduce yourself, "How are you? Pastor of Victory United Church. That's who I am."

But when you come to Victory United Church, you're not preaching because you're not the pastor. That's how the kingdom of heaven will be. That's what God is saying.

"When it comes time for heaven, anybody who loved me and accepted me"—and remember God says everyone who calls on the name of the Lord will be saved—"will be in at the feast. Everyone who didn't really love me—no matter what you said or called yourself—you're out."

(God's Overflowing Kindness Towards Us)

Finally, in verse 13, we read, "Then Jesus said to the centurion, 'Go! It will be done just as you believed it would.' And his servant was healed at that very hour."

Has not our God told us that if we ask according to His will anything we want, it will be given to us? Has not our God told us that He loves us so much that it's His joy to share with us the kingdom of heaven?

The word of God says He is pleased to give you the keys to the kingdom. Go. It will be done, just as you believed.

But for the Grace of God

I was with a buddy of mine the other day—someone I've known since we were teenagers—and he said to me, "I'm going through some really tough times."

"What's going on?" I asked him.

He said, "Well, I'm still struggling with drug and alcohol addiction."

He's doing a lot of cocaine, and that's a bad drug. They're all bad, but trust me on this one, cocaine is brutal. My buddy has a wife and kids and he's a professional guy. I was sitting there talking to him and he said how hard it was, telling me how he'd disappear for days and lock himself in a hotel room on a cocaine binge.

I've been there so I can relate to that, and I said, "Man, this is so sad. Listen, I have this number of another friend of mine you can call if you need help—he owns a rehab place."

But he said, "No, no, no, I don't want it now."

He obviously wasn't ready. So, I just sat there in the chair and I thought, "Lord, thank you so much that I'm sober."

I mean, forget money issues; forget worries and cares, and responsibilities and all that other stuff. I was just thanking God that I'm not dealing with that anymore!

(God's Overflowing Kindness Towards Us)

We have so much to be grateful for, no matter what we're dealing with. Just to have this opportunity to have a life and be alive is enough reason to be eternally grateful.

I wish that he was ready to get the help he needs because you don't have to stay addicted to drugs or alcohol. You don't have to stay addicted to anything. There's help if you want to take it, but it's a narrow road to recovery and you have to go down it to get to sobriety. There is absolutely help, but my friend wasn't ready. I hope and pray he will be soon.

It was a huge reminder to me to be grateful for the little things—for the air we breathe, the food we eat, the friends we have, just to be grateful for so many little things we have.

We get so caught up in all these "big things," but in the process we often take the biggest things for granted—like God, life and salvation.

A .300 Hitter

I was talking with a friend of mine about some personal stuff and the trials and tribulations that we had both been going through. Then we stopped and talked instead about taking a minute to remember how much God loves us. Sometimes we are unnecessarily hard on ourselves.

When I was a businessman, I used to think that being critical was a great characteristic. I would tell people everything they were doing wrong, quite frequently in fact. At one point my partner and I had two hundred people working for us, so as a boss, you would think that was a good thing. I tell our employees, "Hey, it's great that you're doing all these things right. That's wonderful, but let me help you in the areas you're not doing so great so that you can be a better employee, we can all make more money, and we'll all live happily ever after."

As a batting coach or an acting coach, that would probably be a good thing. You could say, "Hey, you're doing all these things right, but let's fix these things you're doing wrong so you can be perfect." Except that nobody's perfect; even in baseball, if three out of ten times you succeed, you're one of the best there ever was, you're a .300 hitter, and you're amazing. In

(God's Overflowing Kindness Towards Us)

football, if you can complete 70% of your passes, only seven out of ten times, you're one of the best that ever lived.

What about the other three times they missed? Why aren't these guys going home and clubbing themselves unmercifully saying, "I stink. I'm the worst ever. You should just get rid of me." No, if they did that, they would be miserable all the time. They wouldn't be able to enjoy the times they get it right.

Don't we live like that sometimes? Don't we sometimes look at our parenting, our husband-ing, our wife-ing (those are new words I created, hope you like them!), our employees, our relationships, our finances, our health and all we see is what's wrong and where we failed, and we become miserable? Instead of saying, "Yeah, there are a couple of things I haven't done perfectly, but look at all these wonderful things I have done," we focus on the failures.

When it comes down to it, there's only one wonderful thing you have to do—love God with all your heart and soul. If you do that, everything else in your life will flow wonderfully from it. You'll have nothing to worry about, yet we beat ourselves up over the things that we perceive are not good or we're not doing right.

I have three kids, when two of them were young—eight and six—I would get upset at myself if I didn't play with them enough by their definition. In my book I was tired and exhausted. I had played with them for hours. Wasn't that enough?

"No, daddy, we want more." Okay, now I feel like a bad father.

If I don't feel like I'm showing my wife how much I love her, I feel like a bad husband.

5: Generous God

If I'm not making enough money, I feel like a bad provider.

If I'm not keeping myself fit and trim, I feel like I'm not in shape the way I should be.

Holy cow, that's a hard life when we go down that road. I can never get it right. Don't we live like that sometimes? That's not the way God wants you to live. That's not what God created you for. God knows we aren't perfect. We have imperfections and that's okay.

There'll be none of that in heaven. There'll be no pain, no crying, no physical infirmity, nothing like that. In heaven, we'll be dancing for eternity; we'll be perfect in Him forever-more. God knew that man would have shortcomings here on earth, but God told us in spite of that to leap and rejoice, that we should be happy and joyful because our salvation is assured. He told us that we shouldn't put pressure on ourselves and let Satan throw these darts at us—telling us that we're not good enough, that we're unsuccessful, that we need to do this better and that better. How about the things that we do get right?

Guess what? I think those are the things that the Lord is looking at, just like any good father would be. He is our good and loving Father and He's not waiting until we screw up to bash us over the head with a stick. He's watching us with joy, waiting to proclaim our names in front of nations: "This is my son! This is my daughter! Aren't they great? They lived their lives doing their best for me and I love them dearly!"

I realize that I only have one thing I need to do right, and that brings with it such peace and joy. I just love the Lord with all my heart and soul, and everything else flows out of that just fine.

(God's Overflowing Kindness Towards Us)

In baseball, we don't always hit the ball the way we want. Sometimes we hit it hard, and the guy catches it, and we're out. That's okay. That's just part of being alive. We're supposed to be celebrating the fact that we're alive. Celebrating! Have you celebrated the fact that you're alive today? Or did you instead just wake up and look at your daily struggles and all of the things that you have to do? Did you wake up overwhelmed at the things you haven't done, or things you don't have, or where you fell short? And did you get all upset and disappointed with yourself? That's just what Satan wants. It's not what God wants though. That's not what you want for your kids, is it? It's definitely not what God wants for you.

It's Finished

A buddy of mine—a young man, seventeen years old, is someone who I would consider a mighty man of God. He comes from a single-parent home and his mother is raising him. His father has been long gone. He's a kid who has been on fire for the Lord since he was ten years old. I've seen him grow up in the church, and some of the men in the church—myself included—try to really encourage him in his dedication to the Lord. It's just amazing to watch God work in his life. He moved up North recently, and I spoke to him on the phone. I asked, "How are you doing, buddy?"

He said, "Oh, good, Jack. The people here are really nice. But I've got to tell you one thing."

I said, "What's that?"

He said, "Well, I sometimes feel like I'm not doing everything I should. I make these promises to God about how I'm going to witness to those people and then I don't do it. And I really, really feel horrible about myself."

I told him, " Satan is just trying to trick you. Satan is trying to make you think that it's about your accomplishments, that if you don't do certain things God isn't going to love you as

(God's Overflowing Kindness Towards Us)

much, or you're letting God down, or you're failing God. That's not the case. That's a trick of Satan to try and knock you to the sidelines so that you'll be ineffective for the Lord. Hey, this may be a time in your life God wants to minister just to you so that He can train you and shape you and mold you to use you later. I've watched you be a light amongst your high school friends and your junior high friends, and I don't know what specifically God is doing right now in your life, but I know God knows, and your job is just to trust Him."

I hope I encouraged that young man, and I hope I encourage you in that same thing. It's all about trusting in the finished work of Jesus Christ. It's about believing that when God said on the cross, "It is finished," when He hung from that cross and He died bloody, beaten, killed by the people of this world for our sin, that price for your sin and my sin was paid forever.

When He said, "It is finished," He meant it. There is nothing that you or I can do to take away or add anything to our salvation. There is nothing that we can do to have God love us any more or any less. God has already demonstrated His love for us on the cross. Our job is to accept that love, to revel in that love, to enjoy that love.

An "A" in the Class

The Bible says we're to leap and rejoice for our salvation is assured. It says, "This is the day the Lord has made, we will rejoice and be glad in it." (Psalm 118:24) When we don't do that, we miss the blessing of the abundant Christian life that Christ died for, that He paid the price for. Oh, of course, we should do good things for the Lord. Of course, we should witness where we can, live a life that glorifies God, go and bear fruit that will last, and make disciples. We're to do all of these things out of gratitude in our hearts for what God has done for us. Remember that, it should be out of gratitude, joy, and thankfulness; not out of guilt, shame, fear, or anxiety.

God's Holy Spirit, deposited in your heart upon salvation, will teach you all things. God will tell you what you're supposed to do and where and when and to whom. Your job is to listen to the Holy Spirit. Your job is to drown out the noise of the world and hear the Holy Spirit so you'll be able to respond as God wants you to.

There's a time in your life where God says, "Be still and know that I am God." There's a time in your life where God says, "My grace is sufficient for thee. You don't need anything

(God's Overflowing Kindness Towards Us)

else. You just need me. You have everything you need." And when we listen to His Holy Spirit, we're reminded that God is pleased to give us the kingdom.

There is a great story and I hope it will apply to your life. It's a story I read, and it went something like this: There was a young girl in her senior year of college. She was a straight 'A' student and a real whiz in science and math. She was signed up for an honors English literature which was required for her to graduate. And she went to the class, and the first day she realized, "Whoa, I'm in way over my head. This is too much for me. It's just too much. I can't learn this English literature. As a matter of fact, it's going to kill my beautiful straight 'A' average. My 4.0 is going to go down fast. So you know what I've got to do? I've got to get out of this class fast. I've got to drop this class."

If you've been to college, you know you can add or drop classes early on. So the girl calls her father and she says, "Dad, please come with me. Come to the school, so I can explain to the dean tomorrow how I've got to get out of this class. It's going to kill my average. I can't handle it." The father says, "Of course, sweetheart."

He comes down with her to the college the next day and he says to the dean, "Dean, listen, this is my daughter. And she's very, very conscientious, dean. She's a straight 'A' student, a 4.0 student. She can't handle this English literature class. It's just too much. Can you put her in a regular English class instead?"

The dean says, "Sure, but can I talk to you guys privately?" She dismisses the rest of the people around and she says to the father, "Now, may I talk to your daughter?" The father says, "Of course."

The dean looks at the daughter and she asks, "Young lady, if I guarantee you right now that I will give you an 'A' in that class, if I give you an 'A' right now today guaranteed—you've earned your 'A'—will you go and take the class?" The daughter says, "Well, yeah. Sure." And the dean replies, "You got it. I've guaranteed you an 'A'. Now go take the class." Then the dean said to the father, "Hey, look. I'm removing the fear, the reason she has not to succeed. I'm giving her that 'A' so now she can go and learn about English literature and not have to worry about it. The thing that was preventing her from learning, this fear of how she will do, how she will measure up—is now taken away. She doesn't have to worry about that. Now she can go and learn." And she went and got an 'A' on her own in the class.

Here's the great news for you. Jesus has given you an 'A'. You're done. You're finished. You've got an 'A' from the Lord. Now you can go and live and learn and enjoy what this life is all about from God. That's a tremendous blessing many Christians miss in their life. They still think it's about what they can do. "I've got to do this to be happy, and I've got to do that to be happy, and God won't love me if I don't do this; I'm falling short here, and I'm falling short there."

No, that's not how it goes. You've got your 'A'. Jesus earned it for you on the cross. Jesus gave it to you for free before you earned it so that you can have all the benefits of it. Now go enjoy... live free... That's the desire of God's heart.

Scot-Free

God told Joshua to be strong and courageous. God tells us the same thing in Psalm 16:8-11: "I have set the Lord always before me; because He is at my right hand I shall not be moved. Therefore my heart is glad, and my glory rejoices; my flesh also will rest in hope. For you will not leave my soul in Sheol, nor will you allow Your Holy One to see corruption. You will show me the path of life; in your presence is fullness of joy; at your right hand are pleasures forevermore."

So the answer is in God's hands, in His presence, and at His right hand. I got a traffic ticket years ago for running a stop sign. So I sent it to my lawyer. I've probably gotten four tickets in the last fifteen years. And I sent them all to this guy. He's very good at beating tickets on technicalities. He got this one beat because the cop was going to be late to court, and I got off scot-free. I committed the crime, but I got off scot-free. With that event I was reminded of something God wants to remind us of every day—we got off scot-free. The penalty of sin is death, and we got off scot-free.

Hebrews 8:12 says, "For I will forgive their wickedness and will remember their sins no more."

5: Generous God

Isaiah 43:25 says, "I, even I, am he who blots out your transgressions, for my own sake, and remembers your sins no more." Thank God that Jesus is our advocate, our lawyer—and He has never lost a case!

The Claim Ticket

Have you ever gone to a really nice restaurant where you leave your coat at a coat check? They give you a ticket so you can grab your coat after the meal. That is the kind of place where, whether you want to or not, you have to valet park your car. They give you a ticket to come pick up your car when you're ready—a claim ticket, a ticket to get what is yours. When it comes time to hand in the claim ticket, you don't fail to turn in that ticket and get back what belongs to you. You wouldn't leave that restaurant without your coat and you certainly wouldn't leave your car there and walk home.

Whether or not you have ever been to one of those restaurants, you have a claim ticket in your hand today. The presence of God, the Holy Spirit, was yours the moment you asked Jesus to enter your life. You possess the "claim ticket" to God's kingdom of heaven. You have it. You own it. It's yours. No one can take it away from you.

Your claim ticket is proof that something is yours. However, what you do with that claim ticket is up to you. I pray that you are not only certain of His kingdom within you, but that you

5: Generous God

have decided to use your "claim ticket", (Jesus himself living in your heart) to lead many others to the best and most lasting thing they could ever lay hold of—eternal life in heaven.

Opening Gifts

Sometimes at Christmas or your birthday, you'll hear this question: "What did you get? What was your present?" The next question often is, "Well, what did you want?"

Let's imagine you wanted a brand new car. Now that's an ambitious request, but that was what you wanted. Instead, you got this tiny little box. You saw the box and you said, "Well, obviously, this cannot be the car. I wanted a car. Clearly, it's not the car. This is terrible. People don't understand me. They don't love me enough to give me what I want. Oh, that crummy little box? Yeah, I'll get to that later. Oh, yeah, happy birthday to me."

Sometimes we're so ungrateful. Our gratitude is so selfish, based on what we think we want. That little box? Oh, you mean the one with the diamond in it that was worth twenty cars but you thought was valueless because it didn't look like what you thought it should be?

The third question is: "What did we deserve?" A birthday gift, a Christmas gift, a graduation gift? What part of the word "gift" is unclear? You deserve none of it. It's not a birthday paycheck. It's not a birthday reward for something you have done. It's a birthday gift. What did you deserve? Nothing.

5: Generous God

We don't deserve the glory of God, we don't deserve the grace of God, and we don't deserve the kingdom of God. We don't deserve heaven; we deserve hell—even the best of us. Even my sweet wonderful grandmother who died at the age of 104 years old, the best woman I ever knew, didn't deserve to go to heaven because heaven is where perfection is. It is the perfect place of God and you need to be 100% perfect to deserve admittance to heaven. And we've yet to see the man or woman or grandmother who can do that.

Each of us is born a descendant of Adam and Eve—that's where we can trace our lineage. We don't need a genealogical tree or a website to show us. We have the Bible. Adam and Eve, as you know, sinned in the Garden of Eden by eating from the tree that God had told them not to eat from. They disobeyed God, and every single person born since that day has been born a sinner because their blood comes from Adam and Eve. It's not based on how many good things you've done in your life because you would have to have done everything in your life perfectly.

We're all born sinners. None of us qualify to get into the kingdom of heaven. None of us qualify to have our ticket stamped "Paid," go on in. Of course, we know Jesus died on the cross. He paid the price for our sin, and now our ticket is stamped. Come on in, paid in full, entry guaranteed. Now when God looks at you and me, He doesn't see us clothed in our sin as descendants of Adam and Eve. He sees us clothed in the full righteousness of Jesus Christ.

It's by the gift of Jesus, the ticket of Jesus—which we didn't deserve—that we are allowed in. He has given us the

(God's Overflowing Kindness Towards Us)

key. We are in the kingdom of heaven. Sometimes we take it for granted, but I want you to think about this because your perception of this, the greatest gift ever, will determine how you live your life. Either you will be grateful and joyful, as it should be! Or you will be miserable.

Missed

I remember hearing a sad story about a young man who graduated from college. He expected only one thing for graduation from his parents—a new car. He knew he was going to get it and he was thrilled and excited on the day of his graduation. He walked up the aisle, decked out in his graduation robe and cap. He received his diploma, amidst a bunch of cheers. He headed to his grad party, where his family and friends were waiting to celebrate. But all this time he was waiting for one thing. That car.

His father approached him and he knew it was coming. Finally. Then his father handed him a small wrapped present. "In this," his father said, "is everything you will ever need."

The young man tore it open and found…a Bible. He was furious. He stormed out of the door and never spoke to his father again. A few years later, word came that his father had died, and, feeling stricken with guilt and remorse, he returned to his hometown. He visited his father's house and found that Bible, the one that all this time he saw as the cause of his anger and bitterness.

He opened the leather cover and saw, taped into the front cover, a key. His key. His car key. The car had been waiting in

(God's Overflowing Kindness Towards Us)

the garage and his father had been waiting for him to open the book and discover his surprise.

So remember, God says, "I know the plans I have for you, plans to prosper you, not to harm you, to give you a hope and a future." He means it and we should trust him.

A Fresh Breath of Perspective

One time I felt like I was dying a slow death. I was in a lot of pain. I had been playing ball with my nine-year old son's baseball team and I pulled a muscle or something in my rib cage. I was hurting so much that I couldn't take a full breath. I don't know if you've ever experienced this for any reason, but not being able to get a full breath of air was frightening. I laid in bed for two days on an ice pack just trying to catch my breath, breathing really slow and easy. Finally, a few days later, I was able to take a full breath without being in pain. It felt great!

I'm back in the game, but here's what God showed me in those couple of days when I couldn't take a full breath. He said, "Jack, you know all that stuff you've been worrying about and thinking about—the future, your family, finances, your health, your kids, all the plans you're trying to make, what will happen, what won't happen, what might happen, what should happen, what could happen? You know all that stuff you've been thinking about and it's causing you a little bit of worry?" These days we call it more sophisticated words: anxiety or stress. But it's worry.

(God's Overflowing Kindness Towards Us)

So I said, "Yes, Lord, I'm very familiar with that stuff."

He said, "What are you thinking about now?"

I said, "The only thing I'm thinking about now, Lord, is being able to take a full breath without my chest feeling like there's a bomb in it that has blown up, that there's a knife in it every breath I take. It just hurts so much."

And God said, "Exactly. That's exactly right. The only thing important to you now is being able to take a breath without being in any pain."

I got the point. And on that day, when I was able to take that breath without being in pain, I was so grateful for the breath. I'm still on that high. I mean it. It hasn't worn off. I hope it never wears off because I'm telling you, the same concerns are still in my life—the same "what will be, could be, should be, may be"—nothing's changed except the way I look at it.

I'll deal with all those things in God's time. He has them all in His hands anyway, and I am so grateful for that. To God be the glory. It was a very personal lesson for me, but it's for all of us. We take for granted the very breath we take—until we can't take it anymore. But we don't want to make that mistake. We want to be grateful to God for the things that we have, and trust Him that everything else will work out. God says put Him first—seek Him first—and all these other things will come.

Revealed for You

The words in First Peter, Chapter 1, are strong. Verses 17-20 say:

Since you call on a Father who judges each person's work impartially, live out your time as foreigners here in reverent fear. For you know that it was not with perishable things such as silver or gold that you were redeemed from the empty way of life handed down to you from your ancestors, but with the precious blood of Christ, a lamb without blemish or defect. He was chosen before the creation of the world, but was revealed in these last times for your sake.

It was for your sake that Christ was revealed. And I can tell you personally, I know that is the truth for me. I truly believe that Jesus died on that cross for Jack Levine and for you and for every person in the world. It's God's desire that all should repent and come to the glory of the Lord, that none should fall short. So when Peter says, "Look, you call on a Father who judges each person's work impartially. Live out your time as

(God's Overflowing Kindness Towards Us)

foreigners here in reverent fear," we need to take note. Our citizenship isn't on earth. It's in heaven. We're foreigners. We're strangers here.

You have God working through you. You have the grace and peace and joy and glory of God. It's unbelievable. It's the greatest. It is so great because you know that when this is over, when this carnival ride ends, it's not over for you. It's not, "Oh, the amusement park is closed. I've got to go home."

No, it's the beginning of an even better life—an eternal one—that God has promised you'll have forever. So, clearly, I want to do what I can to please God and get all the blessings God has in store for me now and later. It's like a doubleheader—it gets better and better. You get them now and you'll have them forever.

But you do affect your blessings in heaven if you're not obedient to God now. Your journey here affects your rewards in your destination there, in eternity. You can certainly lose out on some of those rewards.

Let's look at a moment in the life of Abraham to understand how this works. The word of the Lord came to Abraham in Genesis 15:5-6 and it says:

> *He took him outside and said, "Look up at the sky and count the stars—if indeed you can count them." Then he said to him, "So shall your offspring be." Abram believed the Lord, and he credited it to him as righteousness.*

That's a pretty famous passage. God tells Abraham, "The seed is going to come through you. Go look up at the stars.

5: Generous God

You see them? You couldn't even count them, but that's how many people are going to be your descendants."

Abraham says, "Lord, I believe you." And it's credited to Abraham as righteousness. Why? Because he believed God. We need and should do exactly the same!

Angels Ahead

When the Israelites were at the edge of the Red Sea, stuck between an impassable sea and the edge of the sword, we read in Exodus 14:19: "Then the angel of God, who had been traveling in front of Israel's army, withdrew and went behind them."

The angel of God. There are angels—Michael, Gabriel, and other angels. They're real. It's not a joke. God has angels. God had angels with the Israelites. God has angels in your life and mine. I don't know who they are or where they are, or whether I see them or not. I don't know if it's like *It's a Wonderful Life* with Clarence and bells ringing. I have no idea how God does it. But God clearly says there are angels on behalf of you and me. God has assigned them to protect us, to take charge over us. Thank you Jesus!

Ordering Food

One day in my quiet time, the Spirit of God very clearly quickened my heart. I recognized the Spirit of God speaking. I hope you recognize it too, when God is speaking to your heart and into your life. Very specifically, He said to me, "Go read about Elijah."

It's amazing to me how the pure truth of God can just explode in a paragraph, in a verse, all throughout the scriptures. Anywhere I go in the Bible, truth is there, whether it's Colossians or James or Elijah. Anywhere you go, you can find it in every sentence, in every paragraph.

Well, I found it in the life of Elijah. It starts in 1 Kings 17:1:

> *Now Elijah the Tishbite, from Tishbe in Gilead, said to Ahab (who was then the king of Israel), 'As the Lord, the God of Israel, lives, whom I serve, there will be neither dew nor rain in the next few years except at my word.'*

Elijah was a prophet. He was speaking on behalf of the Lord, and he told the king, "Hey, it's not going to rain until I say it's going to rain."

(God's Overflowing Kindness Towards Us)

Then the word of the Lord came to Elijah: 'Leave here, turn eastward and hide in the Kerith Ravine, east of the Jordan. You will drink from the brook, and I have ordered the ravens to feed you there. (1 Kings 17:2-4)

How great is that? God is in charge of everything, the whole world. He ordered the ravens to feed Elijah. "Hey Elijah, I've taken care of your food, I've taken care of everything. I ordered up the ravens to be there and to feed you." He took care of it.

God says that every hair on our head is numbered. God says he has a perfect plan for our life—that he knew us before we were formed in our mother's womb. God is in charge, as He always was since the beginning, as He is today and always will be. Our confidence in that promise grows when we look back and see that God has always had everything under control. Yet we sometimes sit there and say, "Lord, Lord where are you?" and God says, "I'm right here. I have everything under control."

He is Willing

While Jesus was in one of the towns, a man came along who was covered with leprosy. When he saw Jesus, he fell with his face to the ground and begged him, 'Lord, if you are willing, you can make me clean.' Jesus reached out his hand and touched the man. 'I am willing,' he said. 'Be clean!' And immediately the leprosy left him. (Luke 5:12-13)

God was, is, and will always be willing to cleanse us of our sin.

Always.

This man with leprosy said to Jesus, "If you're willing, you can cleanse me," and Jesus responds by saying, "I am willing."

We know this applies to salvation. Christ was willing to die so that our sins would be forgiven forever and ever. He died so that we would be cleansed with His blood. He died for us to be adopted as a child into the kingdom of God. But that wasn't all. He also died to enable us to have that abundant, joyful life that we can't get from the world. An abundant life here and now, and then an even better life for all eternity, with God in heaven.

(God's Overflowing Kindness Towards Us)

I got saved at thirty-three years old. When I turned fifty-five I realized the past twenty-two years of my life had been a thousand times better than the first thirty-three. He didn't just save me from my sins and promise me heaven in the hereafter, but He filled my life with joy and meaning. It was something the world could never give me, but God had it and was waiting for me all the time.

Living our lives on earth should be this wonderful, exciting journey. Now, let me clarify, I'm not saying there won't be any pain and suffering. If you've lived the Christian life for any length of time, you know that's not the case. God Himself said there would be trials and tribulations. He said it James chapter 1. He said it in First Peter. But He also said that there's a purpose for those difficulties. He said He's using all of those trials and tribulations to mold us and shape us into the men and women He would have us be...so that our joy would be complete.

God is telling you right now, "I am willing." He's willing to forgive the unbeliever and adopt him into the kingdom of heaven as His son. And for the believer, God is willing to forgive your shortcomings and sins and help you get on the path that He's made for your life, so that your heart can be filled with joy.

Just like the prodigal son, God wants you to turn back immediately to Him so He can hug you and love you and bless you, not so He can punish you for what you've done wrong. Quite the opposite. It's so He can be with you and walk with you and show you how much He loves you. God is always willing. So what are you waiting for?

Grants and Applications

On an airplane, there are pilots, there are flight attendants, and there are guys who come clean the bathroom after the plane lands. Everybody is part of the team. They are all trying to accomplish the same goal.

Back in 2009, I spent a few days in Jasper, Florida which is located in Hamilton County. It's a very small town. There are 15,000 residents in the whole county. We have some land up in Jasper that we've invested in for years, and we're trying to do some creative things like put a solar energy farm on it. So, I was meeting with the then Hamilton County Economic Development chairman, who I happen to know, to see if we can get an application for a County grant for the project. This man is also a bi-vocational pastor, which gives us a lot to talk about. We talk about the grants and applications for our solar project, and of course, we talk about God. He shared a little about his life with me, and he's had some struggles. Anyway, he said to me, "Most people don't get salvation."

I asked, "What do you mean? Everybody gets salvation. We know Jesus died for us. He lives inside of us. We have an abundant life now, eternal life forever."

(God's Overflowing Kindness Towards Us)

He says, "Yeah, yeah, yeah, most people get the sin part. They get that Jesus paid the price for our sin, but they don't get the righteousness part. They don't get the part that now we're righteous in Christ. Now, we're covered by Christ's blood; most people don't grab on to how righteous they really are is not based on anything that they've done, but based on Christ. They kind of miss that, and they miss that blessing." He's right. Don't you miss it!

Bloodbath

I've been saved since 1991 and I was thinking how I just take it for granted that Christ actually shed His blood. We all know it. We hear it so many times. We take it for granted. Of course, I know His blood was shed for you and me. Yet I was thinking, no, no, no, it really happened; the blood of Christ has really cleansed me. Satan was throwing some darts at me. I started getting down on myself and beating myself up, yet it was me beating myself up. How stupid is that? I should be free from all of that because I'm cleansed by Jesus' blood. I'm free of all that and I need to focus on the blood of Jesus Christ and what it means to my life.

What does it really mean? The Bible says, in Ephesians 2:12, "Remember that at that time you were separate from Christ, excluded from citizenship in Israel and foreigners to the covenants of the promise, without hope."

Before the blood of Jesus you were foreigners, excluded, without hope. Now, through the blood of Jesus, we have great hope.

But now in Christ Jesus you who once were far away have been brought near through the blood of Christ. For he himself

(God's Overflowing Kindness Towards Us)

is our peace, who has made the two one and has destroyed the barrier, the dividing wall of hostility. (Ephesians 2:13-14)

We were without hope, without God, and Jesus shed his blood so that we could be with hope and with God—hope that everything we believe in is real, hope that we can claim this heaven that God has promised and told us about. Because God, the Holy Spirit, Himself, has come to live inside of every believer, we now have hope through the blood of Jesus.

Not only do we have hope but we have redemption!

You were redeemed from the empty way of life with the precious blood of Christ. That is who redeemed you. I was getting all down on myself, thinking I should be cleansed now, how I should be better than this. I...I...I. Me...me...me. But God was telling me, "Jack, you're focused on the world, on yourself. You need to focus on me. You need to focus on what I did, my blood was shed on the cross."

He said, "Don't you know—haven't you learned by now that every time you get upset or discouraged or depressed or anxious or upset it is always, always—100 % of the time—because you've taken your eyes off me and put them on the world. There is something in the world that has caused you concern or anxiety."

All the time that my eyes are fixed on God, I am joyful, happy. I'm far from perfect in happiness, but if I can bat .300 in the game of happiness, or I can truly say I am happy 8 or 9 out of every 10 days, (in other words MOST of the time!) I'm up there with the greats. That's how I want it to be, and that's how it should be. It's because of the blood of Jesus, shed for you and me.

Getting to Know Him

In the book of Luke, Jesus tells a parable of a guy who threw a feast and people made excuses not to come. One said, "I just got married. I've got to go tend to my new wife." Another said, "I bought a field." Another said, "I've got to check out some oxen." They made excuses, and they missed the feast. They completely missed the blessings that were going to be theirs.

Do we make excuses to God? Do we make excuses for not living the way God wants us to live?

Jesus asked in Matthew 8:26, "Why are you fearful, oh you of little faith?" I think that many people believe in God, yet they do not have complete faith in Him. You may believe in God, but do you trust Him? If you knew Him, you would trust Him. If you don't trust Him, it only can be for one reason. You don't know Him.

You can know someone but not be willing to trust them very much. You know how I can tell how much you trust somebody? By what you entrust to them. If I give you my kids to look after, I must trust you a lot because I value my kids a lot. If I give you all the money I have in the world to hold on

(God's Overflowing Kindness Towards Us)

to, I must trust you a lot because we put value on that here on earth. Trusting a person implies committing something you hold dear into their care.

We can have an intellectual belief of God in our lives but deny Him daily in our actions. We live as if He is far away. Yes, we have faith in Him, and we generally believe He rewards those who diligently seek Him. Yet we still live as though He's far away and unavailable. We deny Him.

The great prerequisite to a perfect trust in God is a perfect acquaintance with Him. There is no other way to come to know the Father but by the way of the cross where self is crucified and life comes forth from death. If you want to know God, come meet Him at the cross and then you'll know Him. Trial after trial, God tries to get your attention in life. He tries to mold you and shape you and bring you closer to Him.

You go through a trial and God says, "Can you hear me now?" God is trying to bring you closer and closer because He loves you so much. He wants you to know how much He loves you.

He talks in Luke chapter 12 about you being of so much more value than birds whom He cares for as well. God knows when a bird falls from a tree and dies. He says, "How much more valuable are you than those birds? You're so much more valuable than the birds because you are God's kids."

God wants you to know how much He values you. In Luke chapter 11 He says you, who love your son, know how to give him something good. If your son asks for bread would you give him a stone, or if his son asks for a fish would he give him a snake. And you're not a perfect father; you're only human. He says, "How much more do I know how to love you?"

5: Generous God

How much more? God is just trying to tell you—begging you to see—how much He loves you, how much He wants to bless you abundantly and exceedingly more than you can ask or imagine. So there is no reason to be afraid! Live a strong and courageous life for God

Betrayed

Years ago, I was investing in real estate with a guy I knew, and business went well for a while...and then not so well. I'm sure you can relate. I left that behind years ago, but in 2010 it came to light there were still some taxes due from our business dealings and it was time to pay up.

I tried calling up this guy and I couldn't get ahold of him. It took me a little while to realize, "Hold on a minute, he's blowing me off!" I felt betrayed. It's the only word I can use to describe how I felt. We were partners in this real estate thing! How could you do this to me now?

I realize we had taken different roads in life and we are now in different places. I'm in ministry full time, and he's somewhere else. But come on, man! We had obligations together. I felt betrayed.

I was thinking about the situation as I drove along in my car the next day, and a couple names came to mind. Bernie Madoff and Scott Rothstein. You may have read about them and their legal troubles in the paper. I thought about the people that they betrayed, and I thought, Man, how must that news have felt that morning? "Hey man, you lost everything. You're not getting it back." Wow.

The difference for me was that, I could cover this guy's taxes. I had the money and thankfully my name wasn't going to be ruined. I wasn't going to be wiped out. Him blowing me off, well it might have hurt a bit, but I could cover it and on we'd go. I didn't like it, but it didn't destroy me. But I thought about those poor people who didn't have that luxury, who were truly wiped out, who were betrayed by people they trusted and had bet their life on.

Then the thoughts got a bit more personal. It came to my mind that, you know what, I betray Jesus every day. I don't betray Jesus purposely. I want to do the best I can. The apostle Paul said in Romans (7:15-17), "The things that I want to do I don't do, and the things that I don't want to do I do, and I've come to realize it's not me, but it's the sin living inside of me." And that's right. The sin is living inside of each one of us—every single one of us.

But that sin has been paid for. There is no penalty left for us to pay for our sin. Jesus died so that you and I can live and have life abundant and life eternal. And man, I was just so, so grateful at that thought. I said, "Thank you, Lord, that you love me so much that you gave your life on the cross, that you shed your blood so every sin I've ever committed has been paid for by your blood and forgiven by you. I have nothing to worry about." I mean, honestly, how lucky are we? It made me very focused on living a life that matters for God. How about you?

6

DOING IT RIGHT
(Obeying God)

No Small Things

A buddy of mine, who I've known for years and is not saved called me up on the telephone to let me know that his thirty-year-old son died in the middle of the night. I don't know if he had a heart attack or if it was drug related; I didn't ask. But nonetheless, his son had died.

I was surprised that this man would call me, but then the thought came to me. I am probably the closest guy to God that this man knew. He was looking for some support and encouragement. This guy is not saved and I was surprised, but grateful, that he would think to call me and want to talk to me. I also sensed, as we talked a few times in the weeks following, how his whole world was now upside down. I have other friends who have had a child who has died, and I can't even fathom what that would be like.

My friend's whole question of what makes sense in life and what doesn't all of a sudden changed because his son had passed away. Now, in an instant, life didn't seem to even be worth living. Nothing made sense anymore.

The sad thing is that, because he didn't know God, it was true. How could anything make sense to him? It is so sad

6: Doing It Right

because we would never want that to happen to anyone we know or love, but if it did happen and they were Christians, we would know that our children were going to heaven and that we would see them again. That assurance would give us a sense of comfort even beyond understanding, knowing that we'll one day see them again. It wouldn't make all the pain go away, it wouldn't answer all our questions, but at least it would be a source of hope for the future. Thank God for His promises of heaven and hope for the future.

In praying about my friend, I realized something important. It's an inspiring and sobering thought: you may be the closest person to God that someone knows.

There are probably people in your life like that today. You are the closest person they have to God. They have friends they can party with or who they work with. They have relatives they spend their holidays with, but when something goes wrong, they don't know who to turn to. Nobody seems to have the answers and no one they know can give them the comfort that faith in Jesus can bring them. Their spirits tug on them to find truth, and they may come to you! So it's good to keep a line open to these friends, and when they face difficulties, to be available to them. You never know what kind of influence you can be on their faith and eventual relationship with God.

I had another buddy who called me up the very day after the call from my friend whose son had died. This second friend, a Christian buddy, said, "Listen, do me a favor."

I said, "What's that, pal?"

He replied, "Can you please pray for my son?"

(Obeying God)

Of course I said, "Absolutely. What's going on?"

He said, "Well, he's thirty, and he had a DUI, and he has to get this restricted driver's license to be eligible for work. He's kind of struggling to find himself, and he just needs direction and really needs a lot of prayer."

Well, I stopped my friend right there and I said, "Listen man. I know this is important to you right now and I will definitely pray about it. But I just have to tell you, you need to count your blessings. I mean, this is the greatest thing that we're praying for your son to get his license. I have another friend who called me just yesterday to let me know his son died."

We need to count our blessings—what we have and what's important. To my Christian friend, this problem with his son's license was actually a major thing—small in comparison to losing your son, but major to him because it was something his son, whom he loves, was dealing with.

A beautiful thought struck me. There's nothing in your life that's a small thing to your Father, God. Every detail of your life is important to Him! The Bible says that He knows each hair on your head!

If you are a parent, you know nothing is "a small thing" when it comes to your children and their happiness. You are God's beloved child and there's nothing in your life that's too small for God.

A Fine Line

In 2013, I read a heartbreaking article out of The New York Post. The title was "Futile Bid to Save Leaper," and it said:

> A security guard desperately tried to talk a twenty-three-year-old Yale student out of committing suicide moments before the young man lept from the 86th floor observation deck at the Empire State Building Tuesday. The guard shouted, 'You don't have to do this!' Cameron Dabaghi, the son of two doctors from Austin, Texas, ignored the pleas and plunged to his death at about 6:30 p.m. Cops found a note in his dorm room that said he was sorry and he intended to either jump from the Empire State Building or the Brooklyn Bridge. The death of the junior who majored in East Asian studies at the Ivy League school stunned pals because he seemed happy. Dabaghi's younger sister, also a student at Yale, said, 'It's so sad. I always thought he was somebody who would change the world.'

Here is this twenty-three-year-old kid who seemed so happy. Not only that, but the people around him thought he

(Obeying God)

was a magnificent person who had the ability to change the world. Yet the thoughts going through his head were, "I gotta get out of here. I can't take this. It's not worth it." He was so depressed and hopeless that he felt there was no future for him.

How can that happen? Two completely opposite views of this man. Here's what I think can happen sometimes: there is a balance, a fine line—a tight rope if you will—between insanity and genius. If you're a follower of the arts, you'll certainly agree with that idea. There is a fine line between insanity and genius, and it's a fine balance to see which side you fall on. One slight move and you're insane. One slight move the other way, and you're a genius. Perhaps they even cross sometimes.

There is also a fine line in life between happiness and sadness. One incident and someone could be sad forever. It could be the loss of a job, a difficult relationship, a financial wreck, a drug addiction, or a health issue. Something can suddenly change our perception of what life should be like, and all of a sudden we're miserable.

There is a fine line between darkness and light, and a fine line between heaven and hell.

I believe that we get to pick which side of those lines we're on.

You might say, "Well, how do I do that, Jack? I want to pick the side of the line I'm on. How do I get to pick the happiness side, the light side, the genius side? How do I get to do that?"

I believe it's about focus. It's about what you're going to focus your attention and thoughts on each day.

6: Doing It Right

God and His Holy Spirit will not fail us. God's love will never fail us. The simple, undiluted, pure love of God is in my life. It's there in your life as well—the knowledge that God loves us so much and He wants us to know and feel and share that love.

God must be so hurt at those times we turn our focus to everything going on around us that we forget the one thing that really matters. Just one little change in perception can mean the difference between joy and sorrow, between heaven and hell. That difference is what we are focusing on.

It's like that hymn: "Turn your eyes upon Jesus, look full in His wonderful face, and the things of earth will grow strangely dim in the light of His glory and grace." Focusing on Him will cause everything painful and confusing to simply fade away; it will bring the peace and comfort that comes from knowing He's in control and that He loves us.

Jumping for Joy

My wife and I attended my aunt's 85th birthday party in 2009. We took my kids Jackson and Talia who were seven and five at the time. We went to my cousin's house for the party and Jackson and Talia were out of control…but in a good way! They were going completely nuts. They were doing cartwheels, jumping up and down, and dancing. And I thought, "Man, they're happy for no reason. They're happy to be happy just for the sake of being happy."

I want to ask you—when was the last time you just jumped for joy? When was the last time, like a little kid, you got to shout and be joyful just because you were full of happiness? When were you last completely in the moment and you felt nothing but joy? We need to get caught up in more moments of happiness and joy like that.

In Private

The Bible says:
When you pray, don't be like the hypocrites for they love to pray standing in the synagogues and on the street corners to be seen by men. I tell you the truth that they have received their reward in full. (Matthew 6:5)

Prayer is private between you and God. God knows your heart. It doesn't matter what you say. It matters what you do. It matters what your heart thinks. Hey, I could say, "I'm president of the United States," but when I get to the White House and try heading to the Oval Office, they're going to throw me in jail for trespassing because I'm not actually the president. It doesn't matter what I say. It matters what's true. It matters what's in my heart. We're not supposed to pray or fast to be heard or seen by others. That's a holy time just between us and God.

Frequent Flyer Points

Think for a moment on Matthew 6:19: "Do not store up for yourselves treasures on earth where moth and rust destroy and where thieves break in and steal." Could God be any clearer? All this stuff that we see and feel around us doesn't really matter.

We tend to say, "Yes, it does. My bank account matters. My car matters. I want to be able to send my kids to college. I need treasures on earth. As a matter of fact, the more I get, the more I can give to you, Lord."

God says, "No, man, you don't get it. That isn't what it's about!"

You need to earn your frequent flyer points for heaven. That's where the ultimate reward is. What you do here—your obedience to God—is earning you blessings and rewards in heaven that will be eternal, that no thief can break in and steal, that no rust or moth can destroy and corrupt.

Every year or two we clean out our house—my wife, Beth, will testify to this. We get rid of so much junk, so many toys that were at one time new for the kids, and they loved them. We spent money on these things and there is lots of other stuff we get rid of too—not just toys.

6: Doing It Right

We just give it away. It's lost all of its value to us. It's lost all of its luster. All the shine is gone. It rusted away. It "mothed." It decayed.

God says in Matthew 6:25, "I tell you, therefore, do not worry about your life, what you eat, drink, about your body, or what you wear." Do not worry about your life.

You say, "God, if I don't worry, who's gonna? I've got to worry about me. I've got to take care of me."

God says, "No, I've got your life in the palm of my hand. I've got it in control."

Every hair on your head is numbered. Two sparrows don't fall down from a tree apart from the will of God, and God says, "Don't I love you more than all those birds and more than anything?" If you want to know how much God loves you just look at the cross. We're not to worry about our life. God takes great pleasure in providing for His children. Relax. Don't worry.

Friends in Low Places

God says in Romans 12:16, "Don't be proud, but be willing to associate with people of low position. Do not be conceited."

How comfortable are you associating with people of low position? It's not about job title; it's not about bank account. It's about heart.

There's no difference between us and people who are homeless or otherwise underprivileged. We might have a nicer address and a nicer house and probably a nicer bank account than they do; compared to them, we're probably the richest people in the world. But you know what? That could be me. That could be you. We could get sick tomorrow, or lose our job and then our house. It could all happen to any of us. It's just the cards that God dealt us.

God is the potter. We are the clay. Who are we to say to the potter, "Look what you've done?" God is using us for His purposes. We're to be grateful for that, but we're to make sure that we never look down on someone else based on their position, their color, their bank account, their job, where they live, how they talk, or what they look like.

Reaping What You Sow

Galatians 5:13 says, "You, my brothers, were called to be free, but do not use your freedom to indulge the sinful nature, rather serve one another in love."

Wow. Do not use the freedom you have in Christ to sin. You could. I could rob a bank. I could steal. I could cheat on my wife. I could lie. I could cheat on my taxes. I could do anything I want, and it's not going to affect my salvation in heaven because I'm already saved. That's a one-time supernatural transaction between me and God. However it would be hard to believe a true believer in Jesus Christ, someone who loves God with all his heart would engage purposely and sin.

But you know what? If I use the freedom I have in Christ as an excuse to sin, I will be subtracting credits from my "account" in heaven. I will be reducing my reward in heaven substantially. I'm never to use my freedom in Christ as an excuse to sin. Ever.

Galatians 6:7 says, "Do not be deceived. God cannot be mocked. A man reaps what he sows." What you give, you get. The life you live is what you're going to get back from God.

(Obeying God)

Are you going to live a life of the spirit or a life of the world? Is your treasure going to be focused on the world? Then God says, "Enjoy it...because that's all you're getting." If you live for the spirit, God says you're going to be blessed thirty, sixty, and a hundredfold more than you can ask or imagine.

God's very specific. He can't be mocked, so don't worry. If you think somebody is getting away with something now—mafia guys, Goldman Sachs guys, guys you know down the street who aren't paying their income tax, guys who are cheating on their wives and they think it's all good—think again. They're not getting away with anything. The word of God says that some men pay for their sins right away, others seem to get off scot-free. But they aren't, their sins are just trailing behind them. Everybody pays on judgment day.

There is not one dead person who doesn't believe in Jesus Christ. I can't tell you where they're spending eternity though. Some are spending it in heaven because they believed in Jesus while they were on earth, and some are spending it in hell because they chose not to believe when they had their chance on earth...but they definitely all believe now.

God's Requirements

God gives Moses plenty of instruction. For example, read Exodus 31:13:

Say to the Israelites, "You must observe my Sabbaths. This will be a sign between me and you for the generations to come, so you may know that I am the Lord, who makes you holy."

God had requirements. Observe the Sabbath. The book of Leviticus has over six hundred laws that the Israelites had to observe. I asked myself a question when I read through Leviticus, and it really bothered me because I couldn't believe how the Israelites were being disobedient to God. They weren't doing what He said after they had seen all sorts of miracles. Here's the question: With more than six hundred rules in the book of Leviticus, and the Ten Commandments, and all of this stuff, does it matter what God asked them to do? In other words, what if God had simply said, "All right, look, there's a football field next door. Just run up and down it ten times." What's the difference what the requirement was? The point is, they wouldn't have done it anyway. Do you think they would have run up and down the football field ten times if

(Obeying God)

God had told them to do that? If that was the requirement, do you think they would've done it? That might've been a little easier than the six hundred laws of Leviticus, but they still wouldn't have done it because they didn't want to.

How come we don't do what Jesus Christ asks us? No, seriously, I don't understand. I know I have a limited brain. Scientists tell us we only use ten percent of our brain's capacity, but I don't understand why we don't do everything Jesus Christ asks us to do. I don't understand why every Christian doesn't reflect the glory of Jesus in everything, all the time, all their lives, with everybody, everywhere. I don't get it. That's what God told us to do.

Now, I know my own flaws. I know I'm far from perfection. I know I've got to work at this. I've got to practice to be a good Christian. I like to play softball, and I've got to practice to be a good softball player. There are a lot of guys who have a lot more natural talent than me. They simply climb out of their cars and they hit home runs. They don't have to practice. I've got to practice just to be decent. These guys are great without doing anything. But, I want to play so badly. I don't want to be left behind. I want to be on the team. I want to play so badly that I do whatever I have to do so that I can at least be at the minimum level to play on their team. You should do whatever you need to do so that you're at least at the minimum level where you can look at Jesus Christ and you can say, "If I die today, I'm going to hear, 'Well done, good and faithful servant. Come and share your master's happiness.'"

God had requirements then. What's God's requirement of us today?

6: Doing It Right

Imitate Jesus. Be holy. Bear fruit and fruit that will last.

God was serious to the Israelites. And I think God is serious in what He is asking of us today.

Here's what He said to them. It's Exodus 31:14-15:

> *Observe the Sabbath because it is holy to you. Anyone who desecrates it is to be put to death; those who do any work on that day must be cut off from their people. Whoever does any work on the Sabbath day is to be put to death.*

Man, that's serious. Do you think God was kidding? "I want you to be holy. And, by the way, just so you guys know that I'm not kidding—seriously—anybody who does work on the Sabbath, kill them. Put them to death. That's what they deserve. They should be cut off because that's how disgraceful it is." I think God is serious to us today in our job description when he says clearly in John 6:29 "This is the work of God: believe in Him who He has sent." Thankfully, we know today God is dealing with His people through the free gift of grace found solely in Jesus Christ. Yet clearly He desires for us to live holy and bear fruit that will last…for He knows this is the lifestyle that will release His life, peace and fulfillment in our lives and allow us to live a life that truly matters for God.

Get Out Of Jail Free

A friend gave me a "read the bible in a year" book, so I'm reading the Old Testament and I'm saying, "Wait a minute!" Now, I'm Jewish and I'm proud to be Jewish, but I was not brought up religious. I didn't go to Hebrew school or anything and I had a question while reading, so I called my cousin up who is very knowledgeable and a practicing Jewish guy. I said, "Listen, I'm a little confused. I'm reading through Genesis, Job, Exodus, and this stuff. I only know the Bible, I don't know the rabbinical law or Hebrew books that aren't in the Bible. Is there anywhere in Jewish history or religion that exempts the Jews from doing this today? Is there any free pass or 'get-out-of-jail free' card or something that says they don't have to do this?"

I know that we Christians don't have to follow these laws because now we have the grace of Jesus Christ in the New Testament, and our obedience now is our acceptance of Jesus Christ. That is how we show God that we love Him. We don't have to follow those old laws. We accept Jesus Christ. We believe in the one who was sent. God says the work of God is to do this: Believe in the one who was sent. That's our one

6: Doing It Right

requirement. Of course, we should love the Lord God with all our heart, soul, and mind, and love others as ourselves because God tells us that those are the most important things to do.

I was thinking about the Jews, and realized that nowhere in the Bible do I see that they don't have to follow the law anymore. So why aren't they still following all of these commands? When I asked my cousin, he said there is nothing that would exempt them from those laws. There is no "out." There is nothing that would exempt the Jewish people from doing all this today. They're still waiting for the Messiah. In their minds, the Messiah hasn't come. We know the Messiah has come. He is Jesus Christ. Jews don't believe that. That's the major difference between the religions. Because they don't recognize Jesus as Messiah, they're still bound by the Old Testament law.

I said to my cousin, "Okay, let me get this right. The Jews created these sects—orthodox, reformed, conservative (and there are probably others I don't know about)—so that they don't have to do these things." See, some of these groups say, "Oh, we love God, but God clearly didn't mean what He said back then to apply to us today. Today it's impossible to follow all of God's laws because of societal, political and technological changes, and besides its just such a hassle. So we'll just kind of love God over here and do what we think is best." And the other sect says, "Oh, we'll do this and not that." And the other guys, "We'll do that and not this."

Now, I give the orthodox Jews a lot of credit because at least they're trying to do everything they still can do. It may

(Obeying God)

seem insane to the rest of the world, as may an Amish way of life, but they're sold out. They're trying to still follow the laws.

Now before you look at the other sect and think, "Look at those idiots. How dare they reclassify, requalify, rethink, respeak, rewrite history and decide what God meant and didn't mean," we Christians do the same thing. We just call it denominations. We have all these excuses of which parts of the Bible we like and which we don't and what God meant and what God didn't mean.

I get that there are different theological perspectives on the Bible. I get that. If you have a dispute over a particular point of theology and you want to dispute that with somebody, fine. But at the very least do every single thing else that you know there is no dispute over, and let's take it from there. We're just as guilty as the Jews who have taken their requirements and put them aside for convenience, for modern-day living. Call it what you will. The bottom line is they're not doing what God told them to do.

In our case, when we fail to do what God has asked us, we can call it denominational preference, or individual interpretation. Or we can call it the "reality" of the 21st century, but the bottom line is the same. We're not doing what God asked us to do. What has he asked us to do? It is made clear in John 6:29 when Jesus said, "This is the work of God, that you believe in Him who He has sent."

Set Apart

We are set apart by God. When the apostle Paul begins some of his letters, he says, "I, Paul, a slave to Jesus Christ," and, "I, Paul, a servant of Jesus Christ." That should be the introduction of every one of us in our lives. "I, Jack, a slave to Jesus Christ." "I, Jack, a servant to Jesus Christ," and my actions should reflect it in my life.

We shouldn't be lovers of ourselves and disobedient to God's instruction. In Exodus 33:2-3, God tells the people: "I will send an angel before you. Go up to the land flowing with milk and honey. But I will not go with you, because you are a stiff-necked people and I might destroy you on the way."

God was angry with the people for their lack of obedience. God couldn't bless them the way He wanted to bless them. In essence He said, "Look, I'm going to take care of you. I'm going to send an angel before you. You go, but I can't go with you because I'm still so upset with you that I'm scared I just might destroy you on the way. You really have to be the stupidest people in the world because I told you what to do, I showed you who I am, I revealed myself to you, and still you chose the world over me." God was upset.

(Obeying God)

Jesus related a parable in Luke 13:6-7 that should serve as a warning and wake up call to every believer:

> *A man had a fig tree growing in his vineyard, and he went to look for fruit on it but did not find any. So, he said to the man who took care of the vineyard, "For three years now I've been coming to look for fruit on this fig tree and haven't found any. Cut it down! Why should it use up the soil?" "Sir," the man replied, "leave it alone for one more year, and I'll dig around it and fertilize it. If it bears fruit next year, fine! If not, then cut it down."*

God is looking to us to bear fruit. God doesn't want to cut you down. That's not God's desire. God's desire is to bless you and love you and nourish you, but God does have requirements. And we are to follow them if we want the blessings of God to flow uninterrupted in our lives.

Here is Moses' prayer back to God when God said he was upset with Israel's lack of obedience. It's in Exodus 33:13 and Moses says to God, "If you are pleased with me, teach me your ways so I may know you and continue to find favor with you."

Have you asked God that? Is that the prayer of your heart? "God, teach me your ways so I can find favor with you, so I can know you."

Or is it, "God, leave me alone so I can go do the things I want in the world, and then bless me later because I'm your son and you don't want to hurt me?"

Moses says to God in verses 15-16—I love this:

6: Doing It Right

If your Presence does not go with us, do not send us up from here. How will anyone know that you are pleased with me and with your people unless you go with us? What else will distinguish me and your people from all the other people on the face of the earth?

Hey, Moses got it. He said, "Lord, I need your presence. I'm going to go out in the world. If you don't come with me, how will anybody know I'm different? What will distinguish me if you are not with me?" That was Moses' prayer.

We have the presence of God in us. He is our distinguishing factor, God's Holy Spirit living in our hearts. We don't have to ask like Moses did. We've received it already in the form of the Holy Spirit. We have it. Are we going to use it for the glory of God, or are we going to bury it for the selfishness of our flesh?

Knowing and Living

We all have our favorite Bible verses and our favorite life sayings, whatever they may be. You've heard some famous ones. You probably know this one: "You've got to know when to hold them, and you've got to know when to fold them." Or how about, "Quitters never win and winners never quit." And, "When the going gets tough, the tough get going."

Man, those are great phrases, as are some of our favorite Bible verses. You know what? They don't mean a thing if you don't live them. It's not enough to know them.

"Hey, quitters never win and winners never quit." That's great. Which one are you going to be?

"You've got to know when to hold them and when to fold them." That's great. Which are you going to do?

"You know, when the going gets tough, the tough get going." That's great. What do we do when it gets tough? Do we get going, or do we fold?

It's the same thing with the word of God. It's not enough to only know the word of God, we need to apply it each and every day to our lives.

Tree and Fruit

In 1 Corinthians 15:1-2, Paul is talking to the church at Corinth, and I believe he's talking to you and me right now. He says this in the first couple of verses:

Now, brothers and sisters, I want to remind you of the gospel I preached to you, which you received and on which you have taken your stand. By this gospel you are saved, if you hold firmly to the word I preached to you. Otherwise, you have believed in vain.

Paul added a disclaimer: "…if you hold firmly to the word I preached to you. Otherwise, you believe in vain." Now don't get fooled by that statement. It doesn't mean you will have to work to continue to earn God's salvation. That is not what that statement says. Salvation is a one-time gift. It's an irrevocable transaction between you and God that can never be taken away. God says in Romans that His gift and His calling are irrevocable. God says that He took out your old heart and He put in a new heart. You're a new creation in Christ.

Paul is reminding us that if we don't see evidence of Christ in your life you were never saved. No matter what you think

(Obeying God)

or say. God knows the truth. Hey, yeah, if you don't continue in the way of the word, then you believed in vain. Of course, we see people who claim to have been saved, profess to know Christ, and then turn right back to the world. There is no significant evidence of salvation in their life, no fruit we can see.

For any real believer, you have accepted Jesus, you believe in your heart and you are saved. God says we see evidence of a tree by its fruit. If someone claims to be a Christian, we should see evidence of it in their life. They should have a changed life. The old is gone. The new is here. I should be a spiritual man, not a worldly man. I should be a man of the kingdom, not a man of the flesh.

It should show in our lives.

Red Dye

God gives us a warning in 1 Corinthians 15:33-34. Paul says:

Do not be misled: Bad company corrupts good character. Come back to your senses as you ought, and stop sinning; for there are some who are ignorant of God—I say this to your shame.

Paul is challenging us to realize what they have done, what has happened here. He is essentially saying, "Listen. Come back to your senses because clearly you're missing it. Stop sinning. Come back to your senses. Bad company corrupts good character."

When I explain to people about salvation, when I'm talking to non-believers the first time, I'll often take a big pitcher of water and I'll say, "See, this is heaven." I'll put one tiny drop of red dye into the water, and the whole thing will become red. And I'll explain that's why even a little sin can't be allowed in heaven—because God is pure, like the perfect water. Even if a little sin gets into it, it pollutes all of it.

That's what God is trying to tell us. He says, "Look, bad company corrupts good character." We need to be thinking

(Obeying God)

about the things of the Lord. We need to take every thought captive and give it to Jesus. We need to be focused on the glory that is to come—on our hope, on our salvation. We are to be sure of things we hope for and certain of what we cannot see. That's our faith in action. That's what people should see in our lives.

If you don't feel that way right now—you know what? That's not a crime. It's just a warning. It's a message. It's as if a flare went off in your life, as if you got slapped up the side of the head. It's God saying to you, "Look, let's you and I spend some time individually, one on one. I'll be glad to explain it to you. I love you so much. You're my son. You're my daughter. I want you to understand all of it. Come, so I can spend some time with you."

Go open the gospel of John. Start reading in the New Testament about John, one-on-one with God. I don't believe you will tell me that God hasn't spoken to your heart because I've yet to meet that man. I've met many men who come and tell me, "I won't look." Well, that's a whole separate issue. But I've yet to meet the man who came and told me, "I went to meet God one on one, and God didn't show up."

He promised, "Ye shall seek me and find me, when you search for me with all your heart."

Keep in Step

I want to share with you God's reminder in Galatians 5:25: "Since we live by the Spirit, let us keep in step with the Spirit."

We live by the Spirit. Let us keep in step with the Spirit. We're to walk side by side with Jesus. We're to be walking with Him—not behind Him twenty lengths, not twenty lengths in front of Him. We're to be side by side. We're to walk in step with the Holy Spirit of God. That's our job.

Ask yourself, "Am I running behind you, Lord? Am I running in front of you?" That's not where we want to be. We want to be walking with Him. I took my little daughter, Talia, to the supermarket, and I held her hand from the car to the store. I wouldn't let her walk in the parking lot alone. I said, "No, you've got to hold daddy's hand. I've got to make sure that you're safe." I want her walking with me.

The question is—Are you walking side by side with Jesus?

If not, Jesus is stopping right now. He was walking, and He's stopping. "Wait a minute. Is that you behind me, son? Hey, come on. Catch up. Is that you in front of me daughter? Hey, come on back a few steps so we can walk together." I

(Obeying God)

hope and pray that you'll take this opportunity to make sure that you're back in step and in line with Jesus.

If you can't do that, you need to go to Jesus and you need to let Him carry you. If the burden of life is too much, if you've been beaten down too hard by Satan or by life, then you need to cast all your cares upon Him. You need to lay it at Jesus' feet. He says, "My burden is light. My yoke is easy." If you can't carry it, then put it down at Jesus' feet and let Him carry it.

God knows things you don't know. God has plans for you that you don't even know about. If you stand on Romans 8:28 that, "All things work together for the good of those who love God and are called according to His will," then your faith in God is enlightened and enhanced, and you can see that you don't need to worry about anything. You just need to trust God.

I hate flying, and I fly a lot. I only hate it because of the turbulence. It really bothers me. I hate bumping up and down violently, and it scares me. Now, I'm pretty sure the plane isn't going to crash. I mean it could, but really the odds are against it. But, man, it's an uneasy feeling. One time, a pilot buddy of mine said to me, "Jack, if you understood what turbulence was, if you really understood it, you would never be scared about it."

He explained it to me, I guess it's a scientific thing. It's like waves in the sea. The boat is not going to sink from the waves. It's going to ride the waves. And supposedly the wind and the air turbulence is the same. The plane is not going to crash. It's just going to ride the waves of the wind. Now I understand it and am not scared of it. I still don't like the feeling, but I'm not scared of it anymore.

6: Doing It Right

If you understood it, you wouldn't be scared of it. We need to apply that to our lives. If we understand God and His promises and His Holy Spirit and His word, and we believe Him, then we have nothing to fear.

I pray it's the desire of your heart to be holding the Father's hand, to be walking in step with Him, so that you will be safe and free to live this life with joy.

Practice Makes Perfect

When my son Jackson was seven years old, he played coach-pitch baseball, which was very exciting, not just for him, but for me as well. Before the beginning of the season, in February, he had undergone hernia surgery, so he couldn't practice with the team. He started playing with the team in their first game.

Jackson would sit out there on the field not really paying attention, crossing his legs, kicking the dirt, looking up at the butterflies. I was nervous that he'd get hit in the face with the ball. Now, Jackson was small, but some of these kids were big, and they could hit. A line drive in the face could really hurt him, so I was concerned about that. Needless to say, I prayed a lot during that time—every game, every batter. Come on, Lord, don't let him get hit.

The weeks went by and all of the team members' skills had gotten much better, including Jackson's. His hitting was getting much better. His fielding had come a long way. All of the kids on the team had developed tremendously, and I thought, "Wow, how did this happen?"

6: Doing It Right

There were two things that made it happen. One was their coach. Their coach was an intense, great guy. It was clear that he loved the kids. He was there at all the practices. He taught them. He trained them. He worked with them. He coached them. He really took time to develop them as ball players.

The other thing that made it happen was they practiced. Jackson actually practiced what he was taught. He kept doing it and doing it, so he got better and better at it.

You say, "Well, what's the big deal about that, Jack?" The big deal is the way it parallels our Christian life.

Here we have God, this amazing teacher and coach, who loves us and wants to teach us and show us everything every step of the way. He takes His time and His life and comes to live inside of us and shows us what to do. But there's a requirement on our end. We should be practicing it.

Of course, it's wonderful to get some practice time on Sunday mornings, but that's not enough. We need to practice during the week. Professional football, basketball and baseball players don't just show up for the games. They practice all week long, even in the off-season, so they can be the best they can be.

We, too, need to practice our Christianity and our daily walk with Jesus. Of course that's only if you want to be better!

Quizzing God

We're all accountable to God for our own actions. Cain had just come back from murdering his brother. God intercepts him, saying, "Where is your brother Abel?" "I don't know," Cain replied. "Am I my brother's keeper?" (Genesis 4:9)

Cain lied outright. By the way, not answering is a lie. And when God asks you something, ignoring it is also a lie. But Cain basically says, "Why the heck are you asking me where Abel is? What am I, his keeper? Am I his guardian? Am I responsible for him?"

God knew where Abel was. God knew Abel was dead, just like God knew where Adam and Eve were in the Garden when they sinned and He called out, "Adam, Adam where are you?" He knew. He was just asking them to see what they'd say. He was giving them the opportunity to tell Him the truth and get it right.

God knows your heart. He knows exactly what you're thinking. All things are uncovered and laid bare before the eyes of the Lord. Yet He asks us about our own sins to see what we will say. Cain lied to God and he tried to dodge it by

6: Doing It Right

asking a question. Do we do that? God asks us about our life, our service, our walk, our love, our faithfulness, our forgiveness, and we shoot back, "Well, God, what about Joe over there? Look at the way he's living his life! God, by the way, how come you're letting America go to hell in a hand basket? What are you doing? I have questions for you, God. Forget me. I have questions for you and about what you're doing."

We quiz God on His leadership, His wisdom, and His will as a way to deflect our own shortcomings, our own lack of obedience, in the hope that God won't notice what cruds we are. What a joke! God has offered us the answer: Just do what is right, and you'll be accepted. (Genesis 4:7)

There is no requirement for Jesus' love. That was a gift to you based on nothing you did. The Bible says, "It is by grace you've been saved, through faith, not by works of your own lest any man should boast." That is a gift from God, but you do have to take it. If the gift is here and you don't take it, and you don't open it, then I guess it's not yours and you never got the benefit which God intended when He gave you the gift.

God will accomplish through you whatever He chooses to accomplish, whether you're working in Home Depot, or you're the president of the United States, or a teacher, or a housewife. It doesn't matter what job you have. It doesn't matter what your bank account has. It doesn't matter what you look like. It doesn't matter if you're a republican or democrat, a Yankee fan or a Red Sox fan. None of that matters. The only thing that matters is were you obedient to God with the blessings and gifts He gave you? Did you make the most of your life for God?

Whose Signature?

Throughout the Bible we read of great Bible characters, but they definitely weren't perfect. Abraham was willing to sacrifice Sarah to save his own neck. He was a coward. He was willing to give up his own wife to protect himself. Jacob was cunning and deceptive. Moses was a murderer. Noah was a drunk. Peter denied Jesus three times. Rahab was a prostitute. Samson was a womanizer. David was an adulterer and murderer.

Man, they could've said, "Oh, I can't do anything for the Lord. I stink! I've got to go home. I've got to quit. I'm done." But they didn't! No. They had flaws. They were human just like you and me, and still they went out and did the best they could for God. When they put their uniform on that said "Team Jesus," they went out and played the best they could. David and the others are all praised by God. So much so, that God said of David, "He's a man after my own heart." (Acts 13:22)

"Well, how could that be, God? You're up in heaven, in this clean, pure place. Yeah, I get that you paid the price and sent Jesus on the cross. I'm cleansed by the blood. I'm clean now

6: Doing It Right

too. I get all that, but how could you call David a man after your own heart when he's an adulterer and a sinner?"

Because God knew that David loved Him. The question is: Do you love God? Because that's all you've got to do. You've just got to believe. You've just got to love Him, and you've just got to let the actions of your life reflect the love that's in your heart. It's our love for God that gives us the ability to love others and be an example of His love to them.

As the poet once said, "We see the signature of our souls reflected in the actions of our lives." The question is: What does God see reflected in the actions of your life? Whose signature is on your soul?

God sees your heart. It's about progress, not perfection, and the more you progress in the knowledge of God, the more of God's blessings you're able to get upon yourself. So just do your best; that is all He asks of you.

The Audit

One of my favorite movies is *It's a Wonderful Life*. It's an old Christmas classic with Jimmy Stewart. I'm sure most of you know it. In the beginning, God (in the movie) is talking to Clarence the angel, and they decide to go down and help this man, George.

Imagine if God was talking to Clarence saying, "Clarence, let's go down and do an audit of Jack Levine's life." Audit? Oh, yes. You guys know what an IRS audit is? You know, the one thing you don't want? Root canal, okay. Prostate exam, okay. But don't let me have an IRS audit. That's when the IRS opens up everything and examines everything about your taxes, past and present. Not a pleasant thing. It shouldn't be an issue for any Christian because we should have nothing to hide. But by the world's standards, let's assume it's not a pleasant thing.

Well, what if God wanted to audit our lives to see how righteous we really were? Could we withstand that audit from God? Would we come out unscathed? What would it show? That question motivates me and drives me because I believe God is looking and keeping record. I believe that not just now but on judgment day I'm going to be accountable for the actions of my life. I get blessed abundantly and exceedingly more than I can ask or imagine each and every day when I try to live a godly life by being like God. The more I try to walk closer to God, the more blessings of God just pour down on my life. It's a wonderful thing.

Losing it All

I have three kids. They're pleasing to me even when they bum me out and tick me off. I love them so much. Of course, I would rather they not do the stupid stuff and that they do the good stuff, but they're still pleasing to me no matter what. Well, we are God's kids. And once He shed that blood for you and me and mankind. Rest assured He's pleased with us. We are clothed in His righteousness. We should revel in that and rejoice in it all the time. We are to do the best we can, but we're not to let the world get us down.

Job is described in Job 1:1: "In the land of Uz there lived a man whose name was Job. This man was blameless and upright; he feared God and shunned evil."

Blameless and upright. Feared God. Shunned evil. Man, what would the description of you and me be today? Because that's what I want mine to be. You know what? That was God's description of Job. Job earned it. Do you and I earn that? Are we blameless? Are we shunning evil? Are we righteous? The first thing I have to do is look at myself and ask, "What would God describe me as today if He looked at me?" Because that's what I want, and if there are things that I have in my life that are not making me righteous and upright, if I don't fear God, and I'm not shunning evil, then I need to change. Or I need to accept the fact that that's not going to be the description I get from God. We have a choice of how we live our lives for God.

The Bible says God then gave Satan the authority to test Job's faithfulness. He said, "The way we're going to do that is to take all his stuff away and see if he still loves you, Lord. Let's try that."

And God says, "Go ahead. Test him. Take his stuff."

Job wakes up one fine morning, and his whole life goes from "Oh Happy Day" to "Oh Crappy Day." (Job 1:13-19)

So, let's get this right. Every possession you had is now gone, burned, stolen, or taken, and your family is dead. That's the synopsis. What does Job say? We find out in the next three verses:

At this, Job got up and tore his robe and shaved his head. Then he fell to the ground in worship and said: "Naked I came from my mother's womb, and naked I will depart. The Lord gave and the Lord has taken away; may the name of the Lord be praised.' In all this, Job did not sin nor charge God with wrong." (Job 1:20-22)

What about us? Man, maybe if you lost all your money you'd be miserable, but maybe you wouldn't charge God with wrong. Maybe you'd say, "Hey look, I get it. I made it, and now I lost it. The Lord gives. The Lord takes away."

But tell me if it was your wife or your family, would that still be your attitude? By the way, it should be. All you have is the Lord's in the first place. His to give and take away.

You're a Teacher

In Matthew 3:1-2, John the Baptist is preparing the way for Jesus Christ to come: "In those days John the Baptist came, preaching in the wilderness of Judea and saying, 'Repent, for the kingdom of heaven has come near.'"

The first message John gives to everybody: Repent.

Why should I repent, John? Repent, for the kingdom of heaven is near. John was sounding a warning. It's time to repent. It's time to turn from your evil ways. It's time to turn to God while there is still time, and it's getting urgent because the kingdom of heaven is near. Absolutely, because John knew Jesus was coming right behind him.

In the next chapter, it gets interesting. When Jesus heard that John had been put in prison, he withdrew to Galilee. From that time on Jesus began to preach, "Repent, for the kingdom of heaven has come near." Jesus is saying the exact same words that John the Baptist said. Now, of course, Jesus knew He himself was the kingdom. He knew God had sent Him down. And sure enough, He was near. He had arrived. The kingdom of heaven had indeed come near.

Have you ever been at a point in your own life where God has come near to you? And if so, what has your response been

6: Doing It Right

to God? Has it been to embrace and receive this wonderful gift from God or has it been to go the other way and turn your back to the world? We see in the New Testament that many chose to embrace Jesus, yet many chose not to embrace him. But He didn't give up. Matthew 4:23 tells us, "Jesus went throughout Galilee, teaching in their synagogues, proclaiming the good news of the kingdom, and healing every disease and sickness among the people."

The first thing Jesus did was proclaim the good news of the kingdom. That was Jesus' mission. That was Jesus' purpose. You and I have that same mission and purpose today. We need to be proclaiming the good news of the kingdom of Christ.

Jesus tells us, in Matthew 5:19, "Anyone who breaks one of the least of these commands and teaches others accordingly will be called least in the kingdom of heaven, but whoever practices and teaches these commands will be called great in the kingdom of heaven."

God is saying, "Listen, there is a ranking in the kingdom of heaven. There is least to great." God is trying to tell us, "Look, you can have the ranking of greatest in the kingdom of heaven. Here's how you do it. Practice and teach my commands and you'll be called great in the kingdom of heaven."

When Jesus tells us to teach, he doesn't just mean from the pulpit or in Sunday School. He means for you and I to be ministers and priests of the gospel, in everything we do, that people see God correctly reflected in us and in our lives. That's how you do it.

Focused

In Matthew 9, Jesus is going about His Father's business. He's not distracted. He's focused. Can you and I say the same of ourselves today? Are we focused? Are we going about our Father's business? Verse 35 says, "Jesus went through all the towns and villages, teaching in their synagogues, proclaiming the good news of the kingdom and healing every disease and sickness." He just continues to do the will of His Father. He is focused only on the will of the Father.

My wife pulled a muscle in her back one Friday afternoon. She had been suffering from a sore back for a few days, and it was getting better. Then she went to chase a lizard out of the garage. She bent down and pulled something in her back and that was it. She began having intense back spasms, screaming in pain. She was in agony all Friday night and could barely move an inch.

I called our son Ricky, then twenty-three years old, and he came over to help lift her. Somehow we got her into the bathroom and then into bed. And I'm figuring, all right, we'll give her some medicine and hopefully she'll be fine in the morning. Nope. The next morning she woke up with the

6: Doing It Right

same thing. She couldn't move without excruciating pain and needed an ambulance to get to the hospital.

The ambulance came—Coral Springs Fire Rescue department—five firemen and rescue people came to the house. And you know what? They were focused. They were very intent. They weren't distracted. They knew what they were doing. They had practiced what they needed to do. It wasn't a question of, "Are they going to drop her?" or "Are they going to be able to help her?" No, they were very focused. Each one was doing their part. They moved her and transported her accordingly. They knew exactly what they were doing. They didn't make chitchat. They were focused on their mission. I was very impressed.

You and I need to be the same way for Jesus Christ. We need to be focused on our mission, not distracted by the things of the world. Can you imagine if they had come into my house and they were cracking jokes to each other, talking about the previous night's ball game, not paying attention, and dropped my wife on the floor?

We do that with other people's lives, don't we? God has called us to be a witness—a light in a world of darkness, salt to a tasteless generation—and instead we're going through life distracted, talking about meaningless things, cracking stupid jokes and other non-kingdom building stuff. Those people who we need to interact with and need to proclaim the good news of the kingdom to are just walking right by us. We're talking to them but not about the kingdom. We're not doing our job. We're not doing what we've been called to do, what we're trained to do, what God wants us to do.

(Obeying God)

And we wonder why we are not filled with the spirit of God. We wonder what God is talking about when He says there will be rivers of joy flowing through us, and we don't feel them. Then, we wonder why we don't have the peace that transcends all understanding that God has promised all believers in all circumstances.

We say, "I don't have that." Right, you don't have that because you're not following God's instructions. You're not doing what God has called you to do. You're doing something else. It's like calling a cook to be a butler. It's like calling a doctor to be a receptionist. Hey, can he do it? Yeah. Maybe he can even do it efficiently. Is it where his skill and talent lies though? No. Is it where his passion lies and what he's called to do? No. He's not called to be a receptionist. He's called to be a doctor and save lives.

You're called to be a lifesaver too. You're called to call the lost to the kingdom of heaven. And all you've got to do is tell them about it.

An Order from the Commander

Can you imagine the commander of the US Army giving a mission brief to go attack an enemy and he says, "Okay, here's the mission. This is what I need you to do. Fly this plane over this hill and bomb that target. That's specifically what I need you to do so we can win the war."

And the pilot says, "Okay, that's a good mission but I think I'm going to fly to California and visit my family." No. He's a soldier in the Army. That's his passion, his life's training, his mission. He's focused on serving his commanding officer. "You tell me what the goal is, Commander, and I'm going to do it. You tell me to bomb that building there, that's what I'm doing. I'm bombing that building."

Jesus gets His soldiers together and He says, "Go and talk about the kingdom of God." And He says the same thing to you and me today. The message has not changed.

God says, "Freely you have received. Freely give." (Matthew 10:8) You and I have received freely. Our salvation costs us

(Obeying God)

nothing. Do we freely give it? Sometimes we live our lives allowing ourselves to be overcome with the busy and hectic nature of the world. These are the very things Jesus talks about in the parable of the sower when He gives the third example of God's word being choked out by the riches and deceit and worry of the world. Our lives are getting so engrossed in the world. It's not that we don't have the kingdom of God. We have it, but we don't give it freely. As a matter of fact, we don't give it at all.

We're so busy being selfish, worried about our own lives—how we feel, what we think, what we want, what we believe, what other people shouldn't believe, and what is right and wrong—that we don't give any of it at all. We take a lot. But we don't give. We're stingy with our money, we're stingy with our time, we're stingy with our life, and scarily enough, we're stingy with our God, as if we get to decide who is worthy of God and who is not.

Let me put it plainly here. You're not worthy, and I'm not worthy. Freely we have received. Freely we are to give. Those are the marching orders from God.

Good Fish

God gives examples. He talks about the kingdom of heaven, and He gives examples of the kingdom of heaven being like a treasure hidden in a field. A man found it, and he sold everything he had and went and bought the field because he knew the value of it.

He said that the kingdom of heaven is like a merchant looking for a fine pearl. He found the pearl, he got everything he had together and sold it, and bought that pearl because it was of such great value.

He talks about the kingdom of heaven being like a fisherman who let down a net, and he collected the fish. You know what the fisherman did with the net after he got all the fish? He separated the good from the bad. The bad fish he threw out. They were worthless, of no value. The good fish he kept and sold.

He talked about the kingdom of heaven being like a farmer who sowed good seed, and a bunch of tares (weeds) got in the seed. His servant asked, "Should I cut the harvest down?" And the farmer said, "No, no, no. Let them both grow together. When it's harvest time, we'll take the tares, we'll bundle them

(Obeying God)

up, and we'll throw them into the fire. And then we'll harvest the good wheat, and we'll bring it into our barns."

God says that's exactly what your life is like. God is looking. God knows your actions and your hearts true intent and the thoughts of your mind. Nothing is hidden from God. He is letting everybody grow together. On judgment day we will see which category you fall into.

There's a great parable in Matthew Chapter 21:28-32 where God gives an example of a father who had two sons. He asked both of them to do something. The Bible says one son went and told the father, "I'm going to do what you said, Dad," but he didn't do what the father asked. The other son said, "Dad, I'm not doing it. This is ridiculous. I'm not doing it." And then later he had a change of heart, and he went and he did the father's will.

Jesus asked, "Who did the will of the father?"

The disciples responded, "The second one. The one who said he wouldn't, but then he really did."

Right, because it's not based on your words. It's based on your actions. It's not based on what you say. It's based on what you do. You can say you love God with all your heart. (And, man, I hope you do!) Well, God has said that if you love me, then you'll obey my commands. What are His commands?

"This I command you. Love one another as you love yourself."

If I love you, I'd want to share the best things I have in life with you—my funniest jokes, the best pizza place I know and everything else I thought was great and awesome. Also I'd want to share all the joy I have with you. If you love somebody, you want to share that stuff with them. If you love your neighbor, you'd want to tell them about the kingdom of God. You share it with them. That's your calling.

Prepared in Advance

In Matthew 19:23-26, we read an interesting story. After a rich man turned away from following God because he had great riches and valued his money more than God, the disciples say to Jesus that it's hard for someone who's rich to enter the kingdom of God. Jesus agrees and replies: "Truly I tell you, it is hard for someone who is rich to enter the kingdom of heaven. Again I tell you, it is easier for a camel to go through the eye of a needle than for someone who is rich to enter the kingdom of God."

When the disciples heard this, they were greatly astonished and asked, "Who then can be saved?" Jesus looked at them and said, "With man this is impossible, but with God all things are possible."

With God all things are possible. Who can be saved? And how? Ephesians 2:8-10 gives us the answer:

> *It is by grace you have been saved, through faith—and this is not from yourselves, it is the gift of God—not by works, so that no one can boast. For we are God's handiwork, created in Christ Jesus to do good works, which God prepared in advance for us to do.*

6: Doing It Right

I think it's funny when people say, "Hey, I've got to go find myself. I need to take a weekend or a week or a month or a year. I need to drop out of life for a while because I don't know who I am and I've got to find myself."

Really? You don't know God's purpose for your life?

"No, no, I know the Lord put me on this earth for something, but I'm searching for what it is. And I need to go away and find my purpose for my life in the Lord?"

Well, God gave me my purpose for my life, and I believe He gave that same purpose to you and every believer. Let's look at it again to be sure we get it. It is laid out in Ephesians 2:10: "For we are God's handiwork, created in Christ Jesus to do good works, which God prepared in advance for us to do."

God prepared in advance these good works for us to do. What are the good works? Go and tell people that the kingdom of heaven is at hand and love others as you love yourself. If you go tell people about Jesus Christ and love others, you will be doing the work of God and then you can be certain you will have lived the life that mattered for God.

The Players

We have to know that Abraham, Moses, Isaac, Jacob, David, Noah, Job—all these guys were just like us. They were the players of their time. In my day Willis Reed and Kareem Abdul-Jabbar were the best basketball players. In my father's day it was Wilt Chamberlain and Bob Cousy. Today it's LeBron James and Dwayne Wade. Every time has its players, whether they are actors, politicians, athletes, or people just like you and me.

We're the people of this day. We're the people God wants to use today to change our families, our communities, our cities, our world—just by simply being obedient to Jesus Christ, by letting the world see God in us and through us.

When Isaac was leading Israel, the Bible says, in Genesis 26:23-24:

> He went up to Beersheba. That night the Lord appeared to him and said, 'I am the God of your father Abraham. Do not be afraid, for I am with you; I will bless you and will increase the number of your descendants for the sake of my servant Abraham.'

6: Doing It Right

God is saying to you and me today, "Do not be afraid, for I am with you. I am with you forever. I will never leave you or forsake you. I've created a perfect plan for your life."

"I know the plans I have for you," says the Lord, "plans to prosper you and not to harm you." All things work together for the good of those who love God and who are called according to his purpose. It doesn't get any better than that one promise for you and I and all believers. History, we either learn from it or we're destined to repeat it. Which one is it going to be? Will we treasure every breath we take and act like it by following God's commandments every step of the journey? Or will we fail to do so, and thus forfeit some of our glory in eternity?

No Free Pass

When Moses doubted God, what did God do? He proved it to him. He asked, "Moses, what's that in your hand?"

Moses said, "A staff."

God said, "Throw it down."

Moses obeyed and it turned into a snake. God told Moses to pick it back up and the snake turned back into a staff.

Moses said, "Okay, I get it. You really have the power to do what you say. I believe it. I'm going to do what you told me to do."

But he still needed a sign. He needed more proof from God after God spoke. And I pray that you and I today don't need any more proof from God than the cross of Jesus Christ and the moving of the Holy Spirit in our lives. That's all the proof we should ever need, the Holy Spirit deposited in our heart by Jesus. That's the reality of God in your life. If you don't have that, you don't have God in your life. If you do have it, you know for sure. Why would you doubt it? I mean, really, if we want to know if you're male or female, there's a way to find out. You can look and check for yourself. You're not going to doubt that after you've seen proof are you? Are you? No. So don't doubt what God has already done in your life!

Now Moses was scared—like Abraham, like Jonah, and like you and me. Moses had a stuttering problem. It's a known fact that he didn't speak too clearly. He says to God in Exodus 4:10, "I can't speak clearly."

God answers him in verse 12, "I'll help you speak. I will teach you what to say."

But Moses says to God in Exodus 4:13, perhaps one of the most amazing lines in the Bible I've ever seen, "Pardon your servant, Lord. Please send someone else."

What's that Moses? You are telling God, "I pass. You know what, Lord? I thought about it. I'm out." God asks, "Deal or no deal?" You say, "No deal."

We do that sometimes, don't we? God knocks on our hearts. The Holy Spirit comes with a destiny, with a word, or even just a thought for that moment. Hey, share my good news with that person. Hey, pray for that person. Hey, be a witness. Hey, I know the wait is long, the line is long. I know you're upset. I know the circumstances, but would you just glorify me with forgiveness and mercy and peace to the people around you so they might get a little glimpse of who I really am through you, the only Jesus they may ever see? You are my son, my ambassador, my representative, my soldier, my warrior here on earth, light to a generation of darkness, salt to a tasteless generation. Can you just be what I created you to be at least most of the time?

God says this to you and me, probably every day, whispering to our heart. Yet, here's Moses bowing out. He wanted

(Obeying God)

a free pass. Thank God that Jesus, when He hung on the cross, didn't take a free pass or say, "Send somebody else." He said, "Lord, Thy will be done on earth as it is in heaven." I pray we too live up to the calling we've obtained and not ask God to skip over us. How tragic it would be if God said, "Okay, I will send somebody else." And you missed God's calling and purpose for your life.

The Hall of Fame

Every single person in Hebrews Chapter 11, known among most Christian circles as members of the "Hall of Fame of Faith," died before they saw God's promise to them fulfilled on earth. It talks about Noah, Enoch, Moses, Isaac, and many others who did what God wanted them to do. These folks were so faithful to God. They are truly the hall of fame of faith.

If you look at the Baseball Hall of Fame or the Rock and Roll Hall of Fame, we see the greatest who ever played enshrined in their halls. And in Hebrews 11, we can see some of God's greatest. Yet every single one of those people died before they saw the promise of God fulfilled on earth. God used them mightily. We clearly see why as history has recorded it, but they didn't know the future. They didn't know what would happen to them. That is precisely what made them such great men and women of faith.

Clearly, we're grateful for their obedience and their following and their faith as it was an inspiration to us, and an example for us, and we learn from it. I hope we learn from it—from every single one of them, especially during those

(Obeying God)

times that we also do not see God's promises fulfilled to us in this life. Only when we have faith and continue on and keep on trusting Him in spite of what we see and feel, only then can we be counted among those who held fast to their faith in His eternal promises. Only then will we also obtain a "good report" for eternity.

Sometimes we can see it here on earth. Hey, look at Billy Graham. We get it. Wow. There'll be a great reward for you in heaven, Billy Graham. I just use Billy Graham as an example because on the surface he clearly looks like someone who's going to have a great reward in heaven. All we see is what God has done in his life here on earth. Others will get the same reward or better as Billy Graham because it's not based on our accomplishment. It's not based on how many people God chooses to save through you. It's based on your obedience to God. We are all at a completely different place in our lives, each and every one of us. And your only responsibility for your reward and your only requirement for your reward to be equal to or better than Billy Graham's reward, is just to say yes to God, wherever you're at. You are rewarded for your obedience. God chooses what He wants to accomplish through your obedience. You can be a Hall of Famer too…go for it!

Ambassadors

Second Corinthians 5:15 says, "And he died for all, that those who live should no longer live for themselves but for Him who died for them and was raised again."

Who are we living for? Are we living for ourselves, or are we living for the one who raised us from the dead? We should be living for Him. We shouldn't live for ourselves anymore. God says that we're a new creation in Christ. The old man is dead. The new man is alive. If we work for the things of the flesh, they are going to die and rust and decay. They're worthless to God in the kingdom of heaven. But if we work for the things of the spirit, if our life is a sacrifice—if we are imitators of Christ—then blessing upon blessing upon blessing will be poured upon us both now and for all eternity.

Verse 20 goes on to say, "We are therefore Christ's ambassadors, as though God were making his appeal through us. God made him who had no sin to be sin for us, so that in him we might become the righteousness of God."

We're supposed to be Christ's ambassadors. When people see us, do they see God in us? We're supposed to be the righteousness of Christ. We're supposed to be the sacrificial

(Obeying God)

ones—giving, sharing, putting others above ourselves, truly living that way. That's the righteousness of Christ.

The question is: Are we?

Do we live like that? When we come into the room or when people are talking about us after we've left, do they say, "Oh, man, that guy? Holy cow! What an ambassador for Christ. It's like Jesus Himself is here."

That's what people should be saying because that's what our lives should truly reflect. It's like Jesus Himself were here.

We read in 1 Corinthians 15:53-57:

> *For the perishable must clothe itself with the imperishable, and the mortal with immortality. When the perishable has been clothed with the imperishable, and the mortal with immortality, then the saying that is written will come true: 'Death has been swallowed up in victory. Where, O death, is your victory? Where, O death, is your sting?' The sting of death is sin, and the power of sin is the law. But thanks be to God! He gives us the victory through our Lord Jesus Christ.*

Now, because Jesus has overcome death, because death no longer has victory over you, because you can't die, because you're going to live for all eternity because of what Jesus did for you, verse 58 tells us what to do:

> *Therefore, my dear brothers and sisters, stand firm. Let nothing move you. Always give yourselves fully to the work of the Lord, because you know that your labor in the Lord is not in vain.*

6: Doing It Right

What part of "Always give yourself fully to the work of the Lord" is unclear? That's a requirement. It's a blueprint for the abundant Christian life. Here God has given us the recipe. "So whether you eat or drink or whatever you do, do it all for the glory of God. For I am not seeking my own good but the good of many, so that they may be saved." (1 Corinthians 10:31, 33).

We need to look at our lives to see whose good we are truly seeking. Are you really about other people, or are you really about yourself? I'm sharing with you from my heart here. I think I'm a reasonably good guy. I like people and I think people generally like me, but God said it's not about what the world sees. God says, "You can fool the world, but you can't fool me, Jack. I'm looking into your heart, and I want to see if your heart is all about you and what you want or if it's about me and what I want. And if your heart is about me, Jack, if you're really grateful and appreciative for the things I've given you, for this life, for your salvation, for this abundant life of knowing me and walking with me, then you will live a sacrificial life. That's how you can please me."

We are to imitate Jesus. We are to sacrifice our life for others. That's how we can live a life that matters for God.

Going to Class

We have an obligation, a specific mandate from Christ Himself to do the best we can to share with people this good news of Jesus Christ. He tells us in Matthew 28:19, "Go ye and teach all nations." He tells us in John 21:17, "Feed my sheep." His truth has been shared with us. We need to share it with everyone else.

It's like if I told you, "I got accepted to Syracuse University."

"That's great. What did you learn?"

"Well, nothing."

"Why not?

"Well, I didn't go to any classes."

"Why not?"

"I didn't want to go." I would be crazy, right? It's not enough to get in. You have to go to the classes to learn the stuff.

It's wonderful to get saved. That's a great thing. But if you want to walk with God, you need to spend time in class. You need to spend time at the feet of God. You need to spend time seeking God's face so He can teach your heart. You need to lay it all down at the foot of the cross. Everything in our life is an opportunity to get closer to God and learn from God and

6: Doing It Right

walk in the spirit of God. We need to turn our hearts back to that relationship with God.

Here's how you pass the test: go to class and learn what they're teaching. Hear what the Holy Spirit of God is saying to your heart. Spend time getting in the word of God—with God, knowing God, praying to God, fellowshipping with God, walking with God, seeking God's face, and praying to God even more. That's how God communicates with us—through prayer, through the Holy Spirit inside of our hearts, and through the Bible.

The biggest way God speaks to me is one on one, individually, when I'm studying His word. That is when the Holy Spirit—who God promised would teach me all things—is shining a light on the word of God, and it's exploding inside my heart. Finally I get it, and I'm going, "Give me more, Lord." I just want to learn more and more and more. I want to walk closer and closer and closer because this is the greatest feeling. It really is.

It's great to hear God's voice through messages at church, and through music, and through books we read, but there's nothing like getting it for yourself, hearing His voice in your spirit, speaking clearly and directly to your own heart. You get that when you spend personal, quality, one on one time with Him. Don't miss that blessing.

Stay Dressed

Here's the key to the Christian life. Jesus is talking to His disciples and, of course, talking to you and me today, saying: "Be dressed, ready for service, and keep your lamps burning." (Luke 12:35)

Can you imagine a fireman gets the alarm call and he sleeps through it, or he's hung over, or he's out of shape, or he's at an NFL football game when he's supposed to be on call? He's not dressed. He's not ready for service. He's not ready to fight to save lives.

God says, "You who believe in me, your job here on earth is to be dressed, ready for service at all times, and keep your lamp burning." Keep the light burning. The light of Christ that's supposed to shine through you, so that the world is able to see the difference of what a Christian looks like in you and me. Just by the way we behave, just by the way we act, just by the things we say, just by the things we do—they should know that we truly are the children of God. Why? Because we do what our Father did. Jesus says, "I do what the Father commands. I do what I've seen the Father do." That's what we're supposed to do. "The servant is not greater than

6: Doing It Right

his master." We're supposed to follow God, just as Jesus did. We're supposed to be holy because God is holy.

Jesus continues with this parable: "Be dressed ready for service and keep your lamps burning, like servants waiting for their master to return from a wedding banquet, so that when he comes and knocks they can immediately open the door for him." (Luke 12: 35-36)

Dressed and ready like a servant waiting for the master to return from a wedding banquet. Why? So the minute he knocks, he doesn't have to wait one second. "Oh, welcome home, master! Great! What can we do for you, master? We are ready. We're your good and faithful servants."

Can you imagine that master coming home from the wedding banquet and knocking and nobody answers? Nobody lets him in and he's locked out of his house all night. Or he comes in and the house is a mess. It's not clean. The beds aren't made. There's no food. "Man, what were you guys doing?"

"Well, Master, we were just kind of having some fun. We decided we'd play some poker, watch TV, have a few drinks or something."

"What? Don't I pay you guys to be ready? Isn't that your job description? Be my servant. Be ready. Do my bidding."

By earthly standards, that's exactly what the servant's job is. We are God's servants, and we're supposed to be ready at all times. We get to serve God out of gratitude. We get to serve God, not out of bondage but out of joy and obligation because He's blessed our lives with salvation, His presence and His joy. God says that we're supposed to be ready at all times.

(Obeying God)

Why, God? Why do I have to be that way? Why do I have to be dressed? Why do I have to be ready for service? Why do I have to be as a light burning?

Jesus says: "It will be good for those servants whose master finds them watching when he comes. Truly I tell you, he will dress himself to serve, will have them recline at the table and will come and wait on them." (Luke 12:37)

Wow! What a great promise from God. God says if you are ready and serve Him in this lifetime, He will come and serve you. You will recline at the table—at the Master's table, at the feast in heaven—and you will be the one being served by the master Himself.

This parable concludes with a warning. Jesus says: "But understand this: If the owner of the house had known at what hour the thief was coming, he would not have let his house be broken into. You also must be ready, because the Son of Man will come at an hour when you do not expect him." (Luke 12:39-40)

Could God be any clearer? God loves you so much, He's telling you, "I've seen the end of the movie. I wrote the book, so I know the ending." He's making it easy for us, His kids. "Don't be caught with your pants down. I want you to be ready. I'm telling you, be prepared because you don't know when I'm coming back. So be prepared by staying faithful to me." And that's exactly how you live a life that matters for God.

Get with the System

All of the employees of McDonald's wear the same uniform. They'll take your order, put together your Egg McMuffin or Big Mac, and give you your coffee. They have their system down.

When you fly somewhere on an airplane, the pilot has his uniform and his hat on, and he flies the route he's assigned. The flight attendants do exactly what they are supposed to do—give you the safety information with the exact same hand motions every time, walk down the aisle handing out snacks and drinks, collect the garbage afterward, and finally making sure everything is in an upright position for landing. They have it down pat.

We have a world where people are used to doing exactly what they're supposed to do. They work within a system that dictates rules and regulations for them to do, and in return, they get a paycheck for doing it. You don't see an employee at McDonald's kicking over the coffee, throwing down his uniform, and saying, "I'm not doing this your way. To heck with you guys. I will sit here and I will serve the coffee my way." Well, sure, do it your way, but not here. You can have that attitude, but you won't be working here. Obviously, it's the same thing with the airplane pilot, bank teller, department store employee, school teacher, or emergency room physician.

You have to follow protocol, rules, and procedures. That's why the rules have been set up, for the employees to follow. If they do, they're rewarded and blessed, if nothing else, with a paycheck. If they don't follow them, they're gone.

Yet, as Christians, we act like we don't care what God has asked us to do. God, as a loving Father, is coaching, nurturing, and encouraging us so we can have his full blessings. He's lovingly directing us, "Here guys. Here's what you do. Here's how the game ends. Don't worry. You just execute the play. I've got it all under control. I crushed Satan at the cross. You just go and do as I say."

But we go, "No, God. No, I'm not doing it that way. It's out of the question that I imitate you."

Why?

"I'm selfish. I'm greedy. I don't want to. I'm stubborn. I don't believe you, Lord. I don't trust you, Lord. I'll have one foot in the world, one foot in the spirit, and I hope that works out."

God says, no, you've got to be all in. That's how you get the blessing.

No Camping for Me

An acquaintance asked me a theological question. I forgot how he phrased it, but the basic gist of it was, "What camp are you in? Who do you follow theologically?"

Me, in all my wisdom, answered, "Jesus."

But he wanted to go deeper than that, and he started mentioning some names—good names, I think. One was John Piper, an influential Christian preacher. I thought, That's interesting. Hmmm. Maybe I actually need to pick a "team." But then I thought, No, I just want my answer to always be just "Jesus." It was interesting to me how the world has carved out such denominations, and how people have allowed themselves to be placed into these different "camps." He was trying to understand how I thought and what opinions or beliefs I subscribed to, and I said, "I believe that Jesus and what Jesus says is all that I need to know. That's all of it."

And it really is.

Smelling Like Garlic

When a life has turned to God, what does it look like? I love 2 Corinthians 3:18, "And we all, who with unveiled faces contemplate the Lord's glory, are being transformed into his image with ever-increasing glory."

Isn't that beautiful? "Ever-increasing glory." It just gets better and better and better. We're being transformed into God's image continually. At this point I've been married for fourteen years, and I love my wife today more than ever. I've known my parents all my life (isn't that something!) and I love them more than ever too. I've known my children all their lives, and my love for them has grown as well. It has continued to grow and I know it will continue to grow.

That's what God wants you to know. When you are transformed into God's image, it's with ever-increasing glory. How do you get transformed into God's image? You accept Jesus as Lord and Savior. You invite Him into your life. He says He brings new life to you. He transforms you. You don't transform yourself. God transforms you. He calls it a renewing of your mind, a transformation of your mind and your heart and your body and your soul and your spirit.

It's like taking a bath in Epsom salt. If you have some pain

6: Doing It Right

in your legs, you get in the bath. But first you have to put in the Epsom salt! If you leave it on the counter and don't put it in the bathtub, it's of no use. It won't work. You take it and you pour it in the water. And then you get in and you let it permeate every pore in your body and work in you. Then it provides you relief.

That's how it should be with Jesus Christ in your life. You should be soaking Him into your life, into every pore and every fiber of your being. Every moment and every breath should be soaking Jesus into your life. And He should permeate through you in everything you do. We should smell Him all over you like you smell garlic when you finishing eating in an Italian restaurant.

You might ask, "Well, that's great, Jack, but how do I do this? How can I turn to God?" God says, in James 4:8, "Come close to God and God will come close to you." If I were to talk to you face to face, it's pretty easy to know how you feel, to understand what you're thinking. They say the eyes are the window to the soul. Well I know if I can see your heart, I can see your mind. However, if your back is turned or we're talking on the telephone, I can't tell. And if you send me a text or email, I certainly don't know what you were really thinking because all the emotion is stripped out of it. Why do you think poker players wear sunglasses? So nobody can see their face. Nobody can know what they're thinking.

God says He wants you to see inside of His heart and know exactly what He's thinking. He already knows exactly what we're thinking, the thoughts and intents of our hearts. But He also wants us to draw close to Him, to come to understand Him better...to know His heart.

Missing It

God has been pleased to give you the kingdom. Luke 12:32 says, "Do not be afraid, for your Father has been pleased to give you the kingdom." What parent isn't pleased to give their kids good food, good toys, good clothes, and send them to a good school. And we're earthly parents. God is our heavenly Father and He can do it all; and God is pleased to give you the kingdom. How ready are we to reach out and take it? Or are we too busy with the toils and struggles of just surviving that we don't look up and realize He's already handing us all that we need?

Have you ever looked at the TV Guide and saw something you really wanted to watch, and later that week you realize that you've missed it? Or you heard people talking about a lunar eclipse and, before you have a chance to check it out, you missed it. These things happen in life. You can miss a plane. You can miss a bus. You can be distracted and miss it. Or you can oversleep and miss it.

In Prince Caspian—one of the books in the Chronicle of Narnia series—Lucy, the youngest, sees Aslan the lion. She and her sister and two brothers have been venturing through

6: Doing It Right

an unknown forest and they don't know the best way to go. Lucy saw Aslan, and nobody else did. They weren't looking. She was the only one looking. She tells the others and they said, "We didn't see him."

She said, "Well, I saw Him." They didn't believe her. They didn't see, but she saw. She was watching. She didn't miss anything.

It's not difficult to miss things. You can miss God's calling for your life. You can miss the joy of knowing you are following His plan for your life. We definitely don't want to miss that. So pay attention!

The Sweet Spot

This day, this moment, this week, this year, this decade, your life—don't miss it, especially the sweet spot. My son Jackson looks at his little baseball bat and says, "Look, daddy, I'm going to hit it on the sweet spot." It's that fat part of the bat. When you hit that ball, boom, it's the sweet spot. It's perfect. The ball goes as hard and as far and as fast as it possibly can. It's the best place to hit the ball.

When people reach a certain age, they come to realize these things a little more. I am part of a men's ministry—about fifty guys—some of whom are seventy years old or older. These older men value life. You know why? They've told me, "We know our time is short. We've got to make the most of every day."

You might not have even reached your prime yet. You might still be in your "sweet spot." That's wonderful! It's a gift that God has given you, and you need to use it and enjoy it. Don't waste it through worry. Don't miss it through joyless laboring for things that perish.

A lot of people don't understand this, and they miss it. They say, "I'm a Christian," but they don't live like it, and they

6: Doing It Right

miss the blessings that God intended. They can even miss the very life that God had purposed for them to live. If you are asking now, "Well, how do I make sure that I don't miss it?" That's a good question. It's a great place to start.

God gives us some simple instructions. For starters, He tells us, "Be joyful always; pray continually; give thanks in all circumstances, for this is God's will for you in Christ Jesus." (1 Thessalonians 5:16-18)

He lets us know the perspective that we need to have on life and every circumstance that comes our way. Our mindset needs to be joyful, prayerful, and thankful—knowing that whatever happens to us is part of His plan. It's "God's will for you in Christ Jesus." It's also the way to make sure you live a life that matters for God.

Be Ready

God says, if you don't want to miss it, be ready. If you want to see the solar eclipse, then be out there when the eclipse is going to happen. If you want to see the space shuttle take off, it would be a good idea to be standing there at take-off time. If you don't want to miss what God's doing, then pay attention to God. God says in Matthew 24:35-36, be ready, "Heaven and earth will pass away, but my words will never pass away. No one knows about that day or hour, not even the angels in heaven, nor the Son, but only the Father."

When an eclipse comes, or a comet passes by, or a meteor shower happens, we can know exactly when it's going to be. It'll be in the papers or online. But we don't know when Christ is returning. No one knows the day or hour that Jesus will be coming back. Sadly some people will be so full of themselves and everything they have going on, that they're not even going to care.

God says:

> *Just as it was in the days of Noah, so also will it be in the days of the Son of Man. People were eating,*

6: Doing It Right

> *drinking, marrying and being given in marriage up to the day Noah entered the ark. Then the flood came and destroyed them all. (Luke 17:26- 27)*

God has told us exactly what is going to happen. He said there will be trials and tribulations. There will be earthquakes. There will be wars. There will be one currency. There will be the mark of the beast on your head. It's all coming. You can see signs of the end coming closer and closer. You don't have to be a rocket scientist—if it's cloudy and overcast with lightning and thunder, it's going to rain.

Hey, we have the Euro and now we are closer than ever to a one-world currency. We have the Internet. The world is all connected. We have everybody hooked up. We have computer chips going into dogs and kids and people to track their location and movement at all times. We have war. We have earthquakes. We have famine. We have disaster everywhere. It's coming. We definitely know that. God says you don't know the hour and you don't know the day, but you just need to be "on guard, alert and sober! Ready!" That's your job. Be ready.

Wakeup Call

There's a young man named Bill, who is a friend of a friend of mine. He is about twenty-four years old, a young Christian man. He's been fighting drugs since he was eighteen. He's been in and out of rehab. I put him there once trying to help him and he just couldn't get over this stronghold. A very close friend of his was also doing the same thing, trying to quit using. Bill's friend had been taking a lot of oxycodone every day and he tried to stop cold turkey. His heart went into shock. He went into a coma, and he died after seven days. They pulled the plug on him.

This young man doesn't have the opportunity to come back. He went out too far. It's over for him. His life on earth is gone and done. He missed it. He made bad choices. My friends and I all feel sorry for him. You probably do too, hearing a story as sad as that. My friend Bill is out there, still living. He might miss it too. God, I pray that's not the case. But it's up to him. Hopefully the death of his friend will turn out to be his wakeup call. He's had a number of wakeup calls so far, and he hasn't responded to any of them. But I pray that this time he will listen.

6: Doing It Right

I can't control what he does, but I can control what I do. You can control what you do. What wakeup call is it going to take for you?

Being a Picture

Charles Spurgeon is referred to as one of the greatest preachers of all time. He lived from 1834 to 1892. He made the following statement during a sermon he preached in London, in 1855:

> *A Christian should be a striking likeness of Jesus Christ. If we, my brethren, were what we professed to be, if the spirit of the Lord were in the heart of all his children as we could desire and if instead of having an abundance of formal professors we were all possessors of that vital grace, I will tell you not only what we ought to be but what we should be. We should be pictures of Christ. Yes, such striking likenesses of Him that the world would not have to hold us up by the hour and say, 'Well, it seems like they're a likeness of Jesus,' but they would when they beheld us and looked at you and I say, 'He has been with Jesus. He's been taught of Him. He is like Him. He has caught the very idea of the Holy Man of Nazareth, and he expands it out of his every action and out of his very life.'*

6: Doing It Right

Man, that's what I want said about me. That's the benchmark. The British evangelist Rowland Hill, who lived from 1744 to 1833 made a succinct statement, and I challenge you to apply this to your life. He said, "I would not believe a man to be a true Christian if his wife, his children, the servants, and even the dog and cat were not the better for it."

Are the people around you better off for your walk with God or not? I think my family would give me the okay. The cat's a little pissed at me at the moment, but I think my family would be pretty positive about it. The question is, are you a true Christian by that definition? Are the people around you better? Rowland goes on to say, "The only thing that can possibly silence the critics of Christianity is for Christians to act like Christ." Ouch! Does that describe you and me or not?

The apostle Paul says about himself, "First, I thank my God through Jesus Christ for all of you, because your faith is being reported all over the world. God, whom I serve with my whole heart in preaching the gospel of his Son..." (Romans 1:8-9).

The key phrase is, "God, whom I serve with my whole heart." He feels that fact is important enough to tell you, like something he would want to write in his autobiography. "Here I am, Paul, and I serve God with my whole heart."

Do we live like that? Do our actions and our lives and our voice and the way that we live say, "I serve God with my whole heart"? Or do we say, "I serve God when it's convenient?" We certainly serve him in church while other people are watching, but do we serve Him with our whole hearts?

That's a question for you to place deep inside your soul and bring it up on a regular basis to find out where you stand. I've

(Obeying God)

been asking myself that question, and you know what? The answer isn't always yes. But I know one thing. I want it to be yes. I want to do whatever it takes for it to be yes because I love Him so much! I love the feeling that comes from knowing I'm doing His will. When I'm walking with Him, there is nothing between me and God.

And that doesn't mean that I'm perfect—far from it. It just means that I'm doing everything I can to be righteous before God, to be an imitator of Jesus Christ, because I don't want to betray Him after all that He's done for me. When God sees me doing my best, even if I'm not perfect, I think He's satisfied. When you see your kids doing their best, how proud are you? Does it matter if they came in first or tenth? No, it matters that they're giving their all, and that's what God wants from you and me—that we give our all.

Trained and Ready

What will your reward be once you get to heaven? The answer is definitely determined in part by your faith: "With this in mind, we constantly pray for you, that our God may count you worthy of his calling, and that by his power he may fulfill every good purpose of yours and every act prompted by your faith." (2 Thessalonians 1:11)

Faith is what makes God fulfill every act and purpose. God has the purpose already set out for you. He had it before you were born, before you were created, before you were in your mother's womb. He's got the purpose for your life. And if you want it to be lived out, you just need to follow Him. He responds based on your faith, just like the apostle Paul looked at that the lame man in Acts 14:9 and said, "I see you have the faith to be healed."

God is asking you, "Do you have the faith? Do you believe in me? Do you trust in me?" Your answer determines your joy and fulfillment in this life and in the life to come.

A friend called my wife and me. She recently lost a sister to suicide and a few weeks ago she lost her brother to a very untimely death. She didn't know if they were saved or not. She

(Obeying God)

said to me, "Listen, I'm not sure I have the faith God wants me to have."

I said, "You're one of the most godly, Christian women I know. You have tremendous faith, and God said He will test our faith. Certainly God is testing your faith. I am not saying that's the reason that your brother and sister died, to test your faith, but how we respond in situations, both good and bad, is a test of our faith. The world is watching and you need to be the light in a world of darkness. The world is watching how you respond."

The world is watching to see how we respond to everything. Are we responding in faith or not? Faith builds more faith. You know, they say fake it until you make it. That actually worked really well for me in business, and we used to train our salespeople that way. Man, we used to train them hard and give them the information and input they needed to get out there and do the job. When you go through your training and then you get called up to the Major Leagues and it's your first at bat, or you're a doctor doing your first surgery, you don't go out and say, "I can't do this."

"Well, why can't you do this?"

"I've never done it before. I've never played major league ball before. I've never performed surgery before."

That's right. You haven't, but you were qualified to do it. We gave you the training (or you got the training from some proper place) and that's why we called you to do it. That's why we made you the surgeon. That's why we brought you up to the Major Leagues. You have proven to us that you're qualified, so we're giving you the shot.

6: Doing It Right

God has qualified you, and He's calling you out to do the job. He says the same thing to you: "I've called you to be my disciples, my representatives, my soldiers, my ambassadors. Most importantly I've called you to be my children. Children of the light, to be my light shining in a world of darkness." You can see the darkness all around. You know the darkness. It's everywhere. There's more darkness now than ever. We need to be the lights, and how brightly you will shine is based on your faith. Faith builds more faith. Go build!

Choosing Teams

In sports, we know that there are consequences for good plays and bad plays. There are great players regardless of your sports team affiliation. Alex Rodriguez is known as a great baseball player. Lebron James and Kobe Bryant are great basketball players.

They're great players, but there are consequences to their plays. Good plays bring winning results for their team, and bad plays bring losing results for their team.

We're not sports guys. We're Christians. But we're in the army of Jesus Christ. We're soldiers. We're players. We have "Christian" written across our uniforms, and we should be playing like we mean it for Jesus Christ.

Second Chronicles 12:13 gives a summary of Rehoboam's life. It says:

> *King Rehoboam established himself firmly in Jerusalem and continued as king. He was forty-one years old when he became king, and he reigned seventeen years in Jerusalem.*

6: Doing It Right

Verse 14 says, "He did evil because he had not set his heart on seeking the Lord." Had he put his heart on seeking the Lord, he wouldn't have done evil.

If we seek the Lord God with all our heart and mind and soul, He will protect us. If we put on the full armor of God, He will protect us. We have nothing to fear. Satan can't get us. Satan can't win if we don't let him. But it's a choice we have to make. The question we need to ask ourselves is: "Is my heart set on seeking the Lord or not?"

It's a yes or no question. There is no other answer. It's either, "Yes my heart is set on seeking the Lord," or, "No it's not."

If the answer is not what you want it to be, you can change it. You have the power to right this wrong simply by setting your heart on the Lord.

Let God speak to your heart about what He wants you to do. How He wants you to seek Him. How He wants you to live and whatever gift and calling He has given to you to use for His glory and kingdom during your time here on earth. Do you trust God? If you do, if that answer is yes, then why wouldn't you do as He commands and seek Him with all of your heart?

In Luke 6:46, God says, "Why do you call me Lord, Lord, and not do what I say?" I pray that the desire of your and my heart would always be to do what God says.

7

HEAVEN
(The Certainty Of Heaven For Believers)

No Closing Time

In the book of Revelation 21:9-11, God gave us a view of what heaven is like.

> 'Come, I will show you the bride, the wife of the Lamb.' And he carried me away in the Spirit to a mountain great and high, and showed me the Holy City, Jerusalem, coming down out of heaven from God. It shone with the glory of God, and its brilliance was like that of a very precious jewel, like a jasper, clear as crystal.

John the apostle is being caught up in the Spirit in the book of Revelation and he is seeing exactly what heaven looks like. It goes on to say:

> The great street of the city was of pure gold, like transparent glass. I did not see a temple in the city, because the Lord God Almighty and the Lamb are its temple. The city does not need the sun or the moon to shine on it, for the glory of God gives it light, and the Lamb is its lamp...On no day will its gates ever be shut. (Revelation 21:21-25)

7: Heaven

Man, how great is that? There is no day on which the gates of heaven will ever be shut to those who believe in Jesus Christ.

It's not like you go to your favorite pizza place on the fourth of July only to find it is closed. No, no, no! The gates of heaven are open always.

The Word of God in Revelation 21:25-27 goes on to say:

> *There will be no night there. The glory and honor of nations will be brought into it. Nothing impure will ever enter it nor will anyone who does what is shameful or deceitful but only those whose names are written in the Lamb's Book of Life.*

How do I get my name written in the Lamb's Book of Life? That's easy. You believe in Jesus. The best thing about heaven is that God will be there. We'll be face to face with Jesus. All you must do is believe in Him.

No Tears

All the suffering you face now, every tear, is only momentary. It's temporary. Soon it will dissolve into an eternity of joy.

How do we take these tears and turn them around? Neil Young wrote a song called, "Don't Cry No Tears Around Me." A few of the lines go like this:

> *I saw you in my nightmares. But I'll see you in my dreams. And I might live a thousand years before I know what that means.*

Well Neil's lyrics merge into a sort of gray area, but there's nothing gray about the Word of God.

God's promises are not a Neil Young song. They are not full of double meaning or gray areas. His promises are clear and true, and they hold firm and fast, and they will endure forever.

His promise about heaven is, "And God shall wipe away all tears from their eyes; and there shall be no more death, neither sorrow, nor crying, neither shall there be any more pain: for the former things are passed away." (Revelation 21:4) Heaven sounds like such an amazing place and God promises that it is. We know no lie can come from the truth. Jesus is "the way, the truth and the life," (John 14:6) and in God there is nothing that is not true.

God is our loving Father; He would never lie to His children. He is truth and He wants you to know truth and to love truth. If we love God we love the truth. And if we love Him, then shouldn't our lives reflect that consistently?

Breath on a Cold Winter Morning

"Dear friends, now we are children of God, and what we will be has not yet been made known. But we know that when He appears, we shall be like Him, for we shall see Him as he is. "Everyone who has this hope in Him [God] purifies himself just as God is pure." (1 John 3:3). This verse is clear. It says everyone...not some people, not a few, not most—but EVERYONE!

What hope is that? The hope that when He appears, we shall be like Him. Everyone who believes in God purifies himself because we have the belief that we're going to see God and we're going to be like Him.

Any child would love his father for doing great stuff for him and being this great dad. That is how we love God. Because of that, we purify ourselves. Because of that, we don't let ourselves get sucked into the world.

God says that we are to be in the world but not of the world. Our citizenship is in heaven. We're strangers here on earth. My driver's license says Parkland, Florida, but it should say

7: Heaven

"Heaven." That's where I'm from. My home is in heaven. I'm just passing through here on earth.

God says our life is but a mist—these sixty, seventy, eighty years you get? Poof! Like a cold breath on a wintry New York City morning, it is there for an instant and then it's gone. That's your life.

Our permanent citizenship is in heaven, and aren't you so glad it is? Our permanent residence is in a place where there are no tears and God's love lights up the place day and night. Hey, it's nice to have a place to call home!

Raised from the Dead

1 Corinthians 15:12-14 says:

If it is preached that Christ has been raised from the dead, how can some of you say that there is no resurrection of the dead? If there is no resurrection of the dead, then not even Christ has been raised. And if Christ has not been raised, our preaching is useless and so is your faith.

Hey, that's the whole gospel right there. Either Jesus died and He was resurrected, and you're going to die and be resurrected, and we believe that and stand in that and we rejoice in that and we sing in that and we live in that…or everything is useless. It's all garbage. If that didn't happen, everything our foundation and religion is based on is a crock. It's worthless.

We know it's true because we've seen the changed lives. We're living the changed life, and we can count on all the promises of God. They are "yes" in Jesus. All are yes, as is the resurrection and this great salvation that God talks about. However Paul goes on to say in verses 15-17 if Christ has not been raised from the dead then:

7: Heaven

> *More than that, we are then found to be false witnesses about God, for we have testified about God that he raised Christ from the dead. But He did not raise Him if in fact the dead are not raised. For if the dead are not raised, then Christ has not been raised either. And if Christ has not been raised, your faith is futile; you are still in your sins.*

If Christ hasn't been raised, if He is not with God in heaven, then our faith is worthless. It's futile. Then we're still in our sins. The penalty for sin is death, and we should expect it to come upon us swiftly and forever and eternally, and we'll be separated from God because there is no salvation. There is no God if He hasn't been raised—then it's all a lie.

The question is, what do we believe?

Paul goes on to say in verses 18-19:

> *Then those also who have fallen asleep in Christ are lost. If only for this life we have hope in Christ, we are of all people most to be pitied.*

How tragic is that? If our belief in Jesus goes no further than this life, then we're to be pitied because that's not what it's about. We're citizens of heaven. We're representatives of God. It's about the kingdom of God. That's the joy. That's the gospel. It's about eternity. It's about us being strangers, passing through in this world on a mission from God our Father, knowing, being certain, that our citizenship is in heaven. Jesus told us He deposited in us the Holy Spirit upon salvation who confirms all the things of God.

Has God confirmed in your heart the reality of the gospel of Jesus Christ, the reality of this great news? If so, we need to

(The Certainty Of Heaven For Believers)

share it with those who don't yet know the gospel. We need to tell them about the miraculous change in our lives that comes from knowing Jesus Christ, the certainty that comes from knowing that we will be with Him forever and ever in eternity and that we will reign with Him. That's the great promise of our God. It is for you and me and everyone. John 3:17 reminds us: "For God did not send his Son into the world to condemn the world, but to save the world through Him."

Jesus wants all people to believe. Luke 19:10 tells us clearly: "For the Son of man came to seek and to save the lost." You and I have it so good! Our prayer should be that of Psalm 107:15 "Let them give thanks to the Lord for his unfailing love and his wonderful deeds for mankind." How about you? Have you been giving thanks lately?

A Butterfly

In I Corinthians 15:35, the apostle Paul says, "But someone will ask, 'How are the dead raised? With what kind of body will they come?'"

That's a good question. How does all this happen?

The apostle Paul answers, "How foolish!" He's basically saying, "Hey, that's a dumb question. Let me tell you why." He goes on to explain in verses 36-38:

> *What you sow does not come to life unless it dies. When you sow, you do not plant the body that will be, but just a seed, perhaps of wheat or of something else. But God gives it a body as he has determined, and to each kind of seed he gives its own body.*

Was a butterfly always a butterfly? No. First it was a caterpillar and then it became a butterfly.

What if you didn't know? What if you just looked at the caterpillar and you said, "You will always be a caterpillar"? Well, you'd be very wrong. The body you have right now isn't the body you will have in heaven. It's like a seed that's been planted. When you're in heaven, you will have a new body. It's

(The Certainty Of Heaven For Believers)

a body the Lord will give you. It's a supernatural body. God says, "I have in store for you the supernatural, a body that will never die, a body that will last forever."

You know, the tire companies have tires that will never go flat. The lighting companies have light bulbs that will never burn out. (Of course, they're not selling them to you, because then you wouldn't need any more tires and light bulbs and they'd go broke. But we know they have them.) God has for you a body that will never wear out for all eternity, but it will not look like the one we have now.

Listen to what the apostle Paul goes on to say, in I Corinthians 15:39-42:

Not all flesh is the same: People have one kind of flesh, animals have another, birds another and fish another. There are also heavenly bodies and there are earthly bodies; but the splendor of the heavenly bodies is one kind, and the splendor of the earthly bodies is another. The sun has one kind of splendor, the moon another and the stars another; and star differs from star in splendor. So will it be with the resurrection of the dead. The body that is sown is perishable. It is raised imperishable.

Hallelujah! How lucky for you and me. This body we have now, it's perishable. It's a return. It's disposable. We're giving it back. It's like a rental car. We're turning it in at the end. It will have no value at the end. God says the one that's raised—the one that's imperishable—will never lose its value. It will shine forever and ever like the stars with God in heaven. Look what God says in verses 43-44: "Our perishable body is sown in dishonor, it is raised in glory; it is sown in weakness, it is raised in power; it is sown a natural body, it is raised a spiritual body."

Of course it's sown in dishonor because we're descendants of Adam, and Adam sinned. We are all born sinners. We know there is not one righteous except Christ. We know that our righteousness is but filthy rags before the Lord. So, of course it is sown in dishonor, but it's raised in glory. It's raised in the righteousness of Christ.

Thanks be to Jesus who paid our sin debt on the cross so that we would be righteous, so that when God sees us He would see us holy, blameless, and above reproach. Oh, man, that's the greatest. Our bodies are sown in weakness, raised in power; sown a natural body, born like we are today, raised in death a spiritual body, like God and to be with God forever and ever.

Perishable to Imperishable

Adam himself was the first Adam. Jesus is the last Adam. I Corinthians 15:46-49 says,

The spiritual did not come first, but the natural, and after that the spiritual. The first man was of the dust of the earth; the second man is of heaven. As was the earthly man, so are those who are of the earth; and as is the heavenly man, so also are those who are of heaven. And just as we have borne the image of the earthly man, so shall we bear the image of the heavenly man.

That's a promise of Jesus Christ to us. Just as we bore the image of Adam in this flesh, so shall we bear the image of Jesus in the heavenly flesh. Just as Jesus died and was resurrected to be with God for all eternity, we shall be also. This is why we rejoice!

This is why we, as Christians, are called to be the light of the world. This is why we bring light to the darkness. We bring salt to a tasteless generation. That understanding, that knowledge, should be reflected in our lives. That's why we're

7: Heaven

so happy. That's why we're so joyful, because we believe everything God said.

Here's one last thought on that. The apostle Paul said in verse 50, "I declare to you, brothers and sisters, that flesh and blood cannot inherit the kingdom of God, nor does the perishable inherit the imperishable."

In other words, it's impossible for flesh and blood to get into the kingdom of God. You can't get to heaven in your present body, in your present state. You can only get dead. You can't get to heaven. But Paul said, in verses 51-52, "Listen, I tell you a mystery: We will not all sleep, but we will all be changed—in a flash, in the twinkling of an eye, at the last trumpet. For the trumpet will sound, the dead will be raised imperishable, and we will be changed."

We will be changed from perishable to imperishable. Whether you're alive and taken up on judgment day to be with God or whether you've been "asleep," it doesn't matter. At that moment, when the trumpet sounds, in the twinkling of an eye, you'll be changed and you'll be like God in His image forever and ever. Man was created in the image of God. Now you will be in the spiritual image of God forever and ever. What a great, great story.

1 Corinthians 15:53-57 says,

> *For the perishable must clothe itself with the imperishable, and the mortal with immortality. When the perishable has been clothed with the imperishable, and the mortal with immortality, then the saying that is written will come true: 'Death has been swallowed up in victory. Where, O death, is*

(The Certainty Of Heaven For Believers)

your victory? Where, O death, is your sting?' But thanks be to God! He gives us the victory through our Lord Jesus Christ.

In verse 58 we read the greatest thing. Paul sums it all up as he counsels us saying, "Therefore because of all this my dear brothers and sisters, stand firm. Let nothing move you. Always give yourselves fully to the work of the Lord because you know that your labor in the Lord is not in vain." Yes, because you were perishable and are going to be raised imperishable, because you were born mortal and are going to live immortal!

Amen. Let nothing move you. Let nothing shake you. Stay focused on the task at hand. Always give yourself to the work of the Lord. You know that your labor is not in vain. You know God will reward you. Live with the certainty and truth you have obtained from God and you WILL live a life that matters for God!

The Great Separation

Since the beginning of time, we have had good and evil working side by side. Satan is here on earth trying to accomplish his will. God has already won the victory in heaven, but this game has to play out. You know the ending. God has already told you the ending, so you don't have to worry because you know the final score. It doesn't matter if your team is losing in the eighth inning. You know you come back and win.

So, there's good and evil, and God allows that. He said specifically, when He gives the parable of the weeds in Matthew 13:30:

> *I'm going to let them grow together—the wheat and the tares that are crushing the wheat—but at harvest time, we'll go bundle them up, we'll separate the wheat and the tares, we'll take the tares and we'll throw them into the fire, and we'll take the wheat and we'll put it in the barn.*

You're the wheat. You are God's wheat. And when you see the evil people in the world who are not Christians and not

(The Certainty Of Heaven For Believers)

living a godly life, and you think they're getting away with something, think again. Unless God is a liar, He says that come judgment day He's separating them all, saved from the unsaved. God is God. I didn't make the requirements. God did. He said, "There is only one way. I am the way, the truth, and the life. No one comes to the Father except through me" (John 14:6) The only way to the Father is through Jesus Christ.

God is in essence saying, "On judgment day, the unsaved will depart from me. I didn't know them. They'll be in hell for all eternity, and those who believe will be with me in heaven for all eternity, reigning in joy, and there will be a chasm—a great space—that you can't cross once you've made your decision." So, that's it. You make the decision now; you can't cross the chasm once you die. You have to make the decision now that you are going to be God's good grain; the wheat and not the tares.

The Super Bowl Trophy

In the New Testament, Jesus only mentioned the church ten times (three times in Matthew and seven times in Revelation.) The first time was in Matthew 16:18. To Peter He said, "And I tell you that you are Peter, and on this rock I will build my church, and the gates of Hades will not overcome it."

In verse 15, Jesus had just asked His disciples, "Who do you say that I am?" Because people were saying He was Elijah or Jeremiah or John the Baptist. Jesus asked something like, "Well, who do you guys say that I am?"

The apostle Peter answered, "Thou art the Christ. Thou art Lord."

Jesus' response was basically, "Peter, that's awesome. Nobody on earth told you that. God Himself told you that. And, Peter, you are the rock on whom I will build my church, and the gates of Hades will not prevail."

The second and third time Jesus talks about the church is in Matthew 18. Jesus was talking about dealing with sin in the church, and He said, "If your brother or sister sins, go and point out their fault, just between the two of you." (Matthew 18:15)

(The Certainty Of Heaven For Believers)

That's still good advice today. There should be no gossip. It goes on to say:

> *If they listen to you, you have won them over. But if they will not listen, take one or two others along, so that every matter may be established by the testimony of two or three witnesses. If they still refuse to listen, tell it to the church; and if they refuse to listen even to the church, treat them as you would a pagan or a tax collector. (Matthew 18:15b-17)*

So ten times in the New Testament Jesus speaks of the church. Yet over one hundred times in the New Testament, Jesus references the kingdom of God. Now, does this mean the church is not important? Oh, no. Jesus ordained the church. Jesus is the head of the church. We are the body. Jesus loved the church. He died for the church. The church is the bride of Christ. We're to love our wives as Christ loved the church.

But understand one thing. The football team is put together to win the Super Bowl trophy. The trophy is much more important than the team. The team's goal is to win the trophy because the trophy is the prize. The kingdom of God is the prize. The church has been put together to lead the world to the kingdom of God. That is the focus of the church. Our mission is to lead the world to the kingdom, to the prize. It's not that the church isn't a critical, important, vital part of the body of Christ. Oh, no, it's very, very important. It's the mechanism by which we lead people to the kingdom of God.

But the kingdom of God is much more important than the church. It's much more important than our very lives. It's

7: Heaven

much more important than everything. It's the prize. It's the kingdom of God. If you want your life to matter for God, you need to live for the Kingdom of God!

The Real Magic Kingdom

To some kids, "The Kingdom" may be Disney World in Orlando, Florida.

So here are some quiz questions for you about your kids' Disney trip:

What do they expect to see when they get to the kingdom?

How do they get to the kingdom?

Who will be at the kingdom?

How much does it cost to get in?

If it's Disney World, kids expect to see Mickey Mouse and Goofy and all the great rides and attractions. If it's Universal Studios, maybe they expect to see Harry Potter and Spider Man too. That's what they expect to see.

How do they get there? Buy tickets and make your way there, either by air, train, land or sea.

Who will be there? Lots of other people who want to see the same thing.

What does it cost? For me, my wife, and kids, about $400, that's just admission to the park for a day. Then, of course, hotel, gas, food, souvenirs etc.

It doesn't matter if the venue is a Miami Heat playoff

game or a Bruce Springsteen concert, you would work out your answers to those same questions. You'd know what you expect to see, how to get there, who would be there, and what it would cost.

Now let's look at the kingdom of heaven.

What do you expect to see when you get there? The Word of God answers in 1 Corinthians 2:9: "No eye has seen, no ear has heard, no mind has conceived what God has prepared for those who love Him." How great is that? You will see such awesome things, better than the best thing that you could possibly imagine or hope for. God has prepared a place, a place wonderfully unimaginable. In God's heaven there is a special place for you. John 14:2 tells us "In my Father's house are many rooms, if it were not so, I would have told you. I go to prepare a place for you." We are so blessed. We are going to heaven…a place where there is no death and no pain. There is only joy and worship forever and ever.

How do you get there? Jesus says, "I am the way, the truth, and life. The only way to the Father is through the Son." We know, as believers, that in order to get to heaven, to get our entry ticket in, we have to believe in Jesus Christ. Jesus said we are to believe in the One God sent. That's in the book of John. That's our job—to believe in the One God sent. That's how we get to heaven.

Who will be there? Every other believer in Jesus Christ, every child of God, every person who has accepted Jesus Christ will be in the kingdom of heaven—regardless of what they did, good or bad; regardless of if they lived up to the calling that they've obtained. We—as children of God, as sons

(The Certainty Of Heaven For Believers)

and daughters of God, as ambassadors and missionaries, as soldiers, as representatives of God, as imitators of God—have been given a wonderful calling, and we should live up to this great calling. But even if we didn't, we're still going to heaven if we accepted Jesus Christ, the Son of God as our Lord and savior.

What does it cost to get in? Nothing.

It cost God everything. God gave Jesus, His Son, so that you could live eternally in a place of beauty and perfection. It cost you nothing. It's by grace you've been saved, by the gift of God, not by works lest any man should boast. (Ephesians 2:8) You did nothing to earn it, nothing to deserve it. God loved you so He blessed you with it.

It is God's kingdom, and it is free and it's yours!

The Pilgrimage

We have a choice, to either be caught up in the things of the world, or caught up in the things of God. If we're caught up in and focused on the things of God, we should expect to live a great life, having an awesome journey with God here on earth and fulfilling His purpose for our life. However if we're caught up in and focused on the things of the world, then we should absolutely expect to have issues, concerns, anger, anxiety, depression, worries and fears. Most definitely.

I believe God is saying, "Look, your job is just to love me with all your heart and soul. That's your only job. Just take each breath as it comes. Suck it in. Be grateful for this life I have given you, this day, this moment. And stop worrying about everything that you can't control."

History is a very important thing. We can either learn from it or be doomed to repeat it. Here in Florida, we have learned, after experiencing a couple of hurricanes, that we better build our houses to a different level of wind resistance, and we need to take better precautions. With modern healthcare, we've learned how to exercise and eat better so we don't die too young. We've learned how to do these things by learning from history. You have probably learned personal lessons through your relationships or perhaps through stock market and real estate crashes. You don't want to repeat them, but want to learn from them instead. I'm going to give you a history lesson here, and I pray it is the best history lesson you will ever learn. How are we, as Christians, to look at our lives? How are we to consider our lives?

Well, in Genesis 47:7, Joseph brought his father Jacob to present him before Pharaoh, and Jacob blessed Pharaoh. Pharaoh then asked Jacob a question. It's a very interesting question—one we don't ask too much in this day. The question was a simple one. Maybe it was conversational. Maybe he really cared about the answer. Pharaoh, the king of Egypt, asked Jacob, "How old are you?" Jacob's answer to Pharaoh is found in Genesis 47:9, "And Jacob said to Pharaoh, 'The years of my pilgrimage are a hundred and thirty.'"

The years of my pilgrimage are a hundred and thirty? If you say to me, "Jack, how old are you?" Today I'd say fifty-five. I should be saying the years of my pilgrimage are fifty-five years. I think I'm looking at it wrong. Jacob had it right.

Life is a journey. The definition of a pilgrimage is a journey. Jacob was going somewhere, so are you and I. He was on a journey through earth. It's a pilgrimage. That's our life. We should be looking at our life as a pilgrimage. We know where we're winding up. We know where the journey leads. It leads to heaven. It leads to the throne of God for all eternity, forever and ever. Have an awesome journey!

Pizza, with Everything

The Bible says to test yourself so that you won't be judged. God's word says it's better you test yourself now and see if you're doing something wrong and fix it, than wait for judgment day to stand before God and hear Him say, "Hey, you did something wrong. I love you; you're in heaven, but here's your reward. It could've been awesome, but it's just okay." And remember, the reward you get when you arrive in heaven is the one you will have for all eternity.

Heaven is going to be awesome no matter what your reward is. It's going to be the most amazing place for us forever and ever and ever. Yet arriving there when you have not taken the journey that God asked you to take would be like—I guess the way I'd describe it to you is if I took you to the greatest pizza place in the world. Let's just assume you absolutely love pizza. So, I took you to the greatest pizza place and you got there and I said, "This is the greatest pizza ever."

And you go, "Oh, this is so great! I'm so happy you took me here! You're the greatest friend ever! You found this amazing pizza place! I can't believe it! This pizza is amazing!"

And I say, "Yes, but you can only have one slice. Oh, but Phil over here, he can have four slices."

(The Certainty Of Heaven For Believers)

That's what heaven is going to be like. You will one day stand before God, so the critical question is, which reward will you get? The Bible talks about a man escaping from fire by the seat of his pants. Obviously referencing one who didn't pay attention to the things of God during his lifetime and who didn't make God the focus of his life, but instead made his own fleshly, selfish desires his focus. That guy says, "Whew, I made it."

Yeah, but only one slice for you.

That's great. Enjoy it. It's cool. But do you want access to more pizza forever? Do you want the four slices? How about unlimited slices? How about the sausage, pepperoni, meatballs? The works? The Bible says to test ourselves, to ask ourselves these tough questions now so that we don't have to face Him later and realize that we're looking at a single slice of pizza for eternity. No, we can know for sure we can have all the pizza we want and of course all God's great and best blessings as our topping!

Seeing the Thorn

God said to the apostle Paul, "My grace is sufficient for thee," after Paul begged Him to take a thorn out of his side. Three times Paul asked God for relief from this. The Bible doesn't identify what that thorn was, or if it was a physical pain, but clearly Paul saw it as a torment of the devil (2 Corinthians 12: 7) Yet God responded, "My grace is sufficient for thee. You just glorify me whatever you're going through, and I will use you mightily."

You may not see it until you get to heaven. You may not see that neighbor who never said a word to you but saw your faith in Christ while your loved one was dying. You might not see that friend, that co-worker who never said a word to you but saw your faith in Christ when you lost your job, when you lost your money, when your real estate went underwater, when your son was battling a drug addiction and through it all you stayed faithful to Jesus. You might not realize how you inspired that person. And then that person moved away and later got saved, lived a godly life, had all these godly kids who had these grandkids who become these amazing missionaries, pastors or witnesses for God. And you're sitting there in

(The Certainty Of Heaven For Believers)

heaven and they go, "Because I saw you had faith in God, that changed my life." Did they you ever tell you while you were on earth? No, but they saw your faith, and you are the reason they made it heaven and lived a life that mattered for God.

Thank God. That's our job. Be faithful to God. He will do the rest.

Homeless

A buddy of mine is doing an outreach for the homeless in the name of Christ. He's a dentist in Fort Lauderdale. He and his brother have opened up their parking lot; they have music and free food and are sharing the gospel. He invited me to check it out, and I did. It was great. There had to be 150 people there and I talked to them. I could see the pain and the earthly suffering in their eyes. You know the story. All they own is one plastic bag or a backpack, downtrodden men and women, young and old. I contrasted it with myself. I mean, my complaint might be something like, "I can't go to Paris on vacation; I have to go to Disney instead." Seeing them like that just brought it home for me. I had a $100 bill in my pocket, and it felt so dirty. The money just felt worthless. I began thinking, what is important here? What is valuable, and what means something?

I was trying to tell these guys to have hope. But how do you tell a guy to hope when he's got nothing? The Lord gave me an analogy to use. I said to them, "Listen, what if Jesus Christ came to you, before putting you on earth and He said, 'Listen, here's the plan. I'm going to send you down to earth, and you're going to be a bum by the world's standards your whole life. You're going to have nothing. You're going to be walking around on the streets, you'll be happy that someone just gave you a hotdog.'

Imagine that Jesus said that would be your mission in life. But then He said, 'When you die, you're going to come with me up to heaven and you're going to reign with me for all eternity. Would that be okay? You're going to be homeless and have pretty much nothing here on earth, by the world's standards "a bum", but you're going to glorify me in everything you do. I'm going to use you mightily. So, what if you're not going to have anything on earth? When you're done, you're coming home with me and then you will have everything."

What about you? Would you have answered, "No, Lord, I'm not doing it. Don't use me for Your glory?"

I think if we knew the plan, we'd say, "Okay. Great." Why? Because we would understand how it's part of His perfect will. Of course, we might offer God a plan of our own such as: "Can't you just use me by letting me be a rich guy in Boca Raton, Lord?"

"Well, there are other guys I'm doing that with. I want to use you here."

"Okay. I'm your guy, Lord. I'm your disciple. I'm your son. Let's do it."

I told these men, "You should be joyful and happy because if you have God and are faithful to His word and listen to His spirit you'll have that certainty that you are doing God's work, that you are in His perfect will and accomplishing His plan."

Shouldn't you and I be the exact same way? No matter where we are or what the circumstances? Whether we have

7: Heaven

some things of this world or nothing at all. The Apostle Paul tells us, "Rejoice in the Lord always." (Philippians 4:4). Shouldn't we do that? Shouldn't we?

Revival

We should be bringing heaven down to earth. The Word of God says, "Your will be done on earth as it is in heaven." God's will. It should be done on earth. You and I with the love of Jesus Christ should be doing God's will here on earth. We should be spiritual beings having a human experience, not human beings having a spiritual experience.

Our citizenship is in heaven. We live with God. We're spiritual beings here on earth with a mission—a purpose from God—to glorify Him in all we do, to bear fruit and fruit that will last. Do that, follow the first commandment to love God with all your heart, and you'll have nothing to worry about. You will be doing "what you can."

I've been saved for over twenty years, and I believe that revival—individual, personal revival—starts very simply. It doesn't start in a tent, or in a camp or crusade. It starts in our heart, with us on our knees and face repenting to God for the sins that we've committed, crying and telling God how when we look up and see His righteousness on the cross—when we look up and see Him blameless, the Son of God, a sacrifi-

7: Heaven

cial Lamb, sacrificed for our lives so we can live—we see how short our glory falls compared to the glory of Christ.

And it breaks our hearts.

It makes us say, "Lord, thank you for saving me. Lord, I want to change. Lord, I don't want to live this way anymore. I don't want to be like this." That's true revival. You look at your life through God's filter and through the filter of Jesus Christ and you say, "God, I don't want to be like me anymore. I want to be like you." Then God's power transforms you to be more like Him and then you are living a life that matters for God.

Your Name in a Book

In the first few verses of Luke 10, we read:

> *The Lord appointed seventy-two others and sent them two by two ahead of Him to every town and place where He was about to go. He told them, "The harvest is plentiful, but the workers are few. Ask the Lord of the harvest, therefore, to send out workers into His harvest field. Go! I am sending you out like lambs among wolves."*

Later in the chapter, verses 17-20, we read:

> *The seventy-two returned with joy and said, "Lord, even the demons submit to us in Your name." He replied, "I saw Satan fall like lightning from heaven. I have given you authority to trample on snakes and scorpions and to overcome all the power of the enemy; nothing will harm you. However, do not rejoice that the spirits submit to you, but rejoice that your names are written in heaven."*

That's what God is saying to us right now. Rejoice in the fact that your names are written in heaven. Those disciples must've been so psyched when they saw those scorpions and snakes and everything submitting under their power. But God said don't be excited about that, be excited that your names are written in the Lamb's Book of Life. That is the ultimate thing to get excited about. That is the true treasure…you have it! Therefore you should be very happy and excited…all the time!

8

HAVING A PIECE OF THE PEACE
(How To Have The Peace Of God In Your Life)

Air Conditioning

The peace of God is like air conditioning. Where I live in south Florida, the minute the temperature rises one degree above our comfort level, we start to sweat. We get uncomfortable. "Oh, I've got to go turn the A/C down. I've got to fix it." If the air conditioning breaks, we immediately call the repair man. As soon as the air conditioning isn't at the perfect level, we know it immediately, and we run out and fix it. We change it.

That's exactly what the peace of God should be like in your life. The minute you get off track a little bit and you don't feel that peace of God, you should be running to the Holy Spirit—like you would your air conditioner repair man—saying, "Fix it! Fix it! Adjust this temperature back because I want to feel the cool breeze of the peace of God in my life. I don't want to be sweating and sticky and uncomfortable."

The peace of God is the most important gift I believe you can get from Jesus, after salvation. So, how do you get it? How do you get God's peace? The first thing about peace is that you need to be able to recognize it. You need to know what it looks like.

8: Having A Piece Of The Peace

Let's say Bill Gates was walking down the same shopping aisle as you and you didn't recognize him. Well, even if you had a great business plan to give him, since you didn't recognize him, and you didn't know him when you saw him, there would be no benefit to you.

If Tony Bennett or Lady Gaga—two musicians, songwriters, singers—were sitting on a park bench a few feet away from you and you had a great song you wanted to give them, but you didn't recognize them, there'd be no benefit to you. And, of course, if Lebron James or Dwyane Wade were shooting hoops in the park while you were walking your dog, and you wanted to be a basketball player but you didn't recognize them, again, there would be no benefit to you.

You need to recognize the peace of God in your life because it's there for you to enjoy. But in order to recognize it you have to access it. It's like Pizza…once you go the pizza place and taste the pizza you know what it tastes like. You don't have to wonder anymore. It's the same with peace of God…so what are you waiting for…go get some!

Tsunamis, Earthquakes, and Market Crashes

I remember a time in 1990, when I literally would've been homeless if my parents didn't send me money from New York to pay the apartment rent. I lost my job, I was out of work for a year, and I would have been homeless. I'll never forget the phone call I got from my father when he told me he was sending down the money. He said, "Listen, you can't fall. I won't let you." I thought, Man, I've got to be the luckiest guy in the world. I have a father who loves me so much.

But I understand that not everybody got the ace of spades with their earthly father. And some of you, by my definition, got ripped off greatly because you didn't have that wonderful love from your parents. But we all have the wonderful love of our Father in heaven. We all have Jesus' wonderful love available to us now and for all eternity, and we all have that great promise from God. Isaiah 26:3 says, "You will keep in perfect peace him whose mind is steadfast, because he trusts in you."

Steadfast means fixed or unchanging, firmly loyal, constant or unswerving. God is serious when He says make sure your faith doesn't swerve. Keep your mind steadfast on Jesus

8: Having A Piece Of The Peace

(focused completely on Jesus) and you'll have His perfect peace. Make sure your eyes stay focused on Jesus and you follow Him only. That's how you get it. If I told you, "I have an endless supply of hundred dollar bills. Just send me an email and I'll send however many you want your way," you'd put this book down (hopefully bookmark your place) and email me before you went any further. Oh, hundred dollar bills, great! But when we're talking about the perfect peace of God in your life, you don't have time? You have other things to think about or other things to do? You should be following God and walking with God constantly to ensure you have God's perfect peace in your life, and it should have much more value to you than any hundred dollar bill.

In John 14:27, Jesus says, "Peace I leave with you; my peace I give you. I do not give to you as the world gives. Do not let your hearts be troubled and do not be afraid."

God's peace is the best peace we can get! His is the best brand there is. That verse has saved my life. My heart isn't troubled. I may not like the situations I'm in, but I have God's peace in all situations. God says, "The peace I leave you, my peace, you can't get from the world."

Jesus said, "I am the way, the truth, the life." (John 14:6) There is no other way. There is no other way to heaven. There is no other way to salvation. And there is no other way to have the peace of God. John 16:33 says, "I have told you these things, so that in me you may have peace that comes from nowhere else."

What has God spoken to your heart about having His peace in your life?

(How To Have The Peace of God In Your Life)

I hope and pray that you hear God clearly speaking to your heart, and this will be the day that you will say, "Yes, Lord, I'm doing it your way. I want that life of peace. I'm not changing your recipe in any way, shape, or form. I'm doing it your way. I want to fulfill my life's call, Lord, and I want to do it with joy and happiness and peace."

That, my friend, is what it is all about. God offers you the best He has...a peace that surpasses understanding. It's the peace that enabled Jesus to sleep in the boat with a storm raging all around, and then to rise and say three simple words, "Peace, be still." He will calm any storm raging within your heart or around your life, and He will bring still waters to your soul. Even if the rain and storm continues, your heart will be at peace.

Don't settle for less than the best God has to offer. You are His child and you can claim it as yours. How about a piece of peace?

An Open Wallet

Do you want to know how God speaks about Himself? See for yourself. This is God describing Himself in Exodus 34:6-7 (as God passed in front of Moses), "The Lord, the Lord, the compassionate and gracious God, slow to anger, abounding in love and faithfulness, maintaining love to thousands, and forgiving wickedness, rebellion and sin."

We should be saying, "Thank you, Lord. Thank you so much." You don't have anger towards us. You abound in love and forgive our wickedness and sin. First Peter 1:3-4 tells us, "Praise be to the God and Father of our Lord Jesus Christ! In His great mercy He has given us new birth into a living hope through the resurrection of Jesus Christ from the dead, and into an inheritance that can never perish, spoil or fade—kept in heaven for you."

God has an abundance of mercy. "You are forgiving and good, O Lord, abounding in love to all who call to you." (Psalm 86:5) All you need to do is call upon God. Psalm 119:64 says, "The earth is filled with your love, O Lord; teach me thy statutes."

(How To Have The Peace of God In Your Life)

Is that the prayer of your heart today? "Oh, Lord, the earth is full of your mercy. Teach me your statutes."

Or, is the prayer of your heart, "Lord, I know I have your mercy. I know I'm saved. Thanks a lot. I have no time for you. I have a lot of other stuff I have to deal with. I have stuff to take care of, Lord. You understand."

God says, "No, I don't understand. Why aren't you coming to me so that I can teach you my statutes?"

Listen to this promise from God. "Let the wicked forsake his way and the evil man his thoughts. Let him turn to the Lord, and He will have mercy on him, and to our God, for He will freely pardon." (Isaiah 55:7)

Your eternal pardon costs you nothing. God gives you His pardon for free. It cost Him everything—the son He loved the most, Jesus Christ. He sacrificed for you and me so we would have life eternal and life abundant. He loves us so much. So the question really is do you want more of God or less of God. It's your choice and your life.

Pressing Forward

Hosea 10:12 says, "Sow for yourselves righteousness and break up your unplowed ground; for it is time to seek the Lord, until He comes and showers righteousness on you."

If you sow righteousness, you will reap the fruit of unfailing love. But there is work to be done.

There's unplowed ground. "Break it up," says the Lord. You have to break up the unplowed ground. There is something to be done on your end.

My wife and I go to Carvel—an ice cream store—with the kids. When my daughter was five or six years old she always had chocolate ice cream in a waffle cone, and she would invariably say to me after she had eaten some of it, "Daddy, make me monster soup."

She'd hand me her hard ice cream and I mix until it becomes soupy and she could drink it. I had to do it and I wanted to do it because it was the cutest thing ever and she liked it so much. But there was work required on my end to do it. I had to take the ice cream and I had to mix it multiple times with a spoon. Then I would hand it back to her, and a big smile came across her face.

(How To Have The Peace of God In Your Life)

But I had to do something, and God says to us that we've got to do something. Break up your unplowed ground for it is time to seek the Lord.

That's what you have to do. You have to seek the Lord with all your heart and all your soul and all your mind. You have to make it a priority. You should start by having a deadline to do that. Make it your goal that by a certain date not too far in the future, you will have sought Him with all your heart. Apply yourself and do it!

If you were looking for a job, you'd be seeking a job. You would be applying yourself to it, studying the classified ads, looking online, making phone calls, setting up appointments for interviews and keeping those appointments. You would be taking time to do it and making it a priority because it's something important. How much more vital is it to seek the face of God—the maker of heaven and earth?

I know people who seek a wife or a husband, money, or health. When we want something badly enough, we're really good at seeking it.

God says, "How come you don't want me? I want you. I love you. I want you to want me. It's time to break up your unplowed ground."

Great Comebacks

Two friends of mine—guys I know from when they were in the real estate business years ago—were doing really well for themselves. I met them through another buddy of mine and saw the deals they were doing, and they were making a fortune. They were young guys—thirty or thirty-five—and they were really flying high.

I've seen them both again recently, separately. Most of the people from their time and era have fallen down and died. And I don't mean physically. I mean mentally and spiritually. You see back in 2008 the mortgage business crashed, the stock market crashed, the real estate market crashed. It was too much. It just buried most of them. They're done and finished.

One of these guys is back in there and he's busting his butt rehabbing houses again. Back where he started at the beginning when he began to build his financial empire. He's working by himself buying houses and fixing them up. He said to me, "I'll never go for the big overhead again. I learned my lesson. But I'm back at work doing what I know how to do, what made me money in the first place." The other guy is in the same situation also, back busting his butt. He started

(How To Have The Peace of God In Your Life)

from scratch again and did what he had to do to claw his way get back. He's not quitting; he's not giving up.

I have a lot of respect for these guys because they're plowing the unplowed ground. They're breaking up the ground. They may not like it, but they're doing what needs to be done.

George Washington Carver was a black scientist, inventor, engineer, and professor in the old days. A student came into one of the classes that he was teaching and said, "Professor, professor, have you heard? The stock market has crashed. You've lost everything."

Without looking up from his notes, Carver said, "Yes, I heard." He continued on teaching because he knew that no matter what he thought or did, he couldn't change what happened. So, all that really mattered was how was he going to look at it. He chose—like my friends in real estate—to go back and put his nose to the grindstone and focus on the things he could focus on. Carver chose not to lament and despair. He chose not to get disgusted and depressed and ruined by an event that he couldn't control anyway. He chose to live instead of die. He chose to be valued not by his bank account, but by his life. Even though he didn't have that bank account anymore, he had his life, and that was the currency and the value.

You and I have that as well. We have a life God has given to us. That's the hallelujah moment.

That's why we should be rejoicing and we should be "amen-ing." That excitement, that joy, that love for God, is admirable and it shouldn't be restricted to just a church service.

It should be evident in all of our lives.

Faith in What

Everybody has faith in something. People talk about religion. A lot of people refer to religion as their faith. They call it faith because that's what they believe to get them something. Most religious people have faith that their religion will earn them favor with God and get them into heaven when they die. But you know what? Religion doesn't have the ability to do that. And what a disappointment it will be for them when they find out they were wrong. God wants a relationship with you, not simply religion.

God is asking you, "Who is it that you believe?" The Word of God (the Bible) never teaches us to have faith in religion. It teaches us to have faith in the Lord Jesus Christ. The question isn't whether religion is agreeable or palatable. The question is whether or not it is truth.

Faith not founded upon truth will result in disaster, for it's not simply faith that saves the sinner's soul but rather faith in Jesus Christ the Lord alone that saves the sinner's soul. We must come to realize that there is only one solution to our problem of sin in this life. That solution is faith in Jesus Christ—not simply belief that He existed but the trust that

(How To Have The Peace of God In Your Life)

He will do what He promised. That's faith based on truth. And if we believe that, we have no problem.

What are you facing right now? Personal problems? Health challenges? Broken relationships? Addiction of some sort? Nothing is greater than God's power to heal and make new. Don't get so caught up in the things that surround you that you lose sight of the greatest gift of all. It is there for you today—the grace of God, the love of Jesus Christ, salvation and eternal life through faith. You have every reason to rejoice.

God wants you to be happy, to live each day filled with His joy. There will be shortcomings and rough patches. But you can leap and rejoice in spite of that, out of pure joy because of your eternal assurance. So be happy! Do it, "for Christ's sake." You will be eternally grateful you did.

A Win-Win

I've already told you about my wonderful Christian friends Theresa and Bill. They are wonderful Christian people, and they have a daughter who has a major drug problem. She eventually dropped out of sight and left behind four kids who were all under ten years old. So, Bill and Theresa have adopted these four grandchildren as their own kids.

When Theresa was dying of cancer—aggressive thyroid cancer. The doctors had basically given her the death sentence. But Theresa, in her Christian faith sent out another great email to all of us. This message said, "First of all, we have hope that God will do a miracle. Second, like Shadrach, Meshach, and Abednego, we are ready for whatever God does. If God is taking me home, then isn't that wonderful? I'll be going home with God."

Of course, she didn't want to leave her husband or her family, and they didn't want to lose her. It's sad and tragic in that regard. But she showed such faith, not just talking about it when times are easy, but she truly walked the walk of Christian faith—like Shadrach, Meshach, and Abednego.

Here's a quick recap of that story. It's in the book of Daniel, chapter three. King Nebuchadnezzar tells them they have to bow down to his god, who is not their God, and Shadrach, Meshach, and Abednego say, "No way!"

Nebuchadnezzar says, "Then I'm throwing you in the fiery furnace."

And they say, "Go ahead, man."

Here's the exact quote. It's Daniel 3:16-17:

> *O Nebuchadnezzar, we do not need to defend ourselves before you in this matter. If we are thrown into the blazing furnace, the God we serve is able to save us from it, and he will rescue us from your hand, O king.*

They didn't mean that God was going to necessarily save them from the fire, but He did. He actually physically brought them out of it unharmed without even so much as a burn mark. They had been prepared to die. Their definition of rescue was, "Hey, Jesus, I'm going to be with you no matter what."

Philippians 1:21 says, "To live is Christ. To die is gain." They're ahead either way, like the apostle Paul said.

That was Theresa's attitude and Bill's attitude, as they walked through the very valley of the shadow of death. That needs to be your attitude and mine as well as we go through this life. You know, whether or not Theresa died from the cancer or lived fifty more years if God had chosen to heal her—either way she was absolutely going to hear, "Well done, good and faithful servant," because she was faithful to the end. And that is what God is asking of you and me. Theresa did die from her cancer and we know and can see for sure that she lived a life that mattered for God. We have to trust

8: Having A Piece Of The Peace

God with everything. Don't let your enemy, who is out there prowling around like a roaring lion looking to devour you, have victory over you. God says resist the devil and he'll flee from you. There's a requirement placed on us. Resist. That is what we have to do.

God will be faithful to do His part and more. As Ephesians 3:20 promises, God will do "exceedingly and abundantly more then we can ask or imagine."

Being the Clay

The following story from the Bible has the potential to serve as a part of the molding process for you. Are you willing to be the clay? This is the story of Cain and Abel, found in the first two verses of Genesis 4. "Adam lay with his wife Eve, and she became pregnant and gave birth to Cain. She said, 'With the help of the Lord I have brought forth a man.' Later she gave birth to his brother Abel."

Notice that Eve said, "With the help of the Lord I have brought forth a man."

Right away, Adam and Eve acknowledged that it was God who helped them. They couldn't have done it on their own. They understood and knew that everything happened according to the will of God, through the hand of God.

Do we do that? Do we live our lives acknowledging that, "Lord, it's because of you that I'm alive. It's because of you that I'm here. I have this breath, this family, this life, this opportunity to live. Lord, only because of you."

God says we can do all things through Him who strengthens us. (Philippians 4:13) All things. Not some. All. And He says, "I am the vine. You are the branch. Apart from me, you can do

8: Having A Piece Of The Peace

nothing." That's the Word of God. "Apart from me, you can do nothing." (John 15:5)

If you've been living your life apart from God, I'd be very anxious to see what you think you've accomplished. I don't mean by the world's standards. You may have a great job. You may have money, a beautiful girlfriend, a handsome boyfriend, you may be healthy. But tell me, in your heart, are you joyful, are you happy, are you at peace, do you love your life? Or, are you anxious, depressed, miserable, upset, sorrowful, regretful, or guilty? God gives peace and joy that transcends all understanding. Just be like clay and let God mold you into His image. Then you can be sure you will live a life that matters for God.

Some Thorns in My Side

I had been seeking God's face for my future and that of my family. As is the case with many people these days, we were facing economic uncertainty and other uncertainties, as well.

I treated this issue as I did pretty much everything else in my life—if there's a problem, I keep going until I solve it. Whether it takes me a day or a year, I've learned in my fifty plus years of life that the way to solve problems is to keep attacking them. You don't quit.

That has generally served me very well in my life because, by God's grace, I've been able to solve a lot of problems and answer a lot of issues and go forward. I have had some degree of success, I think—by my own standards and certainly by the world's standards and I sure hope by God's standards.

As I pondered the future, I knew I just needed to come up with a plan like I'd always done in the past.

Right after that, funny things started to happen. Physical things started to affect me. I was in a lot of physical pain for three months, and it would move from place to place—knees to hips to shoulders. Then for good measure I got a case of

8: Having A Piece Of The Peace

vertigo. I said to my wife one day, about a month and a half into this, "Honey, I think God must have some big plans for me because Satan is definitely trying to kill me."

I finally began to realize that it wasn't necessarily Satan doing this. God said to my spirit, "Jack, you're trying to plan the future. Since when are you in charge of the future? Since when is that your job? You told me at thirty-six years old that you would seek first my kingdom and my righteousness and trust that all these other things will come. You laid down your life for me and you've been fine since then. Why are you worried now?"

Then God made His main point. He asked me, "By the way, these three months that you spent worrying and figuring and planning, do you have the answer?"

I said, "No, Lord."

And He said, "How is your way working for you? How is all that pain and physical stuff feeling? Are you liking that?"

I said, "No, Lord. I'm not liking this at all."

He said, "Well, here's the news. If you continue to try and take control of your life, that's exactly how you're going to feel. You're going to have physical pain, mental pain, emotional pain, and spiritual pain. But you will not have the peace and joy of the Lord."

I realized that God really was speaking to me. And He was telling me that He didn't want me in control. He gave me a scripture, but He added a word. (I understand that nothing can be added to or taken away from the Bible.) But very personally, for me, God said in the Spirit, "My grace ALONE is sufficient for you, Jack. That's all you need. And if you think that anything else besides my grace is going to be sufficient, you're going to have a big problem."

God reminded me that over the last couple of months, my prayers had been all about myself. God was looking at the spiritual condition of my heart, and it had been saying, "What about me? What about my family? How am I going to make sure and this and that? And, Lord, you've got to do this and do that."

God's like, "No, I want your heart focused on other people, not on you, not on your problems, but on others." I should have just listened to God in the first place. I could have avoided a lot of pain.

Silver and Gold

What do people truly want in this journey of life? We want peace and joy, satisfaction and the feeling that our life matters. We want to know that we count for something, and that there's a purpose and a passion for this life we are living. We want to know that it's not just a grind and a problem and a chore. No, it's a joy and a wonder and a unique journey.

I believe God wants everybody to have that feeling. In the world today, there are so many people living without meaning and purpose. They have no faith, no belief in God, no understanding of the concept of God's promise that He has a wonderful plan for our lives.

This is a major reason why the world is in the state it is in right now. Rather than people living and working towards a greater and deeper purpose—that of obeying God and following Him—they are working for themselves, for material gain and things that they can hold in their hands. I can't think of anything more futile. The Bible says those things are the wood, hay, and stubble that will burn away. But when we live for Jesus, our lives are as silver and gold that will not be burned away.

(How To Have The Peace of God In Your Life)

I believe that's what the abundant Christian life in the Lord is all about. Having faith, even beyond understanding at times, that it's all for a reason and a purpose, and God has a perfect plan. And we are part of that plan! Our faith will lead us to that abundant life—our faith in God—because He's the one who gives it to us.

There is nothing you can do, nothing of the world that can give you that sense of joy and peace and purpose. Lord knows I've tried. Before I was saved, I tried everything that the world had to offer—gambling, drugs, power, money, sex. Anything you can think of, I tried, and I can tell you firsthand that none of it satisfied me. Nothing ever left me with a lasting sense of satisfaction. But these last twenty-two years of knowing the Lord have been the best years of my life, and it just gets better and better and better.

Inflated Basketball

Picture, for a moment, a basketball...without air inside it. It wouldn't be too effective, would it? Here's why. It has no air. If you were to bounce a basketball like that, it wouldn't go anywhere. It wouldn't do what it was created to do. As a matter of fact, a basketball like that would never be the one that was shot through the hoop and won the game at the buzzer. No one will ever talk about that basketball. It will never sit up on the trophy case. A basketball like that would be completely useless. It wouldn't fulfill the purpose it was created for.

When we're not filled with the Holy Spirit of God, we can very easily miss our purpose, our unique calling from Jesus Christ. God wants to fill us with His Holy Spirit.

I'm so grateful for what God has done in me and to me. I had been having some chest pain—just a little bit. I didn't think it was a heart attack, but I was getting a little nervous. So I told my wife, "Listen, honey, if I die I just want to let you know that I was having some chest pain." Of course, with my medical degree (just kidding—don't have one) I knew I didn't have to go to the doctor. But finally just to be safe, a few days later and went to the doctor. The good news, it was nothing. Completely fine. But I thought, You know what, let's say I had died, that day. What if I did? Then miraculously I'm alive the next day? Dead one day, then alive the next! Man, I would be so happy. I would be so grateful.

So let me ask you would I be bitter or happy after that? Sad or joyful?

I hope today is the day that you say, "God, you changed my life. I was dead in my sin (destined to die in my flesh) but now I am alive in your spirit (destined to live with Christ in heaven for all eternity). I'm going to look at this world with gratitude, with gratefulness, and I'm going to live that way because I realize it's a gift."

No Pain

God has been breaking my heart with this verse, and I hope He does the same for you. It's from Psalm 32:1-2, and in Romans 4:7-8. Paul repeats it, reminding us of the blessedness of the man to whom God imputes righteousness. "Blessed are those whose transgressions are forgiven whose sins are covered. Blessed is the one whose sin the Lord will never count against them."

That's us. We're that blessed one whose sin will always be forgiven, whose transgressions are forgiven. That's the whole gospel right there. Man, what more could God say to you?

God says, "Can you hear me now? I'm going to forgive your sins. I'm not counting anything against you. You've just have to be adopted into the family of God." That's the requirement—get adopted. God gives His kids the Spirit without limit. You can have as much of God as you want.

I thought of Judas the day he made that deal to betray Jesus. He sold Jesus out for thirty pieces of silver. That day, it must've seemed like a great deal to him. He must've said, "Oh, this is amazing! I'm going to get thirty pieces of silver. Yeah, I'm selling out my boy, but that's okay. Look at the

(How To Have The Peace of God In Your Life)

benefit I'm getting. This is so much better. I'm going to get these thirty pieces of silver. I can buy anything I want. I can have anything I want. This is great." A day later he was dead, he killed himself. He couldn't live with what he'd done. He couldn't live with the fact that he betrayed the one who loved him most, even though it seemed like a great idea at the time.

When Peter denied Jesus, it was just as Jesus had predicted. Peter denied Him three times and the rooster crowed. Jesus was being led from the house of the high priest, and He looked Peter right in the eye. Peter looked back at Him and made eye contact. All of a sudden the guilt, the pain, and the sorrow come flowing through Peter. He couldn't take it, the fact that he had denied Jesus. The Bible tells us that Peter "wept bitterly" because he couldn't handle that he had let down Jesus.

Man, I just can't be at that point anymore in my life. I don't want pain anymore, the pain that comes from not loving God with all my heart and soul, from not doing the simple things that God has asks of me. I'm not doing that anymore. I have to be able to stand before God and say, "Lord, I did what I could."

My prayer is that you will have the faith of a little child, to just fold your hands together, to squeeze your eyes shut, if needed, to get on your knees and say, "Lord, take away the pain—the pain that comes from denial—and continue to fill me up with your Holy Spirit. No matter what is around me, don't let me see anything beyond your love, because there is truly nothing outside the boundless territory of your love." Why should we feel this way? As Psalm 63:3 says so perfectly of God's love, "Because your loving kindness is better than life."

Consider the Lilies

It has been said that gardening is a healthy hobby. You're outdoors, surrounded by oxygen-emitting plants and trees. Your eyes take in the pacifying green below, the heavenly blue above, and the rainbow colors of the flowers and blossoms. You feel alive just getting your hands dirty with the rich soil, knowing that you're planting and watering and bringing things to life.

Well, actually, it's God who breathes life into those things. He is, after all, the original gardener (read Genesis chapter one and see for yourself).

I went out for breakfast with a great friend, a preacher. He's forty-five years old, and he's been an inspiration to me since I met him twenty years ago. He said to me, "Jack, I've had the greatest revelation from God. I've been spending quiet time with God, and God has shown me this one verse that He's had me meditate on. I've seen the verse before, but through it, He's spoken to me like never before. God was just telling me, 'Consider the lilies.'"

There are many things that plants, flowers, trees and gardens can teach us—faithfulness in the little things like watering and weeding, joy in seeing the fruits (and flowers) of our labors, but most of all, we can learn trust.

Apparently, God isn't the only one of His immediate family who was into gardening. Jesus also enjoyed taking His Father's creation and making subject lessons out of them. Here's the passage where Jesus talks about trust and not worrying. He says to his disciples, in Luke (12:22-28):

> *Therefore I tell you, do not worry about your life. Life is more than food. Consider the ravens: They do not sow or reap, they have no storeroom or barn; yet God feeds them. And how much more valuable you are than birds! Who of you by worrying can add a single hour to his life? Since you cannot do this very little thing, why do you worry about the rest? Consider how the lilies grow. They do not labor or spin. Yet I tell you, not even Solomon in all his splendor was dressed like one of these. If that is how God clothes the grass of the field, which is here today, and tomorrow is thrown into the fire, how much more will he clothe you, O you of little faith!*

"Consider how the lilies grow." They don't labor or spin. They don't have to do anything. They just are. When it gets sunny and there is no water, they might dry up a little. But when it rains, they sprout up again and continue to bestow beauty all around. They don't have to do anything but enjoy their existence. The phrase "We are human beings, not human doings" comes to mind.

We're human beings. God did not call us to worry and be anxious and fearful about all these things that we have to do and accomplish. God did not call us to set time tables that would destroy our spirit and fill our lives with pressure and stress. He didn't even say we had to live this life as if we needed to accomplish something by the world's standards. No, God just called us to be obedient sons and daughters, to be children He could bless and, most of all, He could love.

How much clearer could He be? He says consider how the lilies grow. They don't labor or spin. They don't do anything. Now let me clarify, that doesn't mean you shouldn't go to work. It doesn't mean you shouldn't prepare for your kids' future. It just means that you do the best you can. The play is called by the coach and then you execute your part as best you can without any concern or worry about the outcome. The outcome is God's concern. And that's what He is saying.

Here's the amazing part. My friend said to me, "After forty-five years, I'm finally free. I finally get it. There is nothing I have to do. I have freedom in the Lord that I never had before."

A Snake in the Grass

About twelve years ago, in the dead of summer, my air conditioner broke. It was late on a Friday night, and I called a buddy—an air conditioning guy—and he said, "Listen, I'll come down to fix it after the weekend, but you can fix it now yourself. I'll tell you what to do. Take your flashlight, go outside to the back of the house, and I'll walk you through it."

I said, "Man, I'm not going outside. Are you nuts? There could be a snake out there or something. I'm not going out there by myself."

Then I realized that I had a choice to make. I could continue to live in my fear that there could possibly be a snake—even though the odds were against it the mere thought of it disturbed me greatly—in which case the air conditioning wouldn't be back on. I decided that, no, I needed to take this risk. I needed to go out, face my fears even though I didn't want to, because I needed that air conditioner back on. I went out with my flashlight at 10:00 at night and for twenty minutes he walked me through the repair process. The air conditioner went back on. I thought, Man, isn't this interesting? I got so

8: Having A Piece Of The Peace

desperate to have something that I was willing to overcome my fear. That air conditioner being on became so important to me that I was willing to overcome my fear.

I believe, God has asked you, "Am I important enough for you to overcome your fears?"

There is one Bible translation (The Message Bible) of Matthew 6:26, which has a unique phrase that stood out in my mind when I read it: "Look at the birds, free and unfettered, not tied down to a job description, careless in the care of God."

"Careless in the care of God." It's not that we don't fulfill our responsibilities. It's not that we shirk our duties and refuse to keep our promises. It's not that kind of careless. It's opening our arms wide and falling, falling into the hands of God and letting Him hold us and care for us. It's trusting. We are only careless because we are in His care, therefore we have nothing to fear!

The God who created the vast expanse of the whole universe and yet ensures that every bud holds the tiny seed of new life within it is the God who cares for you. He is the God who has counted every hair on your head. He knows every thought of your mind, every feeling of your heart, and He loves you anyway. He has a plan that He created before the foundations of the earth were laid, and you are part of that plan. All He asks is for you to trust...and follow where He leads.

9

STORIES FROM THE STORY
(Digging Into Biblical Stories)

Fake Power

First Kings Chapter 13 tells us what happens when people disregard the commandments of God. Jeroboam had just been given most of the kingdom of Israel and rather than having faith in God's promises, he has two altars made for worship in a place that God had not commanded—bad idea.

So what happened?

> "By the word of the Lord a man of God came from Judah to Bethel, as Jeroboam was standing by the altar to make an offering."

So, a guy comes up and he cries out against the altar by the word of the Lord. Can you imagine this? You're Jeroboam. You're the king. You're at this altar that you created—this fake altar that you created that God is upset at you for creating—and somebody walks up and he says:

> "O altar, altar! This is what the Lord says: 'A son named Josiah will be born to the house of David. On you he will sacrifice the priests of the high places who now make offerings here, and human bones

9: Stories From The Story

> *will be burned on you.'" That same day the man of God gave a sign: 'This is the sign the Lord has declared: The altar will be split apart and the ashes on it will be poured out.' When King Jeroboam heard what the man of God cried out against the altar at Bethel, he stretched out his hand from the altar and said, "Seize him!" (1 Kings 13:2-4)*

Jeroboam said, "No way. You can't talk like this about my altar turning to ashes. I created this. Seize him! Take him away! Throw him in jail!"

The next two verses say,

> *But the hand he stretched out toward the man shriveled up, so that he could not pull it back. Also, the altar was split apart and its ashes poured out according to the sign given by the man of God by the word of the Lord. Then the king said to the man of God, "Intercede with the Lord your God and pray for me that my hand may be restored."*

Jeroboam knew he didn't have the power of God. He knew it was all a crock. He was like the Wizard of Oz behind the curtain and he knew it in his heart.

What about us? What do you know deep down in your heart? Can you look yourself in the mirror, do a spiritual check up on yourself and know how you really stand? It's not too late to change things and make them right.

The story continues, 1 Kings 13:6, "So the man of God interceded with the Lord, and the king's hand was restored and became as it was before."

Now, you would think, at this point, that Jeroboam would get it, right? "Hey, okay, I get it. My hand was shriveled. It took your power to fix that. I'm not going to do this anymore. Lord, I'm going to repent and sin no more."

Well, he didn't get it.

Look what happens in verses 7-9:

> The king said to the man of God, "Come home with me and have something to eat, and I will give you a gift." But the man of God answered the king, "Even if you were to give me half your possessions, I would not go with you, nor would I eat bread or drink water here. For I was commanded by the word of the Lord: 'You must not eat bread or drink water or return by the way you came.'"

He did the right thing. He knew very specifically the commands of God.

Do you?

Do you know very specifically the commands of God in our life? One of my personal favorites is, "Resist the devil, and he'll flee from you." I know I have to apply it to my own life. There's action required on my part. I need to resist. It doesn't say, "Go to the devil, invite him in to hang out and you can tell him when you want him to leave. Or, It's okay to go see what he's up to."

No, it doesn't say that. It says resist the devil and he'll flee from you.

The Old Guy and the Young Guy

So the man of God followed God's commandment (1 Kings 13:1-2) to give a warning to Jeroboam, the king who disobeyed God. This man of God, a young prophet, knew what he was supposed to do. He was told by God to give the warning and then turn back the way he came without stopping and eating anywhere. And he did it. When the king asked him to come in and eat, he walked away. And the Bible goes on to say, in 1 Kings 13:11, "Now there was a certain old prophet living in Bethel, whose sons came and told him all that the man of God had done there that day."

The old prophet saddles his donkey, and he goes to find this young prophet. He says, "Hey man of God, I heard what you did at the altar. That's pretty cool. Listen, why don't you come back to my house, come eat with me. I've got some food. We'll hang out. Two prophet guys talking together. Wouldn't that be great?"

The man of God says to him, "Listen, I can't turn back and go with you nor can I eat bread or drink water with you in this

(Digging Into Biblical Stories)

place. I've been told by the word of the Lord that I must not eat bread or drink water here or return by the way I came."

Now get this: "The old prophet answered, 'I too am a prophet, as you are. And an angel said to me by the word of the Lord: "Bring him back with you to your house so that he may eat bread and drink water."'"

The Bible tells us this old prophet was lying to the young one.

Verse 19 tells us, "The man of God returned with him and ate and drank in his house."

Hey, Satan always, always lies to the children of God. Always. It's what he does. He lied to Adam and Eve in the garden. He's lying to you and me today. God tells us that the thief comes to steal, kill, and destroy. That's his motive. If you're a child of God, Satan wants to steal, kill, and destroy you in your life.

Satan will tell you, "It's okay. God loves you no matter what." God does love you, but there are consequences to our sin, and we're responsible for keeping God's word and God's truths. In order to responsibly keep God's word and truths, we have to know what they are. It's our responsibility to know what God says.

Shouldn't we know the word of God? Shouldn't you be able to know not only in your mind, but in your heart and spirit, what is and isn't the word of God? Then Satan shouldn't be able to lie to you so easily.

So they're sitting at the table and the word of the Lord came to the old prophet and he cries out to the young man of God: "This is what the Lord says: 'You have defied the word of the Lord and have not kept the command the Lord your God gave you. You came back and ate bread and drank water in the place where he told you not to eat or drink. Therefore your body will not be buried in the tomb of your fathers.'"

The translation is: "Tough luck, sucker. You lose." This guy knew what God told him to do. He resisted the first time the king offered him to come back for a snack. He resisted the second time the Prophet invited him, but when the old man prophet lied to him, he said okay.

Why didn't he just stick to what God told him to do? What difference does it make whether the guy was a prophet or not? God told him not to do it. He heard directly from God. "Don't do it."

I admit, the consequence is severe—Old Testament severe. The punishment is, you're out. You're dead. God says you're not going to make it.

Sure enough, as soon as the guy gets back on the road, a lion comes and mauls him, and the young prophet dies. That's his punishment for not obeying what God specifically told him. He dies on the side of the road, and the old prophet who lied to him—much like Judas Iscariot when he betrayed Jesus—says, "Oh man, I blew it. This guy was my brother, a fellow prophet, a child of God and I sold him down the river. I burned him. Now I feel guilty about it."

The Bible says:

> *After burying him, he said to his sons, 'When I die, bury me in the grave where the man of God is buried; lay my bones beside his bones. For the message he declared by the word of the Lord against the al-*

(Digging Into Biblical Stories)

tar in Bethel and against all the shrines on the high places in the towns of Samaria will certainly come true.' Even after this, Jeroboam did not change his evil ways.

What an idiot. Here's King Jeroboam, receiving a warning from the Lord, and still he didn't change his ways.

I scratch my head at that one.

The question is, what about you and me? Man, is God in heaven scratching his head at us? I wonder if He's saying, "Man, I don't get you guys. After all you've seen and all you know, how could you not change your ways? How could you think I'm not worth changing your ways for? How could you choose the world over me? How could you choose the flesh over the spirit? How could you choose death over life?"

And we say, "Hey, I'm not dying. I'm going to heaven. I accepted Jesus."

And Jesus says, "Yeah, but you're missing out on the abundant life that I have for you now—the servant's life."

Jesus came to serve. Jesus said we're to imitate Him. We're to be like servants. He said he who wants to be greatest amongst you should be the least. He said that's how you get blessed. In order to keep it you have to give it away. You're supposed to take all this love of Christ and give it away to the rest of the world. It should just be coming out of you nonstop.

You might say, "Well, then I won't have any left."

That's the amazing power of God. He keeps filling you up. And you have as much as you'll ever need.

Gotta Serve Somebody

Second Chronicles 12:1-5 tells us about Rehoboam, Solomon's son, and how he did not keep God's laws:

After Rehoboam's position as king was established and he had become strong, he and all Israel with him abandoned the law of the Lord. Because they had been unfaithful to the Lord...

Because they had been unfaithful...

The king of Egypt attacked Jerusalem in the fifth year of King Rehoboam. With twelve hundred chariots and sixty thousand horsemen and with troops from everywhere he captured the fortified cities of Judah and came as far as Jerusalem. Then the prophet Shemaiah came to Rehoboam and to the leaders of Judah who had assembled in Jerusalem for fear of Shishak, and he said to them, "This is what the Lord says, 'You have abandoned me; therefore, I now abandon you to Shishak.'"

You know, God says there's a point where He'll just give you over to Satan. At some point, if you're so stupid to not listen, He'll just give you over to your desires. "Go ahead. Just go do what you want." This is exactly what happened here; this Old Testament story set the pattern. God is saying, "Look, you've abandoned me, so I'm going to abandon you. It doesn't mean I don't love you. I love you. You're my kid. But you've walked away from me, so I'm walking away from you. I've had enough."

Verse 6 says, "The leaders of Israel and the king humbled themselves and said, 'The Lord is just.'"

They as much as said, "We got what we deserved." And the next verse says:

> When the Lord saw that they humbled themselves, this word of the Lord came to Shemaiah: "Since they have humbled themselves, I will not destroy them but will soon give them deliverance."

I believe God is telling us, "If you will just humble yourself before me, I will exalt you. If you will just let me increase and you will decrease in your life, I will exalt you."

It's not too late to be the man or woman of God that you want to be and that He wants you to be.

God goes on to say:

> My wrath will not be poured out on Jerusalem through Shishak. They will, however, become subject to him, so that they may learn the difference between serving me and serving the kings of other lands.

How scary is that?

There's a difference between serving God and serving Satan. And for us there is no "in between or middle ground." Jesus says, "If you are lukewarm I will spit you out."

9: Stories From The Story

Satan is your modern-day equivalent of the king of other lands in the Old Testament. Either you serve God or you serve Satan.

As Bob Dylan said, "You got to serve somebody. It may be the devil or it may be the Lord, but you got to serve somebody."

The Patience of Job

Something in the story of Job absolutely rocked me to my core. You know the story. Satan and God made a little wager. It's almost like the movie Trading Places, where two rich old men were brothers who owned an investment banking firm, they did a social experiment on one of their top employees. One of the brothers argued that people change according to their environments. The other one said, no, they are who they are by genetics. So they made a little wager and experimented by trading the places of a homeless street man and their wealthy, uppity nephew.

Well, Satan challenged God that Job would not remain righteous if everything was taken away from him. Satan said, "Oh, it's easy for Job to be righteous, God, because you gave him everything. He's your man. So of course he's righteous. Let's take it all away and see if he still loves you when he doesn't have his wife, his family, his riches, his health." God agrees, and they test Job. We know, having read the story, that Job is faithful. But when Job was in the middle of it, it's not like he said, "Oh yeah, I'm Job, the guy who's destined to say, 'Though He slay me, yet will I trust him.' I know what to do here. It's

9: Stories From The Story

all good!" No, he had no idea what on earth was happening, while he was getting the snot hammered out of him.

Job heard some more bad news, and the Bible says,

At this, Job got up and tore his robe and shaved his head. Then he fell to the ground in worship and said: 'Naked I came from my mother's womb, and naked I will depart. The Lord gave and the Lord has taken away; may the name of the Lord be praised.' (Job 1:20-21)

What a great sister verse to Romans 8:28. Job knew it then, and we need to know it now. The Lord gives. The Lord takes away. May the name of the Lord be praised. Job didn't curse God's name when he didn't get his way. Job didn't say, "Lord, if you love me, you would never do this. How could you, God? I don't understand." Job knew that God was God and Job said, "Lord, I may not understand it, but you give, and you take away. One thing I do understand, Lord, is that you are God, and I am not. I love you, and I worship you. If you've chosen to take something away even though I don't understand it, I praise your name because I know no matter what happens you are mighty, God. And I praise your name."

Can you and I say the same thing to God in our lives as we walk through this earth as His children? Do we say it and believe it? The Lord gives, the Lord takes away. May the name of the Lord be praised.

Later on, Job is defending himself, and he still doesn't understand the situation. He passed that first test of faith, but he's still getting pummeled and he's trying to analyze what's happening. "Why would this happen to me?" Of course his friends are telling him there must be some unconfessed sin

(Digging Into Biblical Stories)

in his life, which we know was not the case, but at the time, maybe that had him questioning himself too. His wife is telling him he needs to deny God because God must not love him if He's letting all these things happen. Job answers them by saying, "I put on righteousness as my clothing; justice was my robe and my turban." (Job 29:14)

He clothed himself in righteousness. He did the exact same thing that we're instructed to do in the book of Colossians. In Colossians 3 we're instructed to clothe ourselves in the righteousness of Jesus Christ. Job clothed himself in righteousness, and we must do the same thing. There is no confusion, no middle ground, no, "Maybe . . . well let me see, do I or do I not do it?" We need to be able to look at our lives and we need to be able to make that same statement before God. "God, I've clothed myself in righteousness. God, justice is my robe and turban. God, I've aligned myself in accordance with your word to the best of my ability."

In Job 31:6, Job says, "Let God weigh me in honest scales and He will know that I am blameless." Here's Job saying, "Look, I don't understand what's happening but I'll tell you one thing, people. If God used an honest scale to weigh me, if He put everything on the scale, He'd know that I'm blameless. If God just looked at the evidence of my life, if He looked at how I lived, what I did, how I think, I don't care what anybody is saying, and I don't care what the newspaper's report (there may not have been newspapers back then, but you know what I'm saying). I know that if God weighed my actions and my life on the scale, on an honest scale, that I am blameless."

9: Stories From The Story

Blameless. Wow! It is almost unbelievable that Job could make a claim like that before God. I'd love to be able to do that. That's what I want, and I hope that's what you want. We should be praying, analyzing and testing—as God said, testing everything and holding on to what is good—to make sure that we can stand before God and say, "God, put me on the honest scale, Lord. I'm blameless."

I don't believe that I'm at a position in my life where I can say that. But that is my goal. I'm striving for it. And I know God is pruning me and taking out the stuff that I need to remove in my life to get to that point. It's painful, but I want Him to do it. I want to be at that point where I can say, "God, weigh me on an honest scale, and you will know that I'm blameless."

Day and Night

You can read scores of self-help books. You can find all these motivational seminar guys, but all they do is come in and fire you up. Here is the greatest motivational speech ever given in the history of man. It's Psalm 1:1-3, three simple verses and it's the greatest motivational speech ever:

> *Blessed is the man who walks not in the counsel of the ungodly, nor stands in the path of sinners, nor sits in the seat of the scornful; but his delight is in the law of the Lord, and in His law he meditates day and night. He shall be like a tree planted by the rivers of water, that brings forth its fruit in its season, whose leaf also shall not wither; and whatever he does shall prosper.*

You want a seminar on how to get wealthy and get ahead? And by wealthy, I'm talking about joy of the spirit. God may or may not choose to bless you financially. I'm talking about joy, something that goes beyond money and fame.

You want peace and happiness? Here's what you have to do—delight in the law of the Lord and meditate on the Lord

9: Stories From The Story

day and night. If you do that, you'll be like a tree planted by the rivers of water. You'll bring forth fruit in your season. Your leaf will not wither, and whatever you do shall prosper.

People sit there and they go, "Man, I don't know how to find peace. I don't know how to get ahead. I don't know how to live life. I need to go to therapy. I need to go to counseling. I need to watch more Dr. Oz or Dr. Phil or Oprah. I need to talk to my friends more. I need some time. I need to go find myself. I've got to keep looking and looking and looking."

Eventually, they die and they have never found anything.

But here it is, so plain and obvious, almost too easy, but it's there as counsel for us to follow: delight in the law of the Lord. Meditate on Him day and night.

When my son Ricky was dealing with his drug addiction, it was an example of my having been down the road and knowing what's there. I'd gone through it myself. I told my son, "Listen, you should go to rehab. There's help. You'll find out why you do drugs. You'll understand." He didn't want to go. He didn't believe that was the formula. So, he went out and searched for something else that would help, until he wound up arrested and in jail. He went kicking and screaming, but finally he said, "Yeah, I'm going to go."

Now he knows that's the formula. Now he has the benefit of experience for that specific instance. God is giving us the formula for our specific lives, and He's saying, "Look, you need to focus on me. Don't forget me. Meditate on me all day long."

That doesn't mean you have to be up on a hill or outcast from the world. It just means that God is first in your heart

(Digging Into Biblical Stories)

and in your mind. It doesn't mean that every word out of your mouth has to be, "Brother, you need to believe in Jesus." You can live your life, but the character of your life and the quality of your life should reflect Christ's love. What comes out of your heart should be your intense love for God based on your gratitude for the intense love you receive from God. It should be reflected in the actions of your life. That's what people should see when they look at you. Just like it says in Psalm 5:11-12:

> *But let all those rejoice who put their trust in you;*
> *let them ever shout for joy, because you defend them;*
> *let those also who love your name be joyful in you.*
> *For you, O Lord, will bless the righteous; with favor*
> *you will surround him as with a shield.*

If we trust God, the world should see us rejoicing. "Let them ever shout for joy." We should be continually shouting for joy. We should be going, "This is amazing! Jesus is the greatest thing going on! I can't believe it!"

Strength from Revelation

In Revelation 1:17, Jesus says, "Do not be afraid. I am the first and the last." God is telling us not to be afraid. We shouldn't have any fear in this world.

I have a friend from church. Her name is Kim. Kim is a wonderful woman who came to the Lord in the last couple of years. Her father died since then, and God has given her great strength to deal with that. She then found out that she has breast cancer. She said to me, "Jack, God has given me this great revelation. I used to be scared of dying and fearful, and God showed me that this is His cancer. I'm His child, and it's His life, and He's taught me to overcome my fear of life and my fear of death. At fifty-four, God has taught me to overcome my fear. He has used this mightily. Kim understands God's will. Do we?"

God says don't be afraid. Whatever it is you're afraid of, God doesn't want you to be afraid anymore.

Revelation 2:10 even goes so far as to say:

> *Do not be afraid of what you are about to suffer. I tell you, the devil will put some of you in prison to test you, and you will suffer persecution for ten*

> *days. Be faithful, even to the point of death, and I will give you life as your victor's crown.*

Don't be afraid, even to the point of death.

I've had surgery, and it's made me better. I knew the pain was going to be short-term, but I knew the benefit was long-term. It was worth it, even though sometimes the cure, what we have to go through, seems to be worse than what now is. Regardless, God still says don't worry.

If we want that crown of life, we've got to hold on to it, even through suffering and difficulty.

Revelation 5:5 tells us: "Do not weep. See the lion of the tribe of Judah. The root of David has triumphed." Do not weep. Do not cry. God has triumphed. This is why we do not need to be afraid.

Jesus' death on the cross and resurrection from the dead is the victory for you and me and every person in the world. It's the victory of life now, it's the victory in heaven forever, and it's a free gift from God. The knowledge of that is enough reason to jump up and down for joy, to be giddy with happiness. We should be going nuts, manifesting our complete joy for the sake of what Jesus did for us on the cross. For we have eternal victory over death and the grave.

When was the last time you jumped, or sang, or danced for joy? Do you think that now might be a good time? Try it; you might decide you want to keep on doing that for the rest of your life.

A Mighty Hand

In Exodus 3:19-20, the Israelites were in bondage and God asked Moses to lead His people away from a life of slavery in Egypt. The story gets really good here when God says to Moses:

> *But I know that the king of Egypt will not let you go unless a mighty hand compels him. So I will stretch out my hand and strike the Egyptians with all the wonders that I will perform among them. After that, he will let you go.*

Who will do it? Who will make it happen? God will make it happen. Who controls circumstances, situations, life, death, beginning, end, this world, heaven, and eternity? Who controls it all? God. He's orchestrating and dictating the events of Moses and Israel's journey as He sees fit for His glory, and He does the same thing with my life and your life. He dictates the circumstances and events as He sees fit for His glory. Our only job, our only mission, is to love the Lord God with all our heart, to say, "Yes, Lord," in obedience and thanks, to trust Him, to be faithful in all things. That's our job. We need to trust that God is doing His job.

(Digging Into Biblical Stories)

But here's Moses answering God in Exodus 4:1. He says, "What if they do not believe me or listen to me and say, 'The Lord did not appear to you'?"

God himself is speaking to Moses, one-on-one, and Moses answers, "Well, God, that's great. Sounds good. You'll take care of everything, but what if I go back to the Israelites and they don't believe me and they don't believe you sent me?" The first thing he does is doubt God. He just heard it from God Himself, and he doubts God. Don't we do the same thing? The Holy Spirit of God speaks to our heart, speaks in our life about something, and we go, "Jesus, that sounds great but what if? What if my wife? What if my boss? What if I can't? What if I shouldn't? What if it is Satan who is telling me this? How do I discern?"

How do you discern? You look at the word of God. How do you discern? How do you know how much air pressure to put in your tires? How do you know what to set your freezer to? How do you discern? You check the user manual. There's God's word...the Bible. It's His user manual for life and it'll tell you everything. It'll tell you if the message is from God or not, loud and clear. If you have any questions, asked the author. He sent you a helper—the Holy Spirit of God—already living inside of you!

The First Sign of Trouble

God is the author and creator of everything—the past, the present, and the future—my life, your life, and every life that will ever be.

In Exodus chapter 14 The Israelites had taken flight from the Egyptians and they'd gotten as far as the Red Sea. Then the Lord said to Moses, "Tell the Israelites to turn back and encamp near Pi Hahiroth, between Migdol and the sea. And I will harden Pharaoh's heart, and he will pursue them. But I will gain glory for myself through Pharaoh and all his army, and the Egyptians will know that I am the Lord." So the Israelites did as God instructed.

God is in control, telling them, "Turn around. Go here." All of it is part of God's plan. There were plagues, there were signs, there were wonders—all orchestrated by God as He chose to harden Pharaoh's heart so His glory could be revealed.

God has just told them to turn back, that He's going to take care of Pharaoh and His glory will be shown and His will be done. Pharaoh finds out that the Israelites have turned back and fled, and his exact quote is, "'What have we done? We have let the Israelites go and have lost their services!' So

(Digging Into Biblical Stories)

he had his chariot made ready and took his army with him." (Exodus 14:5-6)

The Bible goes on to say:

> *As Pharaoh approached, the Israelites looked up, and there were the Egyptians, marching after them. They were terrified and cried out to the Lord. They said to Moses, "Was it because there were no graves in Egypt that you brought us to the desert to die? What have you done to us by bringing us out of Egypt? Didn't we say to you in Egypt, 'Leave us alone; let us serve the Egyptians'? It would have been better for us to serve the Egyptians than to die in the desert!" (Ex. 14:10-12)*

What? These guys lost faith again at the first sign of trouble.

Now we are seeing a recurring theme here. As it's not the first time Israelites doubt God and don't trust him. Unfortunately many times our lives reflect that same theme.

I hope you can see the analogy and thread to your own life today. Do we sometimes bail on God at the first sign of trouble? Do we think, "Oh, Jesus, these words you said, they must be for somebody else. You said you know the plans you have for us, not to harm us but to prosper us, but you couldn't have meant me because look what's happening. I've lost my health, my finances. Look at the housing market, the stock market crash. My son isn't listening; my wife isn't listening. Lord, you've got it all wrong. I better drive because you clearly do not know what you're doing. So I'll just take the wheel back here."

What a mistake.

9: Stories From The Story

The Israelites did the same thing. What a mistake. It cost them forty years. What's it going to cost you or me?

History. We either can learn from it or be doomed to repeat it. Moses answered the people in verse 13: "Do not be afraid. Stand firm and you will see the deliverance the Lord will bring you today. The Egyptians you see today you will never see again."

God says to you and me, "Stand firm, and you will see the deliverance the Lord will bring you."

The Rescuer

God puts circumstances in our life. He throws rocks upon the path of our journey. He allows trials and temptations throughout our pilgrimage. And we're supposed to learn from these. We're not supposed to doubt, question, mock, or turn away from God. No. We're supposed to embrace, love, run to, and bow down before God and trust in faith. That's the type of obedience God is looking for today.

When the Egyptians were in high pursuit of the Israelites, Exodus 14:21 says: "Then Moses stretched out his hand over the sea, and all that night the Lord drove the sea back with a strong east wind and turned it into dry land."

By the way, no criticism of Hollywood, but I've seen the movie. And in the movie, the Red Sea parts in two minutes. That's not how it happened. It took a whole night. Moses stood there all that night, and only then did the Red Sea part completely. The waters were divided. The Bible says the Egyptians pursued them. Pharaoh's horses and chariots followed them into the sea. It tells us right there in Exodus 14:24-25:

> *During the last watch of the night the Lord looked down from the pillar of fire and cloud at the Egyp-*

9: Stories From The Story

> *tian army and threw it into confusion. He jammed the wheels of their chariots so that they had difficulty driving.*

The Lord did just as He had promised. He looked down and He threw their hearts into confusion. He jammed the wheels. He is always—yesterday, today, and tomorrow—in control of all circumstances, things, people and places. God will put people, places, events, circumstances in your life. All intended to bring you closer to Him. All God wants is for you to have a closer walk with Him. "Come closer to me," God says, "and I will come closer to you. Humble yourself and I will lift you up."

The Bible says, in Exodus 14:31, after the Red Sea parted and they watched the Egyptians drown, "The people feared the Lord and put their trust in him and in Moses his servant." Good idea, guys. Now you're thinking.

Jesus, our savior, our sacrificial lamb on the cross, died for you and me for the sins of the whole world. He died so that we would have abundant life now and eternal life forever. Do you think it's a good idea to put our faith in Jesus? Or do you think we should doubt Him and question Him and continue to mock and laugh when God suggests we do something we think is impossible?

Here are God's instructions to the Israelites, from Exodus 15:26.

> *If you listen carefully to the Lord your God and do what is right in his eyes, if you pay attention to his commands and keep all his decrees, I will not bring*

on you any of the diseases I brought on the Egyptians, for I am the Lord, who heals you.

God said to the Israelites, "...if you listen carefully to the Lord." There's a requirement. You need to listen carefully to the Lord. What does God say to us today? In Matthew 6:33 Jesus says, "...all these things shall be added unto you." But there's a requirement. It's—seek first the kingdom of God and His righteousness. When God says in Proverbs 3:5 that He will direct your paths, there's a requirement: "Trust in the Lord with all your heart and do not lean to your own understanding." Could God be any clearer?

Gratitude

A couple of weeks ago I had the privilege to share with a church about one of their dear brothers, a wonderful man named Roman, who had gone home to be with the Lord. Looking at his life, I know without a doubt he was a man who served the Lord. He was a man who I'm sure heard, "Well done, good and faithful servant. Come and share your master's happiness," as he came into the presence of Jesus Christ. That I know for sure. There was no doubt because of the evidence of the way he lived his life. That tree was evident by its fruit.

The question is, if we were to die today, what would our lives look like?

The Old Testament story of Moses and the Israelites, as they left Egypt and crossed the Red Sea, is probably one of the most well known in the Bible. God did amazing miracles. God ordained Pharaoh's every move. He hardened Pharaoh's heart so that God's glory could be shown throughout the journey the Israelites were taking.

Yet the Israelites still didn't believe Him for certain things, which is rather pitiful, all things considered. Let's pick up the story at God's instructions to the Israelites in Exodus 15:26:

(Digging Into Biblical Stories)

> *If you listen carefully to the Lord your God and do what is right in his eyes, if you pay attention to his commands and keep all his decrees, I will not bring on you any of the diseases I brought on the Egyptians, for I am the Lord, who heals you.*

Doesn't that seem like an easy thing to do? You would think so, right? They had just seen this great miracle of the Red Sea. They saw the miracles of the many plagues put upon the Egyptians. They had been fed manna and had just received all these gifts from God. You would think that they would be the most sold-out band of Israelites you had ever seen.

We would think as well that when Jesus comes into our lives we would be the most sold-out band of Christians ever. But no, we really don't see that. Instead we see the world and its issues getting the best of even "good" Christians; our focus still comes off of Jesus Christ and back onto the world.

The Israelites did the same thing. How does that happen? It's found in Exodus 16:2-3. A new issue comes up. A new tragedy comes up. Something strikes us, and how do we respond?

For the Israelites it was a food issue. They were worried about where their next meal was coming from. Let's see how the Israelites responded.

> *In the desert the whole community grumbled against Moses and Aaron. The Israelites said to them, "If only we had died by the Lord's hand in Egypt! There we sat around pots of meat and ate all the food we wanted, but you have brought us out into this desert to starve this entire assembly to death."*

9: Stories From The Story

How ungrateful where they? What little faith. And all I could say when I read that is "woe is me." Is that me? Am I that guy? Are you?

Don't we do this to Jesus? Don't we doubt Him when we don't get our way? Don't we question Him and His thinking and His ability to be God when it doesn't conform with our understanding or our desires or our wishes? We're like drug addicts who won't give up drugs and wonder why they can't get their lives together. Gee, maybe you should give up the drugs.

So here are the Israelites. They just saw the Red Sea part, and they just saw God wipe out all their enemies. God just spoke and said, "Listen, just love me and do what's right in my eyes and pay attention to my commands, and I won't bring any harm on you like I did to the Egyptians for I am the Lord who heals you."

God has healed every single one of us. God has healed our sin. God has paid the price for our sin. God has healed us, and God is still in the business of doing miracles today. God didn't retire. God is not out of the game. He is still in the business of doing miracles today for those who ask according to His will. In order to have the right to ask according to His will, clearly God is saying to us that we should at the very least believe and be grateful for what God has done for us.

It's Raining Bread

The Israelites are grumbling to God, and Moses says, "Okay. God has heard you, so He's going to give you meat to eat."

Those guys were really complaining. They had just seen the miraculous parting of the Red Sea, but now they're turning on Moses and Aaron because they don't have anything to eat. They're saying it would've been better if they didn't come into freedom because at least when they were slaves in Egypt, they got three meals a day. They somehow forgot that when they were in Egypt, they were complaining and groaning that the Egyptian guards were killing them with backbreaking work.

That's just like us, man. We complain about every little thing we don't have, and we forget about these amazing blessings that we do have.

So Moses says to them, "Hey, you know what? God has heard your grumbling."

Do you believe that God hears you? Jesus is at the right hand of God as an intercessor, praying for us. He prays to His Father and His Father hears Him, and He hears us as well.

So here's what happens. In Exodus 16:8:

9: Stories From The Story

Moses also said, "You will know that it was the Lord when he gives you meat to eat in the evening and all the bread you want in the morning, because he has heard your grumbling against him."

God has heard the grumbling of the people, and He responds. He says, "All right. I'm going to give you meat to eat. I'm going to give you bread. You'll have all that you want." And in Exodus 16:9-10, Moses is speaking to Aaron and he says:

Say to the entire Israelite community, 'Come before the Lord, for he has heard your grumbling.'" While Aaron was speaking to the whole Israelite community, they looked toward the desert, and there was the glory of the Lord appearing in the cloud.

So what does God say to them? Well, first He speaks to Moses, and He says, "I have heard the murmuring of the children of Israel." That's verse 12. So yes, He does hear us, that's for sure.

Then He sent manna, and commands them, with instructions he gave to Moses, in Exodus 16:16-18:

Everyone is to gather as much as they need. Take an omer for each person you have in your tent. (This was the measurement they used at the time. Some translations say it was about three pounds.)

The Israelites did as they were told; some gathered much, some little. And when they measured it by the omer, the one who gathered much did not have too much, and the one who gathered little did not

> *have too little. Everyone had gathered just as much as they needed.*

Wow. Talk about the miracle and economy of God. God has always been pretty good in the food distribution business. Like when Jesus took the two fish and the five loaves and He fed four thousand people, and another time after when He fed five thousand under similar circumstances. Man, He has always known just how much to give. And here, no matter what they gathered, they had just enough. God has been good to us in the food distribution business also because He has given each of us, each day our daily bread.

God has said that He is the living bread, and if we eat of Him, we will never hunger again. God has said that He is the living water, and if we drink of Him, we'll never thirst again. Yet we—as do so many countless other believers and non-believers—look to the world to feed our hunger and our thirst. Do we look to the temporal, look to the daily, look to the worthless to feed our hunger and thirst? God has said, "I am your food. I am your everything."

Let me tell you something. If you don't have peace, joy, love, gratitude, grace, forgiveness, and mercy in your life from your appreciation for what you have received from Jesus Christ, you're not ever getting it anywhere else. You can look. You can try, but it's not coming from anywhere else in your life.

God wants you to have it. God wanted for Israel to have it. Moses gives them some more instructions, directly from God in Exodus 16:19. Now, remember they were just complaining they had no food. Here God shows up again and says, "I've heard your grumbling. Okay, here's food." He gives them food and He says, "But one thing. Eat it all today. Don't leave any of it for the morning."

You would think that Israel would listen. You would think you would listen if somebody said, "Look, here's a million dollars. Just one thing. Don't go to the racetrack and gamble any of it." All right. You just got a million dollars. You wouldn't say, "I've got to go to the racetrack. I must!" But we do just that in our spiritual lives. Instead of being grateful, we are selfish and greedy.

It's amazing how conflicting our sinful nature is with the nature of God. We know that. We understand that. That's why when Jesus comes into our lives and gives us that new heart, He said we are to die to sin. We're to die to self. These things are to die—they're not to hang around, we're not to allow them to work in the shadows. They're not to be indulged and not to be encouraged. We're to die to these things. That's a requirement to get the full grace and mercy of Jesus Christ and His blessing in our life.

It's so obvious when we look back on the Israelites and we say, "Look what God told them to do. They have to be the biggest idiots in the world. How could they not do this?"

Is God looking at us and shaking His head, saying, "No, they weren't the idiots. You are. You, church. You, believer, because you live under grace. They lived under the law."

They didn't have the grace of Jesus Christ. They had to do what the law said. We have the saving grace of Jesus Christ. We have the free gift of Jesus Christ, and we still don't do the very things God asked us to do. "Love the Lord God with all your heart and soul, and love your neighbor as yourself." Can you just do that? We say, "Well, I'd like to, God, but you see..."

(Digging Into Biblical Stories)

God says, "No, you need to see! Remember, I gave you everything, and you should just do that out of gratitude." Not out of obligation. Out of gratitude.

Fickle People

We're in Exodus 16 and Moses gave them the message, straight from God, that they were not supposed to keep any of the manna until morning (the manna was the bread God had miraculously given them each day to eat and sustain them). Here's verse 20: "However, some of them paid no attention to Moses; they kept part of it until morning, but it was full of maggots and began to smell. So Moses was angry with them."

How could they possibly take control back from God and do what they want after everything they'd seen and everything God had done for them?

How?

Well how can we possibly do the same after Jesus' death on the cross for our salvation?

God said, "Don't hold any of it until the morning." They said, "I'd better put some away. Maybe God is just God for today. Maybe He's not God for tomorrow. I can't trust God for tomorrow. The food is here now so I'd better put some away. I'll be smart." They still didn't trust God for their provisions. Smart by the world's standards is a fool by the standards of God.

(Digging Into Biblical Stories)

You can't control when you're born. You can't control when you die. You can't do anything. God is your provision.

It gets better. In Exodus 16:28, the Lord says to Moses, "How long will you refuse to keep my commands and my instructions?"

I believe God asks us that question in disbelief as He watches us acting like ungrateful and disobedient children. I have children, and sometimes they're ungrateful and disobedient. And I truly shake my head in disbelief. I think, "You ungrateful, disobedient children. Man, I've given you everything. Your mother and I have sacrificed for you." But I get it. I get that they're young, and I get that they'll grow out of it. They better!

But what excuse do we have before God? We can't say we're seven and nine years old. We are mature. We know the word. We've eaten the word. We have the Holy Spirit inside of us teaching all things. Do we act like it?

The Israelites are still doubting God based on their concept of what reality is, as if God were some slot machine, as if when He pays out, it's, "Oh, God, you're the greatest. Wow, you just killed those Egyptians in the Red Sea. You freed us. You're the greatest. We asked you for food. We were grumbling. And you gave us food. You must really love us. You're the greatest. And oh by the way in case you made a mistake, God, I better save food for tomorrow."

But when they didn't get what they wanted, "Oh, God, you stink. Why don't you leave us here to die? Your servant Moses, he's the wrong guy." Doubting and disbelief.

And it gets better in Exodus 19:1-6:

9: Stories From The Story

> *On the first day of the third month after the Israelites left Egypt—on that very day—they came to the Desert of Sinai. Then Moses went up to God, and the Lord called to him from the mountain and said, "This is what you are to say to the descendants of Jacob and what you are to tell the people of Israel: "You yourselves have seen what I did to Egypt, and how I carried you on eagles' wings and brought you to myself. Now if you obey me fully and keep my covenant, then out of all nations you will be my treasured possession. Although the whole earth is mine, you will be for me a kingdom of priests and a holy nation.' These are the words you are to speak to the Israelites."*

Are we not the same today as followers of Jesus Christ, as His children? We too are a kingdom of priests and a holy priesthood set apart by God. He considers us His most treasured possession.

If you don't believe me, I trust you'll believe God. First Peter 2:9-10 says:

> *But you are a chosen people, a royal priesthood, a holy nation, God's special possession, that you may declare the praises of him who called you out of darkness into his wonderful light. Once you were not a people, but now you are the people of God; once you had not received mercy, but now you have received mercy.*

Are we doing what God called us to do? Are we living like a nation of royal priests, of God's holy kids declaring the praises of Him who called us out into His glorious light?

(Digging Into Biblical Stories)

Clearly, God has told us our purpose. Bear fruit and fruit that will last. Declare the praises of Him who has called you into His glorious light. Go and make disciples. Be holy for I am holy. Imitate me. Run the race marked out for you with perseverance. Forget the past. Focus on the things ahead. Live up to the calling you've obtained.

What is the calling? Live as a son or daughter of God. That's your calling. That was the calling of the Israelites, God's most treasured possession, and that's how God defines you in First Peter. God's special possession.

First Corinthians 4:7-8 says:

> *For who makes you different from anyone else? What do you have that you did not receive? And if you did receive it, why do you boast as though you did not? Already you have all you want! Already you have become rich!*

Every one of us is rich with the spirit of God, rich in the kingdom of heaven, rich with eternal life and abundant life, rich because of our relationship with God. There are many people who might be rich by the world's standards. Many are poor by the kingdom of God's standards. If everything we have is of the world; we will have nothing of the kingdom.

Oh, that we may seek after the things of the kingdom rather than those of the world because that's the life that God has called His special possession to be. That's the life that God says, "I will reward. I will bless. I will glorify. I will use mightily for the kingdom of God."

When you let God use your life, wherever He has put you, wherever you may be, for whatever He has called you to do,

9: Stories From The Story

by just glorifying Him in what you do, by just letting the world see that indeed you are a child of God, it's evident. It shows and people sit up and take notice. They see it's not 50/50. You are not lukewarm, you are on fire for Christ. You are not living as a hypocrite, you are living as sons of God, imitators of God. No, there's no in between. It's clear that we believe in Jesus Christ. We're not perfect. We understand that. That's why Jesus had to die for us on the cross. But clearly there's no question of what team we play for. We play for team Jesus. There's no question of who we love. Our attitudes and actions in our life need to reflect that.

Being God's People

Moses goes up to the mountain and talking about the people of Israel God says, "Look, I just brought you out of the Red Sea. I just fed you when you were grumbling. I've done everything you wanted. Obey me now, and I'll make you my special possession, my treasured possession, my holy people."

Moses does his job and delivers the message. The people say, "We're in." Like the chips at the poker table, they push them all in. Oh, we're in. We get it now. We don't know why we didn't see it before—Pharaoh, the plagues, the Red Sea, feeding us—but we get it now. Where do we sign? We're in. We're followers. We're going to do the right thing.

In Exodus 19:9, the Lord tells Moses, "I am going to come to you in a dense cloud, so that the people will hear me speaking with you and will always put their trust in you."

God is giving Moses a little street credibility. He is saying, "Moses, look, I'm going to come to you in a dense cloud so the people know that I'm with you. They'll never doubt you again." That's pretty strong. God is backing Moses up to the hilt.

9: Stories From The Story

Soon afterward, God gives Moses the Ten Commandments. He gives him the rules. He gives him the tabernacle design. He gives him instructions on the way to live and how to fulfill the law. Jesus had not died yet and been resurrected, so it was not "by grace" that they were saved. It was by following the law. God lays out the law because He loves them so much and because He doesn't want to punish them. He says, "Okay, I'm so glad you guys are in. This is great. Here are the Ten Commandments. Here is how to build the tabernacle to honor me. Here are the laws." And He lays out how they should do it and how they should live.

If you've read about the tabernacle in the Bible, you know it's extremely detailed as God gave very intricate assembly instructions. God was very specific. He wanted to make sure that they knew what to do. Now here's what really amazed me. It amazed me that Noah had no problem following God's instructions to build the ark because he wanted to. The Israelites had no problem following God's instructions to build the tabernacle—this altar to God. And, believe me, it was detailed. The wood, the silver, the fabric—it was like blueprints for the most intricate house you could imagine. They had no problem doing that because they wanted to.

You and I should have no problem showing our gratitude to Jesus Christ, living a life that glorifies Christ because we want to; not because we have to, not because we think we'll be punished if we don't, not because we're scared that we'll miss blessing—which is the truth—but because we want to.

Do you want to? And if you don't, will you trust God enough to do it anyway?

Who Did This?

I love this. It's the first five verses in Exodus 31:

> *Then the Lord said to Moses, "See, I have chosen Bezalel son of Uri, the son of Hur, of the tribe of Judah, and I have filled him with the Spirit of God, with wisdom, with understanding, with knowledge and with all kinds of skills—to make artistic designs for work in gold, silver and bronze, to cut and set stones, to work in wood, and to engage in all kinds of crafts."*

Your parents didn't give you your talents. God gave you your talents. He used your parents as a way to birth you into this world, but God is the one who gave you the talent and skills. God's Holy Spirit, on the spot, fills this guy who had never been filled before. He didn't have the talent before. It's not like God said, "Oh, I'll grab this guy. He has the talent." No. The Word of God says God filled him with the talent he needed to do the job right then.

The Holy Spirit will fill us with the talent each and every day to do the job we need to do to live a life that glorifies Jesus Christ if we let Him and if we want Him to.

9: Stories From The Story

God promises His Holy Spirit will teach us all things. An anointing of the Holy Spirit can come upon any believer at any time. We're all filled with the spirit of God. We're filled with the spirit of God upon salvation. It never goes away. It never gets taken away. It's in irrevocable transaction between you and God upon your salvation. God comes to live inside you. You have His spirit. But the anointing of God, the infilling of God can come and go. It can come for a sermon, it can come for a week, it can come for a month; it can come and go. That's why we have to come closer to God so He'll come closer to us. We want that anointing. We want that filling.

The more we walk with God, the more we get it. The more we walk in the world, the more we don't get it. Don't get caught up in semantics here. It's simple—our talents and gifts come from God. So who are we going to use them for?

Some of God's teachings are painful. But then later we see how God was grooming us and molding us so he could use us. He was building our talents so He could use them for His kingdom. But we couldn't see it while it was happening. As a matter of fact, we were complaining about it while it was happening. "Woe is me."

God makes us strong so He can use us for the kingdom if we ask Him, if we let Him, if we follow His instructions.

Keeping the Faith

When the people saw that Moses was so long in coming down from the mountain, they gathered around Aaron and said, "Come, make us gods who will go before us. As for this fellow Moses who brought us up out of Egypt, we don't know what has happened to him." (Exodus 32:1)

What? Hold it. A couple of chapters ago you just said you're all in. God said He's going to make you His special possession. You said, "This is awesome! We're all in, Lord. This is the greatest!" Now Moses is gone forty days, he's not back, and you're ready to sell out to a new god? As a matter of fact, you insist on it. You go to Aaron, the guy left in charge, a priest, and you say, "Oh, no, no, no, no. You know what? Moses, we thought he was right. We thought he was close to God. We thought he was a friend of God. But now we better take charge here and take control back from Moses, because we haven't seen him in a while."

WHAT? You haven't seen him in a while! What's that about?

Don't we do that to Jesus sometimes? Hey, Jesus, haven't seen you in a while. Let me grab a new god. Let me grab the god of money, the god of pride, the god of anger, the god of addiction. Let me grab something that will just satisfy me for today…as if God has left us—the God who said, "I'll never leave you or forsake you. I am with you always. I have a perfect plan for your life. I knew you before you were formed in your mother's womb. I have a perfect plan for you, plans to prosper you and not to harm you." As if the God who said all of those things is suddenly a liar. As if the God who died on the cross for us all of a sudden didn't know what He was doing. Here are the people who just promised they were all in, and indeed they were all out.

I kind of equate it to when you go to a restaurant and you give your name for your reservation, then you wait for the hostess to call your name and give you a table…and you wait and wait. And you go, "This is taking way too long. I'm going to go up and find out what's going on."

You go up to the hostess and you go, "Excuse me. Where are we? Clearly, there is some mistake. It's taking too long."

And the hostess goes, "No mistake. It's just not your turn yet. There are people ahead of you."

God says he who is first in the kingdom shall be last, and he who is last shall be first. God, according to His timing and His grace, gets to decide. We are the clay. God is the potter. And yet often we act as if it was exactly the opposite.

So there's a rebellion. Moses is gone. The people are asking for a new god. Aaron is freaking out so he says, "Give me all your gold and jewelry," and he puts it into a mold of a calf and sticks it into the fire and says, "This will be our new god. Tomorrow we'll worship him."

(Digging Into Biblical Stories)

By the way, later when Moses comes back and says, "What's going on here?" Aaron lies to Moses. Hard to believe, but true. He says, "Well, the people gave me all their gold and jewelry. I put it in the fire, and this is what came out." Yeah Aaron, sure. Hey, you were the one who put it into the calf mold. Admit it brother, you got scared and caved in. Aaron did have a mutiny on his hands. He had a rebellion. He didn't know what to do. He freaked out. He blew it. He didn't stay faithful to God.

So how scary is this? In Exodus 32:7-8, God actually tells Moses, who's been up on the mountain, what's going on down the hill:

> *Go down, because your people, whom you brought up out of Egypt, have become corrupt. They have been quick to turn away from what I commanded them and have made themselves an idol cast in the shape of a calf.*

What about us? Are we quick to turn away from what God has commanded us to do? Ask yourself in your heart, "Lord, have I been strong, faithful, and courageous as you encouraged, or have I been quick to turn away?"

Moses hurries down the mountain and he takes a stand. It's in Exodus 32:25-26:

> *Moses saw that the people were running wild and that Aaron had let them get out of control and so they became a laughingstock to their enemies. So he stood at the entrance to the camp and said, "Whoever is for the Lord, come to me."*

God is saying that to us, His children.

9: Stories From The Story

"Whoever is for the Lord, come to me."

The word of God tells us all the Levites rallied to him. All the priests of their day came and rallied to God just like we're supposed to, we are to be just like all the priests. I didn't say pastors. I said priests because God said that every one of you is a holy priest, a holy temple for God's pleasure, for God's glory. Can you believe what a moment of truth that was for God's people?

Can you believe that not everyone said, "God, I'm with you"? Not everyone came? Holy cow. Yet we cry about family members and friends and we say, "How could everyone not come to Jesus Christ? How could they not answer the holy son of God?" We should not be surprised. Mankind's nature, his flesh and blood are sin soaked and not in alignment with the spirit of God. Only by the saving grace of God and our acceptance of his Lordship in our lives are we freed from such wickedness and death.

Cain's Mutiny

Genesis 4:3-4 says, "In the course of time Cain brought some of the fruits of the soil as an offering to the Lord. But Abel brought fat portions from some of the firstborn of his flock."

It was time to give an offering to the Lord. So, Cain, he comes with some fruits. "Here God, take some of my fruits out of the basket. Not the good ones, I plan to keep those. Here are some on the bottom. This one's a little bruised. Here, God. Here's my offering. I did give you an offering. God, you said you wanted an offering. Here's your offering."

Abel, out of pure love for God, takes the fat portions—the good stuff, the beautiful stuff, the prime cuts of meat, the beautiful fruit—and he's laying it down at God's feet. Abel does the right thing whereas Cain fulfilled the minimum requirement under the technicality of the law. But that wasn't enough for God. Why not? Cain did what he had to do, Lord. He gave you an offering.

God had a higher expectation of Cain. God says, "To whom much is given, much is expected." God has a higher expectation of you and me. God expects that we would be grateful for

Jesus' death on the cross. God expects that He would matter in our lives and that we would give Him our best—the best of everything we have to offer—our love, our hope, our friendship, our forgiveness, our joy, our peace, our happiness. He expects us to get those things from God and share them with everyone else. God expects our best.

What does God expect from you? I believe the answer is—your best. We have to decide our answer to a very simple question—Am I going to rip God off or not? Because, you know, I have that option. I can rip Him off in my giving. I can rip Him off in my loving. I can rip Him off in my forgiving. I can rip Him off in my worship. I can rip Him off any way I want.

Let's see what happens to Cain, someone who thought that way. The word of God says in Genesis 4:4-5, "The LORD looked with favor on Abel and his offering, but on Cain and his offering he did not look with favor. So Cain was very angry, and his face was downcast."

Get this right. God looked at Abel and said, "Abel, you've given me the best you have." Just like that widow—when Jesus and his disciples were in the temple and saw a widow who put only a few cents in the offering; it was nothing compared to what the rich people of the day put in, but God said, "She has given more because she gave everything. They gave out of their excess. She gave everything she had."

Basically, God is upset with Cain, and He's happy with Abel. God knew the difference in the offering. There is nothing hidden from God's sight. God knows everything. God knows

(Digging Into Biblical Stories)

the intent of your heart when you give and the intent of your heart when you love. How is the Lord looking today at your offering? And I don't mean your tithe. I mean, how is He looking at the offering of your life? This is one of those things you need to get right, for your sake.

Cain was angry that God didn't give him full credit for his cruddy offering. He wanted full credit, and he was mad that he didn't get it. "His face was downcast."

When he was seven years old, my son Jackson lied from time to time, and he got mad at me when I didn't believe his lie.

I'm like, "But son, you're lying."

"No, I'm not daddy. You need to believe me."

"No, I don't. You're lying."

He was upset that I didn't believe his lie, that he couldn't pull the wool over my eyes.

Cain rips off God, and he's mad at God for not saying it's okay. Do we do that in our life sometimes? Do we sell God short, not give God everything He deserves? And then when we go to God and want a blessing or something and we don't get it, we ask, "Oh, God, how can you not give me what I want? Oh, God, I don't understand."

This next paragraph is going to clear it up for you in a big way, in Genesis 4:6-7, "Then the Lord said to Cain, "Why are you angry? Why is your face downcast? If you do what is right, will you not be accepted?"

It would be like me saying to my little kid, "What are you mad about? You're the one who lied. Just don't lie anymore and we won't have a problem."

9: Stories From The Story

God is saying to Cain, "Why are you angry? Why are you downcast?" Then He poses a rhetorical question, the same question he says to you and me today: "If you do what is right, will you not be accepted?" God is saying it's not too late. It wasn't too late for Cain, at that point. God loved him, just like we love that baby even when we walk into the bedroom and get a full-on whiff of a stinky diaper. Just like I still loved Jackson with all my heart when he was lying to me.

God loved Cain and was saying, "Cain, look, I love you, man, but you're doing this all wrong. I don't know what you're angry about, but hey, just do what's right and everything will be okay." Just be like that prodigal son and turn from your sin, repent, and come back to God. And, as He says in James 4:8, "If you come closer to me, I'll come closer to you."

It's not too late for any of us to start doing the right thing with God right now. God still loves you so much. God is not furious. He's just surprised and disappointed. He is saying, "Look, if you do what is right, will you not be accepted?"

You say to me, "Okay, Jack, what do I have to do? What is right?" 1 Thessalonians 5:16-18 tells us, "Be joyful always; pray continually; give thanks in all circumstances, for this is God's will for you in Christ Jesus."

That's what you need to do. That is what is right. Be joyful always, pray continuously, and give thanks in all circumstances—not some, not a few, all. Not just when you get the job, when you get the raise, when you get the girl, when you get what you want. No. Even when you don't.

Romans 8:28 says, "All things work together for the good of those who love God." If we believe Jesus, then we believe that

(Digging Into Biblical Stories)

promise; and that's why we give thanks in all circumstances. If we believe that Jesus is working it for our good, how can it be wrong? It has to be wonderful.

Every Jar Full

If you limit God's spiritual blessings and deposits in your life, you're going to miss it. Elisha was a prophet who took over for Elijah. In 2 Kings 4:1 it says:

> *The wife of a man from the company of the prophets cried out to Elisha, "Your servant my husband is dead and you know that he revered the Lord. But now his creditor is coming to take my two boys as his slaves."*

Wow. I mean, these days they just take your house, your car keys, and ruin your credit. In the old days, they took your family. They took your kids when you owed money and sold them into slavery.

> *Elisha replied to her, "How can I help you? Tell me, what do you have in your house?" "Your servant has nothing there at all," she said, "except a little oil." (2 Kings 4:2)*

Elisha is a prophet! He has the power of God and he wants to help this woman, but all she has is a little oil.

(Digging Into Biblical Stories)

> *"Elisha said, 'Go around and ask all your neighbors for empty jars. Don't ask for just a few.'" (2 Kings 4:3)*

Go around, live your life as a Christian, ask God for His blessings on your life, but don't ask for just a few. God's got a ton of blessings for you that He wants to pour into your life, and into your heart, and into those around you—your family, and friends, and everybody else through you—and He wants to use you mightily if you would get in the game. Just go out and put on the uniform and swing the bat. That's what God wants you to do. Elisha tells her not to ask for just a few empty jars.

> *"Then go inside and shut the door behind you and your sons. Pour oil into all the jars, and as each is filled, put it to one side." She left him and afterward shut the door behind her and her sons. They brought the jars to her and she kept pouring. When all the jars were full, she said to her son, "Bring me another one." But he replied, "There is not a jar left." Then the oil stopped flowing. (2 Kings 4:4-6)*

Get this right. She went out, she went to her neighbors, she got some jars. She kept pouring the oil until every jar was full. When there were no more jars left, the oil stopped flowing.

There was as much oil as there were jars!

That is the key point. Had she gone out and collected a thousand jars, a thousand would have been filled up. Had she got ten thousand, ten thousand would've been filled up. There was as much oil as she had jars.

There are as many blessings as you have faith. It's faith that brings you blessings. That's what God will respond to. That's what God wants to see. It's the equivalent of you getting out and getting the cups and bringing them for oil to be poured in. You take your faith and you lay it at the Lord's feet. He pours His life and blessings into you and your life, and you overflow. Your cup will overflow with blessings, but when you stop living by faith then your unholy living does limit the flow of His blessings here on earth.

We place limits on God in our life and I think God wants us to take those limits off, take off the chains, take off the mental boundaries.

God says, "I have so much more in store for you. There is so much I want to do if you would just let go and believe me."

In 1 Timothy 6:11-12 God says that you need to take hold of the gift that you were given—the gift of eternal life:

"But you, man of God, flee from all this [worldly stuff], and pursue righteousness, godliness, faith, love, endurance and gentleness. Fight the good fight of the faith. Take hold of the eternal life to which you were called."

In order to use a weapon, you need to take hold of it. It's useless sitting on the table, or hidden away in your closet. If you want to use it, you take hold of it.

That's what you're supposed to do with your Christian life. You're supposed to take hold of this eternal call that God gave you.

Whose Neighbor?

It doesn't matter if you've been saved a year or twenty-five years. We all grow as fast as we want to grow with God. As fast as you want to learn, God will teach you. As fast as you want to grow spiritually, God will bring lessons your way.

In Luke 10:25-29:

> *On one occasion an expert of the law stood up to test Jesus. "Teacher, he asked what must I do to inherit eternal life?" "What is written in the law" He replied. How do you read it?*

Jesus was saying "Hey expert, you tell me what it means. How do you interpret the law, what do you think it means?" The verse goes onto say:

> *He answered, "Love the Lord your God with all your heart and with all your soul and with all your strength and with all your mind. And, love your neighbor as yourself." "You have answered correctly," Jesus said. "Do this and you will live." But he wanted to justify himself, so he asked Jesus, "And who is my neighbor?"*

9: Stories From The Story

Jesus gives him an example in the next couple of verses:

A man was going down from Jerusalem to Jericho, when he was attacked by robbers. They stripped him of his clothes, beat him and went away, leaving him half dead. A priest happened to be going down the same road, and when he saw the man, he passed by on the other side.

What's that? A priest? There's a guy with the crap beat out of him laying there half dead, and the priest turns his head, walks away, and says, "I don't think so, it's not my job to help him! I'm not spending my time and effort on this guy."

Can't count on the priest? Man, that's pretty sad.

Verse 32 tells us, "So too, a Levite, when he came to the place and saw him, passed by on the other side."

A Levite? One of the religious guys set apart to do the will of God? They too were priests of God specifically set apart, and he ignores the guy? Wow, man…how sad. This guy's just gonna be left for dead.

And Jesus finally finishes the parable by saying in verse 33, "But a Samaritan…"

You could probably almost feel the crowd getting mad at Jesus for even mentioning a Samaritan. In that day, they were worse than low-class. No one had any respect for them. Nobody cared about them. They were viewed as the dogs of society.

So the Samaritan guy walks by. The last guy in the world you'd expect to care at all. And what does he do? The Samaritan comes up to him, he bandages his wounds and he pours oil and wine on them. He puts the beaten man on his donkey, brings him to an inn and takes care of him. The next day he

(Digging Into Biblical Stories)

takes out two denarii, which is two days' wages, and he gives it to the innkeeper. He says, "Look after this beaten man. When I return I'll reimburse you for any expense you may have."

In Luke 10:36-37, Jesus asks, "Which of these three do you think was a neighbor to the man who fell into the hands of robbers?"

The expert in the law replied, "The one who had mercy on him." Jesus told him, "Go and do likewise."

That is what He wants us to do: "Go and do likewise. Have mercy on others, live a life of sacrifice, give what you have to someone else, and I will bless you."

The Samaritan's heart was in the right place. He knew about sacrifice. And Jesus said, "Go and do likewise." He says the same to you and me.

A Cry is Heard

God's prophet, Elijah, goes to Zarephath in response to the prompting of the Lord. A widow, also in obedience to God, takes Elijah in, feeds him, and takes care of him. After all that, in 1st Kings 17:17, her son gets sick and dies.

Now, can you imagine this woman's perspective? "Hey, I just did the right thing, Lord. I followed you. You sent this prophet. You put it on my heart to take him in and feed him. I did just that. I took care of him. He's here, and now my son is dead. That's great, God. You got any other good news for me? Anything else you'd like me to do?"

She's asking, "Why did this happen?"

Look what happens next. Elijah says in verses 19-21:

> *"Give me your son." He took him from her arms, carried him to the upper room where he was staying, and laid him on his bed. Then he cried out to the Lord, "O Lord my God, have you brought tragedy also upon this widow I am staying with, by causing her son to die?" Then he stretched himself out on the boy three times and cried to the Lord, "O Lord my God, let this boy's life return to him!"*

(Digging Into Biblical Stories)

Guess what? Verse 22 tells us, "The Lord heard Elijah's cry." God's word tells us the prayer of a righteous man (and a righteous woman) is effective. If we're righteous in the sight of the Lord—not perfect, but righteous in the sight of the Lord—then God hears our prayers, and according to His will, He will answer.

The Lord heard Elijah's cry. The boy's life returned to him, and he lived. Here are verses 23 and 24:

> *Elijah picked up the child and carried him down from the room into the house. He gave him to his mother and said, "Look, your son is alive!" Then the woman said to Elijah, "Now I know that you are a man of God and that the word of the Lord from your mouth is the truth."*

John says that if they were to record all the miracles that Jesus did, they would be too numerous to write down, so many that all the books in the world couldn't contain them. That's how many miracles Jesus did, yet we scratch our heads and wonder if we should believe Him sometimes.

"Hey, God, how do I know you know what you're doing?" How? Because He's God, and we should trust Him and believe it. So, clearly, the woman now believed based on what she saw, and we too should believe based on what we've seen in history, and what we claim to believe. If we say we believe that Jesus Christ is Lord, should we not believe that He will make good on every one of His promises?

Now, there may have been times when you wondered, times when you weren't sure if God was moving in your life. Times when you are thinking, "God, I don't feel it. I don't have the vibe. I don't have the happy leaping and rejoicing vibe. I'm a little bummed out, and how could you let all this stuff happen to me, God?" Just like that lady said, "How could you let my son die?"

Even Elijah questioned God, "Why would you let this happen?" And you know what? God was in control the whole time. God is in control the whole time. Trust Him. He's working all the time on your behalf.

God has said all things work together for our good. So knowing that, trusting God, believing that all the books in the world couldn't contain all the miracles God has done, then if He says all things work together for my good, I'm going to believe it.

The Right Team

Elijah, the Old Testament prophet of God, followed God's directions and it led him before the evil king Ahab to proclaim a drought. Then, he followed God's directions to hang out by the brook and be sustained by ravens. After that, he followed God's directions to head to Zarephath.

Then it was time for some new directions from God. We can read about it in the first couple verses of 1st Kings 18:

> *After a long time, in the third year, the word of the Lord came to Elijah: "Go and present yourself to Ahab, and I will send rain on the land." So Elijah went to present himself to Ahab.*

He's been hiding from king Ahab, as Ahab had it in for Elijah because Elijah was turning people toward God and away from Ahab's false gods. So God tells Elijah to go pay Ahab a visit, and Elijah did just that. He didn't hesitate or argue or double check. He doesn't say "You sure you got that right, God?"

Meanwhile, back at the palace, Ahab has sent his right-hand man, Obadiah, to look for springs or streams, to keep their horses and mules from dying, as there was a severe drought in the land. Now Obadiah was a God fearing man who had actually hidden God's prophets in the past from the evil edicts of Queen Jezebel (more about her soon). Well, Elijah appears before Obadiah in verse 8, and he says, "Go to your master and tell him Elijah is here." He's basically calling Ahab out.

Obadiah is not happy about delivering this message to Ahab from Elijah. He's a little scared about this. He says in verse 14, "You tell me to go to my master and say Elijah is here. He will kill me! If I tell him you're here, he's going to come look for you. Then God's going to take you away someplace else because God is protecting you. Ahab's going to come, not find you, and he's going to kill me for saying you were here."

Elijah reassures him, in verse 15, "As the Lord Almighty lives, whom I serve, I will surely present myself to Ahab today."

So, Obadiah went to Ahab and told him, and Ahab went out to meet Elijah. King Ahab says to him, "Is that you, the troubler of Israel?"

Can you imagine that? Here's Ahab going, "Is that you? Are you the guy that's causing all the trouble for Israel? Are you the guy stirring everything up, causing all the trouble? I've been looking for you."

Well, Elijah has a great comeback for that accusation: "I have not made trouble for Israel, but you and your father's family have abandoned the Lord's command and have followed the Baals."

"You have abandoned the Lord's command." Hey, if you want to make trouble for yourself and your family, there's the formula. Just abandon the Lord's command. It's really easy. You'll have plenty of trouble for you and your family. Elijah is very specific. "I didn't cause trouble." He's just speaking the truth: "You've gone to follow other gods. You're the one who's abandoned God."

What an excellent reminder that we're never to abandon God. What better witness could we need than a guy like Elijah? James 5:17 says he was a guy just like us, just as human as we are. The same goes for Job, Paul, Jonah, and everybody in the Bible. All the guys in Hebrews Chapter 11(the Hall of Fame of faith), all the way through their problem-filled lives, they didn't know that they were going to be great people. They didn't know what was happening. They were just trying to serve God, struggling with their flesh and their stinking rotten hearts, knowing there was no righteous man. They all had flaws and characteristics of the flesh, of the mind, of the heart, of the tongue, of the body, all of them. And yet, they just loved God and stayed faithful to the best of their ability.

They did what they could, and when they made an error or struck out they came back, they knew what team they played on, Jesus' team. That's one thing they knew for sure. They might have struck out, they might have made an error, but they were on Jesus' team. They never quit, and they didn't stop playing. Their stories are there as an inspiration for you and me in the lives we are living today. Now, we look back and it's easy to say, "Well, of course they did miracles and great things. They were mighty men of God. Look at them!" That's not how they felt at the time. They were human, but they remained faithful to God and followed His directions day by day. They trusted Him and obeyed. And that's what people should be saying about you and me. And they will. We have the potential to be those same mighty men and women of God, just by remaining faithful to Him.

A God Contest

I'll bet the people who impacted you most in your Christian life were not world-famous people. I doubt it was Billy Graham, as great a preacher as he is. No, it was probably your grandmother, or perhaps your spouse, a godly boss, or a kind godly friend. Maybe it was someone you met one day and they said something and God touched your heart through it. Or maybe it was your local pastor who faithfully preached the word of God every week. Those are the people who have influenced you, right? Normal everyday people who were faithful to God, and they inspired you and helped to make you who you are today. That's what we are to be to everyone else—not someone famous, just someone faithful.

In 1 Kings chapter 18, God's true prophet, Elijah, calls out 450 false prophets, as well as all the people of the town. He says, "Get them all together. Assemble them all. We're going to settle this once and for all. We've got me here on God's side, and all of you prophets and people on the side of Baal."

Elijah stands before them, looks them right in the eyes, and asks, "How long will you waver between two opinions?" He said, "If the Lord is God, then follow Him, but if Baal is God, follow him." But the people said nothing.

The question I have is: what do we say? I believe God says the same thing to us today. "If I am God, then follow me, and if I am not, then don't." In Luke 6:46 He asks the convicting question to our hearts: "Why do you call me Lord, Lord and yet you do not do what I say?"

What answer do you have for God?

How long will we falter between two opinions? How long will we falter between the ways of the world and the ways of Christ, the flesh and the spirit, Satan and God?

Then Elijah says in 1 Kings 18:22-24

> *"I am the only one of the Lord's prophets left, but Baal has four hundred and fifty prophets. Let the Baal prophets bring up two oxen; let them pick one, butcher it, and lay it out on an altar on firewood—but don't ignite it. I'll take the other ox, cut it up, and lay it on the wood. But neither will I light the fire. Then you pray to your gods and I'll pray to God. The god who answers with fire will prove to be, in fact, God."*

The prophets of Baal choose a bull and prepared it. They begin calling on their God, dancing around the altar. They started in the morning and danced and prayed until noon. Nothing happens. (Can't imagine why.) No answer. No fire.

Finally at noon, Elijah's been waiting a while, probably just itching to let God's power be shown. But he had to wait until the people knew nothing was going to happen at the altar of Baal. So now he's going to have a little fun. He says, "Hey, you guys have been dancing for a little while now. Don't you think your god would've shown up by now?"

In verse 27, Elijah taunting the prophets of Baal says:

> "Shout Louder!" he said" Surely he is a god! Perhaps he is in deep thought, or busy, or traveling. Maybe he is sleeping and must be awakened."

Verse 28 tells us, "So they shouted louder and slashed themselves with swords and spears, as was their custom, until their blood flowed." That didn't work either.

In verse 29:

> Midday passed, and they continued their frantic prophesying until the time for the evening sacrifice. But there was no response, no one answered, no one paid attention.

Elijah must have had a lot of patience. He waited until it was time for the evening sacrifice. Then Elijah said, "Now, it's my turn. Gather around, everyone."

They came.

Now it was Elijah's turn. In 1 Kings 18:31-35:

> Elijah took twelve stones, one for each of the tribes descended from Jacob...With the stones he built an altar in the name of the Lord, and he dug a trench around...He arranged the wood, cut the bull into pieces and laid it on the wood. Then he said to them, "Fill four large jars of water and pour it on the offering and on the wood." "Do it again," he said, and they did it again. "Do it a third time," he ordered, and they did it the third time. The water ran down around the altar and even filled the trench.

9: Stories From The Story

Sound like an impossible situation? Those are the best times for God to perform a miracle.

Elijah made it even harder for his fire to start by trenching and soaking everything in water. He did it on purpose to prove the mighty power of God was at work. Here's what happened, it's verses 36-39:

> *At the time of sacrifice, the prophet Elijah stepped forward and prayed: "O Lord, God of Abraham, Isaac and Israel, let it be known today that you are God in Israel and that I am your servant and have done all these things at your command. Answer me, O Lord, answer me, so these people will know that you, O Lord, are God, and that you are turning their hearts back again." Then the fire of the Lord fell and burned up the sacrifice, the wood, the stones and the soil, and also licked up the water in the trench. When all the people saw this, they fell prostrate and cried, 'The Lord—he is God! The Lord—he is God!"*

So much for the false prophets. They all believe now. When they saw it they all believed. No doubt about it. You know what? Every person who has died believes in God right now. Oh, they know it for sure. They may be believing in hell, or they may be believing from heaven, but rest assured they know for sure now who God is and who his son Jesus is. Every single one of them.

I love Elijah's line: "Look, show them this fire, Lord, so that they will know you're turning their hearts back again."

"Lord, you're turning their hearts back again." I believe

(Digging Into Biblical Stories)

that's the message that God has right now. It's His desire to turn our hearts back again to Him—100% to Him. Are you willing to go? That's how you live a life that matters for God.

Missing a Shot

Sometimes we think our life with Jesus is like a roller coaster ride. Yes, there are trials and tribulations. We understand that, but you know, everybody goes through those—not only Christians. Every single person in the world goes through those. And we Christians have the blessing and benefit of the Lord to help us through those times. We have reason and purpose, guidance and comfort. God says you already have all you want. We have the kingdom of heaven within us, and the hope of it forevermore. We're rich. We're heirs to the throne of heaven. We're Jesus' kids. We've got it all. Sometimes we mope around like it's a bad thing when it's a great thing. We just need to pay more careful attention to what we've heard.

In the Old Testament, we read that God's prophet Elijah, after doing some amazing miracles, ran for his life in fear. In 1 Kings 19:4 we see that: "He himself went a day's journey into the desert. He came to a broom tree, sat down under it and prayed that he might die."

That's how bummed out he was. He said, "Lord, kill me." Sounds a lot like Jonah, when Jonah was upset that the Lord

(Digging Into Biblical Stories)

didn't work things out the way he assumed they would. He also said, "It would be better that I die." Here's Elijah doing the same thing: "I've had enough, Lord. Take my life. I'm no better than my ancestors."

Can you imagine Michael Jordan quitting basketball because he missed a shot? Can you imagine Al Pacino saying I'll never make another movie because he blew a line or Eric Clapton saying, "I'm not playing guitar anymore because I missed a note?" That is absurd, and that's exactly what's happening to Elijah.

That's exactly what happens to you and me sometimes. We get discouraged. We get depressed. Things don't go our way—we think they should be one way, but they're another. We all of a sudden take our eyes off God, like Peter. He could have walked right across the water, but he took his eyes off Jesus. As soon as he made that mistake—so easy to make, so easy to do—he got scared. He heard the wind, he saw the waves, and he began to sink. Of course, Jesus pulled him up, and of course, Jesus would do the same for us.

Jesus wants to pull us up as well. Christians are so stubborn we never get it right until we die and are made perfect with Jesus in heaven. Sometimes Jesus pulls us up while we're living and we don't have to die to be shown the truth, which is, I'm sure, what His desire is, as it would be the desire of any parent. But sometimes we do need to hit rock bottom because that's the time we finally look up and realize that He was there all along. We Christians are supposed to die to self—our pride, our sense of personal goodness and rightness—when we do that Jesus lifts us up and exalts us.

9: Stories From The Story

So back to Elijah. Elijah lays down under the tree and falls asleep. Then he is woken by an angel and given food and drink. He journeys to a mountain and goes into a cave. He spends the night and the word of the Lord came to him: "What are you doing here, Elijah?"

Elijah is ready to pour out his heart before God. It almost sounds to me like he rehearsed these lines a few times over: "I have been very zealous for the Lord God Almighty. The Israelites have rejected your covenant, broken down your altars, and put your prophets to death with the sword. I am the only one left, and now they are trying to kill me."

God delivers a message that has to be one of the greatest teaching moments of all time. Look what God does, and see the parallel in your life: 1 Kings 19:11 says, "The Lord said, 'Go out and stand on the mountain in the presence of the Lord, for the Lord is about to pass by.'"

Here is the punch line, in the next verse:

> *Then a great and powerful wind tore the mountains apart and shattered the rocks before the Lord, but the Lord was not in the wind. After the wind there was an earthquake, but the Lord was not in the earthquake. After the earthquake came a fire, but the Lord was not in the fire. And after the fire came a gentle whisper.*

A gentle whisper. That's where God was. It was a hurricane worse than Wilma. It was a fire worse than the Chicago fire, an earthquake worse than Haiti. God said, "Stand outside. I'm coming." There was an earthquake, wind, fire, but that's not

(Digging Into Biblical Stories)

where God was. When it all went away, when all the noise died down, the whisper of God could be heard. Elijah heard the whisper of God Himself.

If you want to hear from God, you've got to get rid of all the noise, man. That same still, small voice lives inside you. It's the Holy Spirit inside of us that speaks today, but you've got to be quiet to hear it. Are you willing to shut up to hear God?

Getting Seconds

The prophet Elijah knows that he's soon going home to be with the Lord. He's at the end of an illustrious career as a prophet, and he's grooming his number two guy, Elisha, to take over.

In 2 Kings 2:1-6, we read:

> When the Lord was about to take Elijah up to heaven in a whirlwind, Elijah and Elisha were on their way from Gilgal. Elijah said to Elisha, "Stay here; the Lord has sent me to Bethel." But Elisha said, "As surely as the Lord lives and as you live, I will not leave you." So they went down to Bethel. The company of the prophets at Bethel came out to Elisha and asked, "Do you know that the Lord is going to take your master from you today?"
>
> "Yes, I know," Elisha replied, "but do not speak of it." Then Elijah said to him, "Stay here, Elisha; the Lord has sent me to Jericho." And he replied, "As surely as the Lord lives and as you live, I will not leave you." So they went to Jericho. The company of the proph-

(Digging Into Biblical Stories)

> *ets at Jericho went up to Elisha and asked him, "Do you know that the Lord is going to take your master from you today?"*
>
> *"Yes, I know," he replied, "but do not speak of it." Then Elijah said to him, "Stay here; the Lord has sent me to the Jordan."*

So, Elijah went to Bethel, Jericho, and Jordan and he kept telling Elisha to just hang out where they were. But Elisha said, "As surely as the LORD lives and as you live, I will not leave you." Elisha is not going to be left behind. He is so faithful to his mentor, and faithful to his God so he refuses to just wait around. He's not going anywhere but with his prophet and with his God.

> *So the two of them walked on. Fifty men of the company of the prophets went and stood at a distance, facing the place where Elijah and Elisha had stopped at the Jordan. Elijah took his cloak, rolled it up and struck the water with it. The water divided to the right and to the left, and the two of them crossed over on dry ground. When they had crossed, Elijah said to Elisha, "Tell me, what can I do for you before I am taken from you?" (2 Kings 2:7-9a)*

Without missing a beat, Elisha says to him, "Let me inherit a double portion of your spirit." (2 Kings 2:9b)

What an amazing request from Elisha to Elijah. He said, "Man, let me get two of what you got because what I see you have is so amazing." And he got it. His request was answered. I pray that our request from God would be, "Lord, can we have a double portion of your spirit." God said that where our heart is, there our treasure will be. If our heart is on the things of the world, that's what we're going to focus on. If our heart is on the things of God, then we can have blessings so abundant our cup will run over. Won't you ask God for that specific blessing?

Elijah was a man just like us. Elisha was also a human being just like we are. But with God's power and anointing, His blessing and guidance, and most of all, with His Spirit, they stood out as extraordinary men of God who were never forgotten. God wants to do the same for you.

Just Two Things

Think for a moment about everything God did to Job. He took everything away; his kids are dead, he's covered in sores, he's afflicted, he's rotting away, and Job says, "Lord, just two things don't do to me. Just two."

Number one: don't withdraw your hand far from me.

Lord, please, no matter what is happening, you are God. I need your hand on me. That is my prayer, and I hope it's yours as well. Lord, don't take your hand off me.

His second prayer was, "Let not the dread of you make me afraid." Meaning, don't let me be scared of you, Lord.

Don't take your hand off me, and don't let me be afraid of you.

God says He'll never leave us or forsake us. Never. Because of Christ, you and I can boldly go to the throne of God. We can go right to God with no fear. God won't take His hand off of us, He'll never leave us or forsake us, and we should have no fear talking to Him. We have the two things that Job wanted so badly, and sometimes we take them for granted.

After all this, Job says, "I know that my Redeemer lives, and that in the end he will stand upon the earth. And after

9: Stories From The Story

my skin has been destroyed, yet in my flesh I will see God." (Job 19:25-26)

Do we know this? Do we know what Job knew? Do we know that our Redeemer lives? Do we know that when our flesh is destroyed we will see God?

If we knew it, wouldn't we behave as the happiest people on the earth? No matter what happened, wouldn't we look to God joyfully, trustingly, lovingly? We would be living our lives as if God talked with us in heaven before He sent us to earth. Giving us our purpose, sharing his plan with us and he said, "Listen, I'm sending you for this mission. This is how I want to use you. You don't know the impact you're going to have on people. You don't know the assignment I have for you. Just trust me that this is what I've given you." Wouldn't you go down joyfully, happily?

It doesn't matter if you're called to impact thousands, or millions, or just one. Live your life fulfilling that call God has given you. You never know who is watching you and might be telling your story one day. "This person's example made me decide to live my life for Christ!"

If nothing else, you know that your Redeemer lives. At the end of days, you will stand before Christ, and He will say to you, "Well done, good and faithful servant. You have been faithful in what I have called you to; I will make you ruler over many things. Enter into my joy."

FINAL THOUGHTS

Thank you for investing your time in reading my book. I hope it was a blessing to you.

I've been extremely touched and motivated by the response I received from my previous books. *Don't Blow It With God* and *Where The Rubber Meets The Road With God* were life-changing books for a lot of people. Many of them got in touch with me and told me the impact the books had on their lives. Of course that inspired me tremendously. I wrote *Don't Blow It With God* as a roadmap to the ultimate Christian life so that anybody who read it would have no excuse to not be living the abundant, joyful life God intended them to have. I wrote *Where The Rubber Meets The Road With God* for every Christian who wants to be certain they will hear, "Well done good and faithful servant" when they get to heaven. That was critical for me and I believe for my readers, as well. My third book *My Addict Your Addict*, deals specifically with overcoming addiction and is based on my own battle with addiction and my experiences as the parent of an addict.

I was motivated to write this book, *Live A Life That Matters For God*, because I saw so many people who didn't have the

Final Thoughts

time, desire or willingness to sit down and get involved in a deep book and read lengthy chapters, even though for many they held the keys to the happiness, joy and the peace of God.

Yet, as I've learned in life, and certainly in business and preaching, it really doesn't matter what I say, what matters is what people hear and see. In other words, what their "take-away" is. And obviously if people aren't listening or looking than they cannot see or hear anything. In our world today things come fast and quick. Many people will not sit down and read books whose chapters are 20 to 40 pages long (like my first two books).With that in mind, I set out to write in a format that today's fast-paced world would embrace, pick up excitedly, and be blessed by. My hope and my prayer is I've accomplished that.

God bless you!

Jack

SPECIAL THANKS

To Erica Alvarez. Thank you for working so diligently in helping me edit and organize this book. I know it turned out to be much more work than you ever imagined, but I appreciate your blessing and your desire to finish the task. I know you did it because your heart is for the kingdom of God and God's people. It was my blessing to work with you.

To John Rabe, "Old Reliable." The man who has been there for me on every one of my books and played a critical part in this one. John, you inspired me with a clear, objective voice as to how to make sense and order of this massive volume of material. Always my number one go to book guy, you never cease to amaze me with your dedication and devotion to my projects and to the Lord. I am so grateful God has seen fit to provide me with such a wonderful friend and man of faith to help with these books.

Sean LeGasse. While it's true I drove you crazy with all my changes and comments. I did ask you to read it for continuity and clarity and of course as any good pastor and brother in the Lord would, you gave me your honest opinion. (The nerve

Special Thanks

of you…smile!) And thus I had to go back to the drawing board more than once…Smile again! I am so thankful to you for all the time and effort you put in. You treated this book like it was your own and worked on it over and above what I could've imagined. I am sorry for all the hassle that went along with it, I think I blew up your computer and probably cost you your job, but what the heck…we had fun. Or at least I did! (Smile again!) You hung tough with me and I know it's the desire of both our hearts that it should all be for the glory of God. Thank you, brother, for blessing me.

Kim Leonard. Kim has done layout and design for the interior and exterior of all four of my books. She brings top-quality professional design work to my projects, but equally as important a passion and heart for the Lord that is refreshing and real. She has guided me throughout the process and has made every one of my books, including this one, a much better product. I'm indebted to her for her dedication and devotion to making sure that God is represented in the best way possible and that through our work together, we can reach as many people as possible for the kingdom of God. I also love the fact that she will always tell me when I am wrong, even when I don't want to hear it. Kim and her husband Allen have been a tremendous personal and professional blessing to me.

Shaun Smith. Well it's becoming a habit with me. I throw my books in Shaun's face and tell him to read them over. I give him complete freedom (and no money) to give me some honest and unbiased comments and thoughts. I also remind him that having to proofread the book is the price you pay

Special Thanks

for being my friend. As always, he gave his heart and soul to this project and I am very grateful.

My wife Beth. Well honey, another round of madness and insanity. And another book that we pray will glorify God. Thank you for loving me and being by my side, encouraging me to continue to write, preach, speak and live a life of ministry for God and His kingdom. That is only one of the great blessings you have given me.

Now I know the 6 people that I've acknowledged above probably think of me like Woody Allen. If you don't know Woody Allen, he's a movie director who never tells the actors and actresses in his movies how the movie ends or what the plot is. It drives them crazy. He only allows them to see the scenes they are involved in. So they never know what the movie was really about until they see it in the theaters. Now, the good news for Woody is a lot of people think he's a movie-making genius (although he has had some personal issues). I'm hoping that those I've acknowledged will look at me the same way. Because they never have any clue what's going on in my head and what the final version of my books will look like. I change things a lot and move them around from the versions they looked at. My hope and prayer is some day (today would be a good day... smile!) they'll think of me as a book writing genius. But right now I don't think I'm so lucky. They probably think I'm a little crazy. I have no rational answer for that and no explanation, except to say "To God Be The Glory." I pray the end product is one that will bless you. I know I always receive a tremendous blessing from writing the books and interacting with everybody involved. Thank You Lord for allowing us to serve You.

www.ingramcontent.com/pod-product-compliance
Lightning Source LLC
Chambersburg PA
CBHW031358290426
44110CB00011B/203